On Human Worth

'Duncan Forrester has interwoven the local with the global, and personal story with social analysis, into a lucid and engaging argument. He shows the task of public theology to be as much about listening as speaking, and offers a case study in how to articulate the basic principles on which a just and sustainable society should rest. This is, as he promises, truly a book to challenge, disturb and enlighten.'

Elaine Graham, Samuel Ferguson Professor of Social and Pastoral Theology, University of Manchester

'Duncan Forrester's book is essential reading on a disturbing topic which most of us acknowledge but with which few of us know how to deal. Like the author, I feel guilty every time I see a beggar on the streets or at the door. I know that in God's sight we are somehow equal, but there is a huge gulf between us. Can it be bridged? What does it require of us? Forrester writes out of a lifetime of wrestling with such questions, and also with passion, clarity, and conviction.'

John W. de Gruchy, Professor of Christian Studies, University of Cape Town

'Duncan Forrester's book could not be more timely. It is a bold and angry challenge to a world which has come to believe in the "freedom" of inequality; a world which daily tolerates and even celebrates obscene polarities of wealth. He persuasively undermines the shibboleths of those whose fatalism reinforces inequality, and affirms the role of intellectuals as servants of the poor, indicating how those who "take sides" come closer to objectivity and the truth. His book represents another nail in the coffin of an economic ideology which serves the interests of the privileged few, and neglects the many.'

Ann Pettifor, Jubilee Plus Programme Co-ordinator, formerly Director of the Jubilee 2000 Coalition

'This is a profound and moving book: profound in its rigorous engagement with some of the deepest questions in social and political theory; moving in that it attends closely to the impact of poverty and inequality on the lives and prospects of ordinary people.'

Raymond Plant, Professor of Politics, University of Southampton

On Human Worth

A Christian Vindication of Equality

Duncan B. Forrester

scm press

0 334 02825 6

This edition first published 2001 by
SCM Press,
9–17 St Albans Place London N1 0NX

SCM Press is a division of
SCM-Canterbury Press Ltd

Typeset by Regent Typesetting, London
and printed in Great Britain by
Biddles, Guildford and King's Lynn

Contents

Part Three: Fruits of Equality: Practices and Policies

Acknowledgements

I am indebted to many friends and colleagues for encouragement, advice, criticism and help as this project has developed. I learned much from Simon Robinson's Edinburgh PhD thesis on R. H. Tawney's understanding of equality, and from Douglas Hicks's fine book, *Inequality and Christian Ethics* which he kindly allowed me to read in proof. In Oxford I was grateful for the generous hospitality of Harris Manchester College and its Principal, Dr Ralph Waller, and for stimulating and constructive discussions with Chris Rowland, Gerry Cohen, Kenneth Nordgren, Mark Hope, Cecile Barber, Stuart White, Raymond Plant, Oliver O'Donovan, and numerous others. Nearer home, I was particularly helped, stimulated and encouraged by Adrian Sinfield, Bob Holman, Kay Carmichael and David Donnison, while three colleagues – Ian McDonald, Nicholas Sagovsky and Andrew Morton – read the whole book in draft and gave me a multitude of useful comments and suggestions. An outline of my argument formed the substance of the Von Hügel Lecture at St Edmund's College, Cambridge in May 2000. I am grateful to the Master, Professor Brian Heap, Fr Frank McHugh and other colleagues at St Edmund's for their welcome and encouragement. Colleagues and students at Edinburgh have been unfailingly supportive, and I am particularly grateful to the Provost, Dr Frances Dow, and the Faculty Group Research Committee for a grant which enabled me to have the expert help of Dennis Lambert while preparing the typescript for the press. Professor John Witte, Jnr., of Emory University gave me encouragement and reading suggestions. Alex Wright of SCM Press and Dr Philip Hillyer were constantly supportive and helpful.

Multitudes of anonymous folk have challenged, disturbed, enlightened and taught me as I have wrestled with the issue of equality down the years. Most of them will never know how much I am in their debt.

Once again, Margaret has not only enlightened, taught and encouraged me more than anyone else, but she has put up graciously with my long obsession with the completion of this book.

All Saints' Day, 2000

Prologue

Why Equality is Important

This book has been germinating slowly over several decades. Its origin lies in my reflections as a young Christian on encounters with poverty and gross inequality in India, in Britain and in the United States. It starts with a practical question: what should I, as a middle class, secure Christian academic, what should we, as citizens of societies which strive to be just and decent, what should policymakers and politicians do when face to face with inequality? And the book ends also with a practical question, and some pointers to how it might be answered: in what ways can we as citizens, as Christians, as church, as society build a more equal, just and decent global community in which the worth of human beings is more adequately affirmed?

My arrival in India for the first time came for me as a culture shock, above all because of the intensity of the visible poverty and inequality, so much more obvious, extreme and horrifying than anything I had seen up to that time in Britain. Beggars were everywhere, often with missing limbs or other physical deformities; women with hungry children in their arms; legless men, hauling themselves around on ramshackle wooden trolleys a few inches above the ground, hungry sick children pathetically holding out begging bowls, teams of beggars systematically working through the suburban trains.

'How should I respond to all this pain and anger and need, to these broken lives all around me?' I asked in great confusion. Some Indian friends pointed out that beggary was organized; that some beggars made a good living; that many of their injuries were self-inflicted in order to arouse more pity, and attract more alms. All these things probably went on. But yet that was but a tiny part of the whole awful tragedy, and it was being used to justify doing nothing with a good conscience. Beggary was but the most blatant and visible manifestation of a radically unequal society and an unequal world. If you went to the villages, or to the urban slums there were fewer beggars, but appalling poverty within sight and hearing of great and often callous prosperity.

To add to my confusion, when I visited slums in Chennai (Madras) or in Madurai – I remember particularly vividly a ramshackle slum built around an open sewer in Madurai – there was an unexpected warmth of welcome, a high-spirited excitement among the children, a dignity that was not born of resignation among many of the adults, a lively sense of community. Perhaps there was a sense in which I and my like, and not these slum dwellers, were the problem, if the language of problem and solution is indeed an adequate way of talking about such matters.

The intensity of the poverty and the inequality in India suggested that we were impotent to do anything. And in a sense that was right: the problem was far beyond the capacity of a few individuals to change. It is not surprising that on all sides, and particularly among the comfortable, there was, and is, a great deal of resignation, of acceptance of things as they are because fundamental change seems beyond the horizon of possibility, because prosperous people like to be content, and because many of the poor accepted their lot without question and without complaint. And such attitudes are often enough reinforced and supported by religion. We ought to be resigned to God's will, some people said; others believed our joys and woes in this life were the fruits of an earlier existence. Both agreed our present condition was a given, beyond scrutiny or remedy.

A beggar, a burnt-out leper, with a clawed hand and hardly any toes, regularly begged on the footbridge over the railway outside the college where I taught. His name, if I remember aright, was Munuswamy. I tried to use my early halting Tamil to speak with him. I gave him small sums of money. I hoped that one day I would have the language and the courage to become a friend of Munuswamy.

And then I began to encounter the reality of the 'great gulf' between Lazarus and the rich man that ultimately became the unbridgeable chasm between the rich man and Lazarus in Abraham's bosom in the story that Jesus told. Munuswamy with his broken life, his physical frailty, his illiteracy, his poor self-image lived in a different world from mine. I lived in a cosmopolitan sphere of security, opportunity, excitement, health, independence, respect – and also in the world of consumerism, where people are regularly measured by the size of their purse, and high levels of consumption are admired. Munuswamy lived in the tiny, circumscribed world of the railway bridge and his little mud hut, full of uncertainties about survival, dependent on the alms of others, his life a constant humiliation. My missionary allowance as a bachelor was a mere £480 per annum, but for all that Munuswamy and I belonged to the opposite ends of the scale of global material inequality.

The Munuswamy I met all those years ago is probably dead by now, life-expectancy in India being what it is. But if I went back to Madras today, I would find his place taken by some other Munuswamy, whose story would be very similar.

I feel I must do something for Munuswamy. But nothing I can do will put the relationship right. Whatever I do, I feel rotten. Anything I do is simply a personal act which at best may ease Munuswamy's lot for a moment. The very act of giving underscores the inequality between us. Charity, alms, doles-out do not establish neighbourliness, friendship or equality. Indeed, they often make things worse, especially if they are impulsive, patronizing, ill-considered. And even if I were to help Munuswamy in a serious way, how many hundreds of thousands of beggars are there in Madras; do they not deserve help as well?

The relationship (if one may call it that) between Munuswamy and me is so structured as to make virtually impossible an authentic, caring friendship between us. I am tempted to give Munuswamy a paltry sum to go away and terminate the embarrassing relationship. There is no way within our encounter of meeting Munuswamy's deeper needs, which are, as with everyone, for care, respect, affection and a recognition of worth as well as for material resources – always remembering that material resources may, or may not, be signs and expressions of care, worth and affection. Neither 'buying off' Munuswamy with a few coins, nor refusing to give alms, eases my conscience. It is the system that creates and tolerates such poverty, and the parody of authentic caring relationships involved in beggary, which are wrong. They offend against the conviction that Munuswamy and I are neighbours, given to one another to love.

I know that Munuswamy and I ought to be neighbours, but seemingly we cannot be. And this hard fact reminds us that the establishment of equality cannot be simply a matter of individual morality and personal responses. The whole community is involved. Munuswamy sits begging on the railway bridge partly, or mainly, because of the way the economy has treated him – and me. And the economy is not an impersonal irresistible force. It can be controlled and managed, and people who lose out in the market may be compensated if society sees fit to do so. Munuswamy is begging on the bridge, dependent on the charity of others, because of welfare legislation and practice – or the absence of it. And I know, because I am educated, that not only is it incredibly hard for Munuswamy and me to be neighbours, but that I actually *benefit* in subtle anonymous ways from Munuswamy's distress. Behind the legislation and the practices, the workings of the global economic system and the more local market economy there lie deep-seated values which suggest priorities and practices, legislation and policies. In a real sense these largely unexamined values are responsible both for Munuswamy's condition, and for my uneasy conscience. Munuswamy probably believes he should be reconciled to his condition, for culture and society tell him that he has in a sense brought it on himself, that it is right and proper in relation to an objective moral order. Certainly the dominant cultural and religious tradition within which he lives suggests that inequality is part of the God-givenness of things, to which Munuswamy should be resigned. My religious and cultural background tends to see inequality as a problem, not part of God's original or final ordering of things, and morally and religiously suspect. My unhappy conscience reflects a Christian upbringing, and immersion from childhood in the world of the Bible. My conscience would perhaps be easier today without that formation.

Our encounter is conditioned by the fact that Munuswamy is poor in a poor, euphemistically called *developing,* country, while I come from a powerful and prosperous Western economy. My prosperity and Munuswamy's poverty reflect this global inequality. Our relationship – or lack of it – highlights in human terms the realities of the world economic system, and illustrates why these inequalities are a matter of moral concern. It also suggests the complexity of responding wisely and effectively to inequality, harmful and unacceptable as it may be. And we must, of course, always remember that there are 'Munuswamys' in the wealthy societies where still, as in India, the reality of inequality is that great wealth exists alongside poverty.

Personal initiatives are hopelessly inadequate to the scale and complexity of the problem. It would be better if some of my resources should be rechannelled anonymously through the taxation system to Munuswamy and his kind. That would be both less patronizing and more likely to have positive results than impulsive individual giving. It would be good if Munuswamy were to be taken care of – and care is one of the things he needs – by skilled, wise and gentle people on my behalf and as representatives of the broader community. But these things would be just a beginning, just palliative measures in dealing with a social cancer. So we must talk about social policy, social attitudes, and the kind of community that we want as well as individual behaviour. We must consider global economic processes such as international debt, and consider, as the Jubilee 2000 Movement has done so effectively, how steps may be taken towards a more just and equal situation.

But above all, we must discuss ways of expressing how, despite our differences (some of which, let us remember, are good and valuable) Munuswamy and I are of equal worth, entitled to self-respect and dignity, secure from being shamed in public because of who we are. Worth needs to be recognized and given substance in action, in policy, in the way our society operates and structures itself. And in today's world these issues inevitably impinge on world economic relations. Equality, fellowship, neighbourliness need to be expressed among other ways in the sharing of material things like money and other material resources.

We are therefore concerned in this discussion with the kind of society, indeed with the kind of world, we want. That the issues are so complex can easily lead to resignation, and the assumption that nothing can be changed. But if Habermas is right to speak of 'an exhaustion of utopian energies' today,[1] a book such as this must be concerned first of all with the possibility of a re-igniting of utopian hopes as the engine of social transformation. For a Christian theologian the authentic utopia is the Reign of God, and this is grounded in existing realities, for here and there we can, or should be able to, see seeds or partial manifestations of God's Reign which show that it is feasible.

I have, for example, in recent years been greatly impressed with residential communities for people with severe learning difficulties – the people in the past stigmatized as 'idiots', 'morons', or 'cretins'[2] – both L'Arche Communities based on the insights of Jean Vanier, and Rudolph Steiner residential homes. In such communities great efforts are made to emphasize that carers and those cared for are both primarily members of the community. They are of equal worth and importance, and each person, no matter how seriously handicapped, has a contribution that can be made to the life of the community. The worth and value of each is affirmed; people learn to care and to be cared for; the community as a whole discountenances 'unacceptable behaviour', and enforces the norms necessary for living in community.

Or consider a Christian congregation gathered around the table to celebrate the Supper of the Lord. Typically, they are a mixed bunch. There is a poor elderly pensioner standing next to a young, prosperous and upwardly mobile banker. Here there is a middle-aged woman with Down's Syndrome, and her sister who cares for her so willingly, standing next to a university professor. A twelve-year-old schoolgirl receives the bread and the wine from a long retired carpenter. A young gay man suffering from AIDS stands next to a mother of four children, a Chinese student who can hardly speak English and a visiting Indian Dalit join the circle. Here all, in their diversity and difference, find one another as equals and as neighbours, their infinite worth is affirmed and expressed. They share equally material things that are necessary for the sustaining of life and for human conviviality, things that are here charged with immense spiritual significance. Here is a little *foretaste* of the equality of the Reign of God, and an enacted commitment to equality.

I want in this book to enquire into the grounds for believing that Munuswamy and I are of equal worth, and that a decent society is one in which there is a recognition in policy, procedures and structures of the equal worth of human beings. There is today a widely diffused and rather vague notion of the equal worth of human beings. But this belief is not universally shared, and in some quarters its is vehemently rejected. Often a vague notion of equality is formally acknowledged as a good thing, but felt to have very restricted applicability in 'the real world'. Where does the assumption of equality come from? Can it be clarified and defended? How can it best be commended?

This book is intended to be practical. It is about the place in the community of Munuswamy and of me, and how the community and its members may properly affirm the worth of Munuswamy as equal to my worth. It is about how such things may be expressed in policy and in social structures as well as in personal and small group behaviour.

I write as a Christian practical theologian. I am concerned with the movement between faith and equality – something that I am convinced is of the greatest importance, but is often totally neglected in discussions of equality today. This means that I will spend time on the *historical theology* of equality in an effort to clarify what Christians mean by equality, and why it is important. I will also spend time on what might be called the *dogmatics* of equality, examining, to clarify things further, how it relates to other central themes and aspects of Christian faith and life. And finally I will be concerned with commending equality – a kind of *apologetics* of equality – exploring quite specific ways in which equality might be made operational today. Equality requires, I believe, to be commended to the public as a true and important social value, and as something that *works*, that has immediate implications for behaviour and for policy. It also must be commended to Christians and people of faith as a unavoidable implication of discipleship.

The structure of the book is such that it starts and finishes with the inequality that keeps Munuswamy and me apart from one another. I begin by trying to place this question in the broader framework of the deep-seated and powerful structural inequalities that dominate today's world at every level, and how these affect people and communities and relationships. An important early section is on the meanings of equality, to clarify what kind of equality I am talking about. I then discuss the contemporary secular discussion of equality today, and the problems – and importance – of making a theological contribution to that debate. Attention then shifts to examining the roots, the development and the fruits of a Christian commitment to equality. And finally I discuss some of the ways in which Christian equality should be expressed.

There is in relation to equality a role for individual initiatives, and equality should also be learned within the family, where most moral formation in fact takes place. I am sure my unease in my dealings with Munuswamy reflects attitudes and values which I assimilated initially as a child through my family. There is also a role for the church, not only in making statements and trying to influence the way things go – although that is certainly important – but also in the exemplary way it may structure its own life and worship, and in the rigorous way in which it examines its own life, perhaps asking the question whether it can sing the Magnificat without striving passionately for human equality. And there is, of course, an important place in the discussion for public policy, since a decent community should affirm and demonstrate a commitment to equality in the way it deals with its members.

I started meditating on the theme of this book in India while teaching in a missionary college that had down the years made determined and partially successful efforts to overcome the divisions and inequalities characteristic of India, and weld students from very different backgrounds into a broader experience of community which would affirm the worth of each. I complete the project in Edinburgh, which now has many more beggars in the streets than when I left for India some decades ago, and in an Oxford distinguished for many things, among them the beauty of the daily renderings of the Magnificat in countless chapels, and the large numbers of homeless and sometimes demented beggars in the streets.

I hope the book will be found to be disturbing. Writing it has been a disturbing experience for me.

Part One:
Equality Today

I

Meanings

Meaning and truth

What do equality and inequality mean? The question sounds simple enough. The common sense answer would be that one assembles the 'facts' and statistics, one then stands back to seek an objective understanding, detached from value assumptions and distracting emotions. But it is not as easy as that in 'the real world'. The scientific model on its own may lead us in the wrong direction, despite the necessity to take the facts of the case, the statistics, and so forth with real seriousness. But these are not the end of the matter, and in some ways they can be misleading.

What I am advocating is something like the 'discourse ethics' of Habermas and his colleagues. For Habermas, speech is not simply our expressing ourselves; essentially it is an effort to achieve shared understanding. 'Reaching understanding', Habermas writes, 'is the inherent telos of human speech.'[1] But the discourse which seeks agreement in understanding is only authentic if it is free and unforced, if, that is, it approximates to what Habermas calls the 'ideal speech situation', in which no one is intimidated or inhibited from sharing fully in the discussion, and contributing insights, experiences and concerns. 'Participants alone', Cronin writes, 'are ultimately competent to adjudicate claims concerning their needs and interests, and only a consensus achieved in argumentation that sufficiently approximates to the conditions of the ideal speech situation can legitimately claim to be based on rational considerations, and hence to be valid.'[2] In Habermas's ideal speech situation there is no intimidation, no pressure, no 'pulling rank'; only the force of the better argument is recognized. Participants do not seek to use or manipulate one another; they do not talk at or for one another, but to and with one another.

In discourse ethics it is the particular responsibility of the powerful to develop skills of listening. A proponent of discourse ethics, John Forester, puts it thus:

Developing the ability to listen critically is a political necessity. Listening well is a skilled performance. It is political action, not simply a matter of a friendly smile and good intentions. Without real listening, not simply hearing, we cannot have a shared, critical and evolving political life together. In listening we may still better understand, explain, and cut through the pervasive 'can't', the subtle ideological distortions we so often face, including, of course, our own misunderstandings of who we are and may yet be. Listening well, we can act to nurture dialogue and criticism, to make genuine presence possible, to question and explore all that we may yet do and yet become.[3]

It is this kind of attentive listening and conversation that I hope will undergird this book as a whole, and this chapter in particular.

The analogy of a court of law can prove illuminating for our project. In the course of the trial of Jesus Pilate famously asked 'What is truth?' In any context the determination of truth is not an easy matter; in a legal system this is the function of the courts. In a court of law, save in the most exceptional circumstances, the proceedings take place in public. Verdict and sentence are not left to judges or experts in the law operating alone and in private; they take place in public so that justice may not only be done, but be seen to be done. And the public forum also provides a way in which new evidence may arise, relevant to the case in hand. Furthermore, where the system of trial by jury is favoured, this suggests that judgment is not best left to the 'experts' but to a group of perfectly ordinary people, with a variety of positions, interests and points of view, who can tell sense from nonsense and truth from falsity as well as anyone. The accused must be present in court, not only to see justice done, but to question the evidence or the proceedings as necessary.

In a court the powerful and educated are represented not only by the judges and the court officials and the police, but by the advocates, whose task is to use their skill in the law and their powers of argument to present as strong a case as possible in order to help the court to determine the truth. But they also have another role, which is this: as educated and professionally articulate people their task often includes giving a voice to those who otherwise would be voiceless, intimidated by the context of the courtroom, and commonly lacking in education as in confidence. The voice of the powerful arguing in their own interests should not be the only voice that is heard. Others must be encouraged to enter the discussion.

The voice of the victims, and of the accused, of those who are normally voiceless, must be heard; the establishment of truth and of meaning should be done in public. This is almost a commonplace of the courtroom, but is often neglected in other contexts where there is a search for truth and meaning. Hence in the writing of history, for instance, much is written from the viewpoint of the victors, of the powerful. They have control of the sources, their voices are clearly heard. But the voice of the vanquished, of the weak, of the poor, of the failures, of the illiterate is rarely heard. And when the 'voice from below' is heard in historiography it is often based on transcripts of court proceedings, or on painstakingly collected oral testimony.[4] In historiography, as in courts of law, there is also a lively sense that although there are stages when detachment is necessary, judgments must also be made and values affirmed. This is a complicated, if necessary part of the process of seeking truth, and must be done responsibly and carefully. The normative element enters not only into judgment and sentencing; it is part of the semantics of practical discourse. It must be determined whether a particular death, for instance, is from natural causes, or suicide, or manslaughter or murder. The language is through and through normative. In its judgments, the court ultimately takes sides, and realizes that taking sides at the appropriate moment on the basis of the relevant evidence is part of the search for truth. Judgments on the part of those who cannot enter emotionally into the situation may be in that respect defective.

Liberation theologians characteristically see a central part of their role as standing with and speaking for the poor and the excluded, the ones who are commonly without a voice, fulfilling the biblical injunction:

Speak out for those who cannot speak,
for the rights of all the destitute.

Speak out, judge righteously,
defend the rights of the poor and needy.[5]

The liberation theologians, I believe, are right in affirming this role of
the theologians, to speak for the poor, and weak and voiceless in a more
demanding and empathetic way than that required of the advocates in
court who speak for the victims and the accused in establishing truth.
Only those who stand with those who are denied a voice can articulate
their voice and contribute thus to the search for truth, not allowing the
meanings of the powerful and intellectual to dominate the discussion
and exclude or despise other voices. A proper objectivity is often compatible with taking sides; indeed taking sides, commitment, can be an
avenue to truth. The liberation theologians' insight at this point is of
broad relevance and importance.

Understanding and experience

It is, I believe, bad in principle and bad in practice to talk about people
behind their backs, particularly if they are relatively powerless people
who are often labelled 'problems', and one is talking about their
problems and how to solve them. I have been involved over a number
of years with the organization, under the auspices of the Centre for
Theology and Public Issues, of a number of conferences on major social
issues like poverty, homelessness, or violence against women. One of
the principles of the Centre is not to talk about people 'behind their
backs', because to do so is fundamentally inegalitarian. It is not taking
the people most intimately concerned seriously as equals. They must
be equal, indeed privileged, participants in discussions which affect
them, and their communities and their future so deeply and intimately.
Without this, the issue is frequently misunderstood, and the responses
are in danger of being inappropriate and ineffective. Accordingly we
always have at a conference, say, on poverty in Scotland, a number of
participants who are themselves poor, and likewise with conferences
dealing with prisons, or homelessness, or unemployment.

We try, with some success, to ensure that some of the formal input is
from recognized experts, often people with major international reputations. Their contribution is invariably excellent, balanced, humane,

incisive and constructive. But commonly in the discussion there comes a point when one of the poor, or unemployed, or homeless people gets up and says angrily to the experts, and to the middle class academics and church people in the audience generally, words that say more or less, 'You don't understand. You don't know what you are talking about.'

Some academic experts take such remarks a bit amiss. After all, they have studied the issue for years; they have established reputations. The accusation, 'You don't know what you're talking about', hurts, and surely it can't be true. Besides, those who make the charge are often extraordinarily emotional, inarticulate and confused, as well as being quite aggressive. So, almost physically, the academics sometimes back off. This is no concern of ours, their very body language seems to express.

Other experts take it on the jaw; they admit there is an inside meaning to social problems that cannot be resolved without remainder into statistics, however carefully garnered and analysed; they attend to the angry outbursts and try to make links between this emotion and its roots in the situation they are professionally expected to analyse with detached objectivity. It is as if they recognize the limitations of their scholarly meanings, and seek the help of the 'insiders' to fill out the human reality of the matter. In a way they seek the angry – and often impressive – speakers from the sharp end as *colleagues* in understanding and response. It is almost as if they regard themselves as the academic servants of the poor, the homeless and the unemployed, allies in striving to do something to make the world a better place.

If we are seeking for what I call 'the human meaning' of inequality, experience – particularly the experience of the weak and poor and vulnerable – and feelings are vital ingredients of meaning alongside the statistics and the sharp social analysis. But it is not easy for people, however intelligent and sympathetic, to attend to the weak, the poor and the excluded. Understanding the human meaning requires what Richard Tawney called 'an intellectual conversion', a change of direction and of priorities, and of self-understanding. It calls for intellectual humility before the complex truth. It demands breaking through some pretty stubborn and resistant social and intellectual barriers, because one cannot attend to people from a distance. It is not a matter of passive listening; indeed people will not speak honestly to one who simply listens, detached like a judge. They will speak to someone who is with them, for them, on their side. It's a bit like the rather strange fact that in the Hebrew Bible the same verb means 'loving' and 'knowing'. If people believe you care for them, that you love them, they are more likely to tell you what lies in their hearts, and what their circumstances have done to them, and their families, and their communities, and how they see the way forward.

Let me give an illustration of this process. A number of years ago in a Scottish city the authorities were concerned about how to respond to a large increase in the number of homeless people on the streets and sleeping rough. They believed the answer to the problem, at least in the short to medium term, was more hostels, upgraded doss-houses, and night shelters. Before implementing this policy, some city officials thought it would be wise to confirm that this is what the homeless men (almost all the homeless are men) wanted. They employed a young sociologist, a woman (and that is not, I think, irrelevant to what happened) to carry out this small research project. As expected, all went smoothly to begin with. Armed with her questionnaires, with lots of little boxes to tick, she was finding that most of the men seemed to want upgraded doss-houses; some of them seemed to have an extra sense, to work out and give the answer that was expected. Then, one day, a homeless man became agitated and talkative. He spoke to the young sociologist about how he had been treated the week before in the social security office, how he had felt humiliated and cheated, his dignity taken away, and the almost visible label marked 'scrounger', pinned on him. As she listened, the young sociologist grew angry herself. At the end of his story, she took the old man by the hand, took him back to the social security office and acted there as his advocate and representative. Unlike the previous week, this time he got the benefits to which he was entitled.

Word spread quickly among the homeless people: this woman is not just a bothersome interrogator; she's on our side! She understands! Then she began to get quite different information, because they trusted her. Now, almost universally, they told her that they felt they could, with a little support, establish themselves in a two-room council flat. They wanted to settle down and return to normality. They felt it was possible, especially if the support they received was understanding, sensitive and unpatronizing. Because many homeless men had shared their inner feelings with her, the young sociologist could now, and only now, write sensitively and faithfully of the human meaning of homelessness. For she had taken a crucial step from academic detachment to fellow-feeling.

Another example is this. In the late 1980s I chaired for the Church of Scotland a working party on the distribution of wealth, income and benefits. Its report was published as a book, *Just Sharing*.[6] We started the book with accounts of two kinds of experience of poverty and maldistribution. Several middle class academic members of the working group described how their understanding of themselves, of community, and of what they ought to do with their lives had been transformed by involvement in situations of great poverty and deprivation. And then we had direct testimony from poor people. What I remember best, and the part of the book which had the greatest impact, was a transcribed discussion with a group of women from Easterhouse, one of the most deprived housing estates in Glasgow. They came across as wonderful people, who were joyfully sustaining community and caring for one another in situations of great poverty, hardship and uncertainty. This section of testimony came before the statistics and the economic analysis, before the theological reflection, and before the discussion of what we should do now as a church and as a nation. It seemed to achieve its object remarkably well, which was to share feelings of joy, frustration, anger, confusion and uncertainty, and to indicate to our largely middle class and comfortable readership that 'intellectual conversion' was possible and had happened to many who had been attentive to the human meaning of poverty and maldistribution.

The human meaning of equality and of inequality suggests the need to put scientific study of the situation at the service of a more affective or emotional approach[7] which enables us to see things through others' eyes and leads to a more adequate understanding of the situation. I am trying to avoid using words like 'sympathy' or 'compassion' because they have been so devalued in common usage. But they both in origin mean feeling together, putting oneself in the other person's shoes and sharing at the level of feeling in order to deepen the understanding and strengthen the will to do something to improve the situation. And this is precisely what I am talking about.

This stress on participation, on consultation, stands in opposition to a once-powerful trend in the British Fabian and idealist tradition which held, sometimes chillingly, that educated, well-intentioned people were adequately equipped to decide what was good for others without the need to consult them. This sometimes led to the idea of a society where poor and weak people and communities could have good done to them whether or not they thought that the policies concerned were desirable. I say that this approach was sometimes chilling, because it was latently totalitarian, and systematically demeaned the people to whom good was being done by failure to consult them or take into account the way they saw the world.[8] It was little surprise that when Sidney and Beatrice Webb, the leading Fabian intellectuals, visited the young Soviet Union they found it a tidy and well- organized egalitarian nation, with people having good done to them – or so they thought. Returning home they wrote a massive volume detailing their enquiries called, in the first edition, *Soviet Russia: A New Civilisation?* In the second edition, the question mark was removed. They felt they had seen Fabianism working!

An even more disturbing case of people 'doing good' to others without consulting them was the way British people of conscience, education and integrity – and often evangelical Christians – handled the Irish Famine of the 1840s. Amartya Sen points out that the British consistently regarded the Irish peasantry as inferiors, who were to a great extent responsible for what had happened. He quotes Richard Ned Lebow as suggesting that the British saw the famine as being caused by laziness, indifference and ineptitude, so that the burden of government was not so much 'to alleviate Irish distress but to civilize her people and to lead them to think and act like human beings'.[9] The Irish were not seen by many in positions of authority as equals; had they been so regarded, the policies adopted to deal with the famine would certainly have been different. Charles Trevelyan, an evangelical Christian and the permanent head of the Treasury, and thus the British official most directly responsible for dealing with the famine, declared, 'The great evil with which we have to contend is not the physical evil of the famine, but the moral evil of the selfish, perverse and turbulent character of the people'. At every point he resisted 'outdoor relief'; even while recognizing the existence of a famine in which thousands would die. At the height of the hunger he warned: 'If the Irish once find out there are any circumstances in which they can get free government grants ... we shall have a system of mendicancy such as the world never saw'.[10] The Irish famine is perhaps an extreme case, but it is not an isolated example of what can happen when there are extreme inequalities of power and wealth, and when the rich and powerful regard others as almost a distinct, and inferior, species, whose views and understandings do not deserve attention.

In a far smaller scale and in a lower key I experienced something of the same process when as a young minister I worked with the theological college's mission in a slum area of Edinburgh, a district with a real sense of community solidarity, and many wonderful people. One day brown paper envelopes began coming through people's letter boxes. On opening and reading them, people learned that a decision had been taken to 'clear' the slum, and they were offered rehousing in one or other of the peripheral council housing estates. Families with a good record of employment were offered houses in a 'good' estate; those with a police record were to be rehoused concentrated in particular stairs in a run-down estate where they could conveniently be supervised by the police. Old folk were offered sheltered housing, often far from their families and friends. People were angry and confused. They felt, correctly, that they had not been consulted. Most of them did not wish to move out of the heart of the city. They didn't want their community to be split up. They felt they were victims of oppressive power. And they felt humiliated.

We, from the Mission, went to the Housing Department. There we met, not ogres or tyrants, but decent, well-educated middle class people who had the welfare of the city at heart, and believed that they were doing good to the people of Lower Greenside. They were surprised and puzzled when we told them that local people were angry; they believed they had been acting for the good of the people of Lower Greenside as well as the city as a whole. The chairman of the housing committee and some of his officials came down, under some pressure from us, to a crowded and angry meeting. They left it still puzzled and now perhaps a little frightened that they might not in fact know in the city chambers what was good for the community of Lower Greenside.

This story does not have a happy ending. The people were moved out, and scattered around the ring of council estates around Edinburgh. Some of the old folk were so confused by their new sheltered housing that they were found wandering the streets and ended up in geriatric hospitals. The children came back for months, to play with their friends, now scattered around the city, on the ruins of their old homes. I wonder if we have learned from episodes such as this about the virtues of equality for a healthy democratic society, about the need to consult people and involve them in the making and implementation of policies which affect them deeply?

The human meaning of inequality is thus often experienced as oppression and exploitation, powerlessness and the destruction of relationships. It is often an experience of shame and humiliation. Adam Smith, as Amartya Sen points out several times, insisted that all human beings should have 'the ability to appear in public without shame'.[11] Similarly, John Rawls gives a significant place among his 'primary goods' to 'self respect'. And Avishai Margalit defines the decent society as 'one whose institutions do not humiliate people ... in which every person is accorded due honour'.[12] Poverty and extreme inequality are inherently humiliating to all parties involved, as we have seen when we considered my relationship to Munuswamy; and some ways of responding to inequality and poverty make the humiliation and the shame worse. We have therefore to consider carefully ways of overcoming inequality and building communities which involve full participation and at every stage affirm the equal dignity of the participants. Pity and condescension are inherently patronizing and entrench inequality. Something like Habermas's 'ideal speech situation' in which all participants speak without fear or threat or 'pulling rank' and without constraint attend to one another as they seek together to resolve the issues facing them might be the way ahead. But to enable Munuswamy and me to enter together into such an 'ideal speech situation' surely involves dealing effectively with the powerful structures of inequality which keep us apart.

The human reality of inequality today: bare facts

The bare facts show very clearly that inequality has been, and is increasing, both globally and in most of the industrialized societies such as Britain and the United States. The latest detailed survey in Britain, using 1997 as its base line, shows

- The gap between low and median incomes has been increasing, because the incomes of poorer households rise more slowly.

- The gap between those living on Income Support and households with income from work has widened considerably.

- More than 10 million people live on incomes less than half the national average.

- Lone parent families are far more likely to have low income than other types of family. There are now one and a half million long-term recipients of Income Support who are of working age.

- More than half the people who receive Income Support are long-term recipients.[13]

There has been a general trend towards greater inequality for the last fifteen years or more. One of the most sophisticated recent studies shows that inequality has grown at a rate that is 'historically highly unusual, if not unprecedented'.[14] In Britain the wealthiest 10% of the population own more than half the nation's wealth; the wealthiest 50% own more than 90% of the country's wealth. The incomes of the wealthiest escalate at a prodigious rate; the poorest 10% get poorer or simply have static incomes. Children and the aged are particularly vulnerable, and open to damage. Among the industrialized nations, only Russia and the United States have higher levels of child poverty than Britain. Lone parent families are the family type most likely to live in poverty. Pakistani, Bangladeshi and Black households in Britain are very much more likely to live in poverty than white families.[15] The charity Age Concern 'is increasingly concerned about poor pensioners becoming excluded from society and the widening gap between rich and poor'. This is because, 'If the range of income, top to bottom, is increasingly wide, then society loses cohesion. It becomes impossible for everyone to mix on reasonably equal terms and to have a sensible share of the normal accoutrements of social life.'[16] The issue is real and pressing, since a recent examination of inequality in the UK found that nearly two thirds of those over 70 are among the poorest 40% of the population, and only half as likely as those in other age groups to be among the richest 40% of the population.[17]

A report for the Joseph Rowntree Foundation published in 2000 reported that a quarter of the population of the UK was living in poverty in late 1999, more than at any time in the last 20 years. This meant that

- About 9.5 million people cannot afford to keep their homes adequately heated and free from damp.

- Approximately 8 million people cannot afford one or more of the household goods now generally regarded as essential.

- As many as 6.5 million adults go without essential clothing, such as a warm waterproof.

- About 10 million adults cannot afford to save £10 a month for a rainy day, or for retirement.

- Nearly 7.5 million people are too poor to visit friends and family, attend weddings or funerals, or have celebrations on special occasions.

- One child in 25 lacks celebrations on birthdays or two balanced meals a day because of poverty.[18]

The human reality of poverty today: testimony

The human reality of inequality is best expressed, not in statistics, but in poor people's accounts of their own lives in their own words, stories of hardship and of courage, of disasters and of triumphs, of generosity and of destructive behaviour, of friendship and of exploitation. Such narratives make no claim to objectivity or comprehensiveness, but they add a vital and often totally absent, dimension to the discussion. They are more than anecdotes or hearsay evidence; they give access to dimensions of reality otherwise closed to us. The voice of those who are usually silenced must be heard in the discussion if it is to be real and authentic. So here is Erica's story, in her own words, from the remarkable book, *Faith in the Poor*, produced by Bob Holman, and reproduced here with her permission:[19]

'Erica'

I was born in Glasgow but I have little memory of my early days. I know that my dad was cruel to my mum and I have no idea what happened to him. There were four children and myself. We were always in need of money and I hated going to school because I did not have the things that other kids had. When I was about eight, my stepdad appeared.

We moved to Garthamlock, Easterhouse. The council told mum she had to take the house because it was the only one on offer and she took it because all her life she had lived in bedsits and it was her first proper house. Things were OK at first. We lived with our step dad and he was fine to live with at first, but then things started to happen. He would touch me in places I didn't like. I was scared of him but I knew it was wrong. It didn't happen too often at first but then it became a lot. If I was standing doing the washing-up he would come into the kitchen and put his hand between my legs, I would ask him to stop but he would just go ahead and do it.

I wanted to tell my mum but I was scared it would kill her because she was very poorly at the time. She was waiting to go into hospital for an operation. She was 18–20 stone and she was told she only had a 50–50 chance of surviving it. When she went into hospital things got worse at home with my stepdad. He would make me get into his bed with him and I would cry myself to sleep at night after saying a prayer to God to bring my mum home safe. Then the worst thing happened, mum died and left me all alone in the world. I don't know what was happening to my brother and sisters at the time. My aunt lived in Easterhouse but I never saw much of her after mum died. She was my mum's sister.

I was now eleven or twelve and my body was growing and I was becoming a woman in my eyes. I didn't know what was going on and I had no one to talk to. We lived across the road from the Little Sisters of Mercy. So I used to go to them just to talk and we prayed a lot. I wanted to tell them what was going on at home but I couldn't bring myself to speak about it. At the same time I couldn't cope at school, so I started to play truant or I would be bad and get excluded. Then I started to run away from home, but my stepdad would come into town with his friend from the next close to us and they would look for me, and when they found me he would take me home and things would be the same again. The last time I ran away I was in a shop and I stole something and got caught, so when the police came I told them a false name and I had nowhere to live because both my mum and dad were dead. So they took me to an assessment centre called Beechwood and I hated it. So the first chance I had I ran away with another girl called Bet. We became good friends.

For a long time I kept running away from different homes. In the meantime I tried to sniff glue, I tried all sorts of things and I started to drink in pubs and clubs. I was only thirteen but I passed for older because I was a big girl. I started to hang about with a lot of gay people and drink in gay bars. One day I walked into a gay bar and my brother was sitting there. It was a shock for both of us. Then he asked me if I was gay but I told him no, which was true. He told me he was and I told him, 'So what?'

When I was about fourteen, I met a girl, a bit older than myself, and we got talking. She told me she was working on the streets. I told her I didn't understand, so she said she would show me. She took me up a couple of streets and then we came to a stop at a corner and we just stood there. All these cars were going by, nodding their heads at us. One of the cars stopped and she walked over to it and opened the door. She was talking to the driver for some time. Then she shut the door and walked over to me and told me he wanted me. I asked what she meant by that and she said if I gave him sex he would give me £20. It was tempting but I said no, so she told him. Then she came back and said he would give me £40. I wanted to do it but the sex thing scared me to death. I told her and she told him. They called me over to the car and he said he would give me £50 and he would be kind to me. I asked him to come back in five minutes so I could think it over and he said OK and went away. My friend said I would be daft if I didn't do it. It was hard but it was the idea of all that money plus I had nowhere to go and nowhere to sleep for the night. So when he came back I went with him. He took me to a hotel. When we got to the room I was so scared I went to the bathroom. When I came out he was sitting on the edge of the bed. He asked me if I wanted to forget it. I was tempted to say yes but I needed the money. So I put the lights out and took my clothes off and got into bed with him. I shut my eyes and let him do what he wanted to do. I was glad the light was out so he could not see the silent tears on my face and I prayed it would be over soon and it was. He got up and he dressed in silence while I lay in the bed crying to myself. He sat on the edge of the bed and gave me my £50 plus he said I could sleep in the hotel for the night because it was paid for. Then he went away and I stayed in the bed for what seemed a lifetime. Then I got up and ran a bath and sat in the bath tub for about an hour. I went to bed and lay thinking about mum, dad, my brother and sisters and what I just did with a strange man. But then I thought about the £50 under my pillow so I put it all to the back of my mind: It was hard but I did it.

From then on I worked the streets. I got caught and taken back to different homes. I ran away and met this boy and fell in love with him. I thought he loved me but he just wanted me to work the streets for him, and he told me if I didn't do it he would kill me. So I did it for him, but I felt I was back to square one again with no money in my pocket. The next car I got into I told the man to drop me off somewhere else and he did. So I was on my own again, but by then I was a bit more mature. I was caught again and taken to an assessment centre. I decided to stay for a bit of a rest and that is when I found out I was having a baby. I was only fourteen, so they decided to send me to a mother-and-baby home run by nuns. It was OK, and when I had turned fifteen, I went into hospital to have the baby. I had a little boy and called him Mick. They took him away from birth and put me into a children's home. They let me see Mick now and then. I had to get on with my life again. All the time I was fighting for the custody of Mick, but I was fighting a losing battle.

When I was seventeen I fell pregnant with my daughter, so I had to adopt-out Mick because I knew I was too young to look after two kids. By this time my brother and sisters were living in England and my stepdad was dead. I had no one to turn to so I had to go to the same mother-and-baby home with my daughter until the council got me a two bedroomed flat and I could move into it.

When I moved in I could not afford to live on what they gave me, so I went back onto the streets to work. It worked for a while then I had to go to prison. They took Charlotte into foster care. When I came out I got her back and I wrote to my brother in England and he came up to live with me and help me look after her. When he thought I could cope on my own he moved to England again. I was back to square one, on the streets, arrested, Charlotte in foster care again. This time it was longer and I lost my flat, so I took to the drink very heavy. But I still went to see her as much as possible.

Then one day when I was twenty years old and pregnant again, I looked at myself in the mirror and I didn't like what I saw. I decided to sort out my life before I lost another child. My next child was born, called Deidre. I got a house in Easterhouse with my brother, and I looked up an old friend who lived nearby and we became good friends and she helped me get some things for my house. Then she introduced me to her ex-bloke and we hit it off right away. Things were going great and I was on my way to getting Charlotte back. Ivor asked me to marry him and I said yes. My brother got a place of his own just around the corner.

Me and Ivor got married. I got Charlotte back and things were looking up for me for the first couple of years. Then Ivor started to drink very heavy. I wanted to pack mine and the girls' bags and leave, but I loved him so much and he needed us to help him through it so I stayed. I needed help too so I started to attend the Salvation Army. It was the best thing I had done in a long time. At first it was just me and the kids going then I talked Ivor into coming with me to see what it was like and he liked it. The Salvation Army meant the world to me. The holidays at Butlins – and we never went on holidays before. The kids going to the Sunday School. Christmas Day at the Sally was great. I was in the women's choir which Annette led. I never missed a Sunday service. Captain and Mrs Buchanan were a part of our life and they still are even though they have retired. I always remember the captain's bushy eyebrows. It helped me to believe in God. It took me a long time to accept. I do believe although sometimes I doubt. I think if there is a God why have these things happened to me, why hasn't he prevented them? But it is not his fault that these things happen.

Ivor was still drinking. Then I fell pregnant with his son Gilbert. My brother moved back to England and we moved to a bigger flat. Things were tight moneywise, plus the girls were being picked on at school because they were of mixed race. Charlotte was getting the worst of it as she was the oldest. Then I fell pregnant again with another girl. A couple of months after her birth, my brother and my sister came from England for a holiday and they saw what was happening to the girls. They suggested that we all moved to England. They took the two girls with them back to England when they went back so that me and Ivor could settle things in Easterhouse.

We moved to a place called Wakefield, and it was hard because we had no money. We had to sleep here and there, then we went into a homeless people's hostel and we hated it. Then just after Christmas we got a letter from the council asking us to leave because we were not entitled to a house because we gave up one in Easterhouse. They just did not understand. So we were out on the streets yet again. We moved in with my brother in his one-bedroomed flat so that was three adults and four kids getting on top of each other. Then a letter came that we had been allocated a house of our own. Me and Ivor were dancing about, hugging each other we were just so happy.

We moved into the house with nothing. We had no money to buy things with. We put in to DHSS, but they could only give us so much and it was not enough to get half the things we needed, so my family chipped in to help us. It was still not enough, so we had to borrow money from all sorts of places. The girls were getting picked on at school again, plus Charlotte was attacked by a man. It was all getting on top of me and I just don't know how I coped.

My friend Bet came to England to live with us in Wakefield. Then she got a bedsit in Bradford and I would go and visit her. When I saw that it was full of different coloured people I thought of moving there so that the girls could be in amongst their own type. By this time, Charlotte was thirteen and Deidre was ten. We were told by Bet's landlord that if we moved into one of his rooms for a couple of days then he would give me the keys to a four-bedroom house. He took us to look at the house and we loved it at first sight. So we moved to Bradford into one room. Then he was called to Pakistan so we were stuck in this one room, six of us in one double bed. Ivor was helping out at the chip shop at the back of our building. But he was getting pennies for it. He would drink a lot because he could not cope with it all. Neither could I so I ended up taking an overdose which almost killed me.

When I got out of the hospital, I got in touch with social services. They sent this woman to our room and she was hopeless and offered no help at all. So when she went away I got in touch with them again and asked for someone else to help me. They sent a lady called Lorraine, and she was a great help to us all. She asked me what I wanted her to do, so we sat and talked for a bit. I explained how I came to be in Bradford, and she asked if I wanted her to take the kids into care till she helped me get a house. I told her it would break my heart but it was for the best. So I let her take the three big ones and I kept the youngest one with me. It was so hard, but I knew the kids were well cared for and I saw them a lot. But Ivor was still drinking. Then my brother moved to Bradford beside me which was a bit of a help. I got an offer of a lovely four-bedroomed house. When we went to see it I was head over heels with it. I would have been daft to turn it down so I accepted it and Lorraine helped me get the grant for it.

I moved in on the Wednesday and got the kids home on the Monday which was a bit quick because I was not quite right in the head. I did not know what was happening to me because not long before we moved into the house my thirteen-year-old daughter Charlotte was raped by some Asian boy and it broke my heart. So when we moved in and the kids came home I could not cope, and me and Ivor were not getting on at all. I asked him to leave, then I started to drink very heavy and I was smoking drugs. It all started getting on top of me, so I asked Lorraine to take the kids back into care till I sorted my head out, and she did. Again I saw them all the time. So did Ivor. I was still drinking a lot, then Ivor came to have a talk with me and asked if we could go back to normal. But I was not ready as my head was still in a mess. I let him move back into the house, but he had to sleep in one of the kids' beds. I could see for myself that I was hurting him in a bad way. But I could not help myself. Then one night I realized how much we were missing the kids. So we talked about getting our lives sorted out and getting the kids back for good. So we did and it was fine for a bit. Then Ivor started to drink again because the job he was doing was not getting paid right. It went on for a couple of years. The worst was when he would come in drunk and speak to me the way he did. I know he didn't mean it but it still hurt me to hear him. I wanted to leave and be on my own, but he needed me bad. So did the kids as they had been through enough, so I had to put up with it the best I could. People would say they don't know how I coped. Neither did I. Then one day he was caught drinking and driving. He lost his licence and

he was fined. With all that was happening, he had a nervous breakdown and he was taken into a mental hospital for a bit. Now things
are a lot better between us. He doesn't drink now although he does
get depressed a lot. But we have learnt to cope with it the best we
can. The only problem we have now is the same as always and that is
MONEY.

*[Erica kept a diary giving details of her determined struggle to make ends
meet, to maintain her self-respect, and provide for her family. This is an
appendix to this book. Erica's diary ends as follows:]*

I am not rich and I am not angry about it. I am the worst off in this
street. Next door has some beautiful things. I don't hold a grudge
against them, I'm glad they have got it. But I don't like it to be
rubbed in like when other people's kids boast to my kids, 'We've got
this, you haven't.' It does make me jealous at times. I don't want to
be stinking rich. I just want to be comfortable so that when my kids
want a new pair of shoes, I can buy a pair. I had to go to a secondhand
shop to get Gilbert a pair so he could get back to school. I've got
central heating but I can't afford to turn it on. I am still in debt
paying for last Christmas. I am still paying for the kids' clothes.
Sometimes you have to borrow to eat. Once I lent from a man and
put down my child benefit book, I worked out that he took £450 to
lend me £220 for Christmas. It was robbery but I had no other
option. I don't have much time for politics, I've got my kids to look
after. But I do think everyone should be equal. I hope my children
have a better future. I would not part with my kids or with my
husband. But if I had my time again I would not have so many kids.
I don't like the poverty, I don't like the kids coming home and
asking for something and I can't give it to them.

What kind of equality?

Why should Christians – and others – be committed to equality and
what kind of equality are we talking about? The two questions, according to Amartya Sen are 'distinct but thoroughly interdependent'. 'We
cannot' he continues, 'begin to defend or criticize equality without

knowing what on earth we are talking about, i.e. equality of what features [e.g. incomes, wealth, opportunities, achievements, freedoms, rights]. We cannot possibly answer the first question without addressing the second.'[20] The first question is perhaps in some ways easier to answer than the first. As I will argue later in this book, there is a long and close relationship between Christianity and the idea of equality which has given the modern notion of equality its distinctive shape, and suggests a connection between Christian commitment and commitment to equality, or at least that any serious Christian social thinking must give major weight to the value of equality.

Meanwhile it is necessary to note the complexity of the concept of equality, and the fact that it is frequently used with quite extraordinary looseness and lack of clarity. Impatient people often believe that concepts as vague and pluriform as this are best replaced by their component parts, or even that there should be a kind of moratorium on their use because they have become little more than vacuous, if soul-stirring, slogans or battle-cries. Such would, I believe, be a mistaken policy. The idea of equality is complex and I have chosen advisedly to speak of the *meanings* rather than the meaning of equality. But there is, I would argue, a coherence in the idea of equality; the meanings and applications cluster around a common core, which is a view of people in society, admittedly of great generality but still exclusive of a variety of alternative views.

At the heart of the notion of equality lies the conviction that each person is of infinite, and hence equal, worth and should be treated as such. This means that being human is far more important than differences of colour, gender, class, creed, wealth, intelligence, nationality and so forth. This conviction should colour our attitudes and relationships and should shape social structures, which are networks of relationship and distribution. We recognize other people's equal worth by our attitude towards them, our treatment of them, our relationships with them and our regard for them, and also, rather more indirectly, but very significantly, in the way a society and its distribution of resources of all sorts are organized. To affirm human equality is both to say something important about what human beings are, and also how relationships and social institutions should be arranged, and how we should behave to one another.[21]

Human beings are entitled to be treated with respect because they are of equal worth, independently of their ability, contribution, success, work or desert. That is the bottom line, the essential affirmation if we are to have an adequate justification and motive for generous and respectful treatment of people with severe disabilities, of the senile, and of the unemployable.[22] But it is difficult to see how this core affirmation can be justified without theological reference. And there is huge disagreement about how best this equality of worth may be translated into policy and practice.

What I have said about equality so far is still rather general and inevitably somewhat vague. But even before discussion of the grounding and justification of equality, and of varieties and dimensions of equality, this general statement is not without force. It excludes an orientation towards *in*equality as a matter of principle. Although some inequalities may be justifiable or even necessary, they still require explanation as deviations from the norm. Equality as such is incompatible with racism, anti-Semitism, sexism, apartheid and other systems that celebrate and enforce human inequality. A general affirmation of equality stipulates in very broad terms the kind of goals for which society should strive, the general direction that social policy should take.

But such a general affirmation is far too broad and imprecise to give direct guidance for policymaking, or for the taking of political decisions, or indeed for individual behaviour, such as my relation with Munuswamy. Before any question of application can be dealt with, the concept of equality has to be unpacked, the complex of meanings that the term carries explored, and its inner tensions and contradictions faced up to. Furthermore, since all societies have multiple goals, the priorities among different kinds of equality need to be examined. Sometimes quite incompatible goals are held together; priorities between goals vary from time to time. Some social goals may be a part, even an indispensable part, of a more comprehensive social ideal.

Consider, for instance, the relation of equality and justice. Justice and equality are not two labels for the same moral reality, although doing justice seems to involve a predisposition to equal regard for people's interests and a tendency towards equal distribution.[23] In family life the children's complaint that something – say the allocation of pocket money – is not fair, meaning by that equal, is a call for justice, tending to confirm Rawls's egalitarian instincts as he develops his theory of justice as fairness. Any deviation from equal pocket money requires a justification. The little girl who receives less than her older brother may well be satisfied when told that she will receive the same pocket money when she is as old as her brother. But she is unlikely to be convinced by the suggestion that boys *deserve* more because they are boys, or that boys *need* more money than girls. That children of the same age in the family should receive the same pocket money is accepted as fair because it does not rest on an alleged inequality between boys and girls entitling boys to receive more; rather, equality here means equal treatment to children of the same age, who are in broadly similar situations as to needs and wants. The case is more complicated in a family in which one child has severe learning or physical difficulties. Differences of treatment in such a case can be justified by the differences in need. The least well off have special claims which ought to be met so that a relative equality may be established between the various members of the family – or of the society, for that matter.[24] Fair, just and equal treatment does not necessarily mean *identical* treatment, but differences need to be justified in a way that does not suggest some inherent inequality between the parties. Fair and equal treatment is the essence of happy family life. A sensible parent tries to love the children equally, and not show favouritism or partiality in the distribution of goods and resources. Not only in families, but in societies, justice based upon a recognition of human equality is fundamental to social harmony.

As we shall see later, the divine justice goes beyond fairness in a radically egalitarian direction.[25] So in Jesus' parable, those who have laboured throughout the heat of the day receive the same pay, the same 'outcome', as those who were called into the vineyard at the last minute – one reminder among many that Christians should take with profound seriousness the basic equality of human beings in their needs if not in their deserts.

And what of the relation between equality and freedom? It is widely claimed today by thinkers such as F. A. Hayek, R. Dahrendorf and R. Nozick that it is impossible to proceed beyond equality before the law and equal citizenship (what used to be called 'one man one vote') without sacrificing liberty. Efforts to move towards equality in distribution, or equality of outcomes would entail a massive loss of freedom. 'In an open and free society', writes P. T. Bauer, 'political action which deliberately aimed to minimise, or even remove, economic differences ... would entail such extensive coercion that the society would cease to be open and free'.[26] George Orwell's *Animal Farm* and Hayek's *The Road to Serfdom*, in their very different ways, hammered home the point – which no one in their senses would wish to dispute – that a certain absolutist and fanatical search for an imposed equality of condition leads to the forfeiture of liberty. What Hayek and Orwell and their like do not demonstrate is that well-thought-through moves towards greater equality necessarily lead to such drastic erosion of freedom as they suggest. And it is interesting that the very people who press this kind of argument also believe that certain kinds of equality – equality before the law and equal citizenship, for example – are prerequisites of a free society. And, as John Plamenatz pointed out, those who suggest that a reduction in inequality is only possible if freedom is diminished rarely, if ever, argue that inequalities must be *increased* so that liberty may flourish and abound. They seem to acknowledge by implication that equality is desirable unless the cost is too great.[27]

Some ways of pursuing equality may indeed diminish freedom, but in itself equality is a condition of freedom. This is now all but universally acknowledged at the political level: a free society is a democracy in which each person has an equal influence in the election of representatives to run the society. That does not mean, of course, that everyone has an equal share of political power – far from it. But it does involve a constraint on the permanent concentration of political power in the hands of a small group, class or party, a limit to inequality of power. In a democracy the ultimate locale of power is the people, each and every citizen; those who exercise power do so as stewards, responsible to the people. Great concentrations of economic power likewise require to be curbed and inequalities reduced if freedom is to be more generally distributed. As R. H. Tawney argued,

> a large measure of equality, so far from being inimical to liberty is essential to it ... Liberty is, in fact, equality in action, in the sense, not that all men [*sic*] perform identical functions or wield the same degree of power, but that all men are equally protected against the abuse of power, and equally entitled to insist that power should be used, not for personal ends, but for the general advantage.[28]

The judicious pursuit of a greater degree of equality, that is, encourages freedom, diversity and individuality. Surely egalitarian policies pursued with an eye to the central importance of liberty extend freedom by offering more options and choices to more people than before at the expense of some reduction in the range of choice for the more privileged. It is only the draconian pursuit of sameness of condition to the exclusion of all regard for other social values which involves the sacrifice of liberty to equality of a sort. The case that equality necessarily involves an increase of freedom and capability has been powerfully argued in recent times by Amartya Sen.[29]

So far I have been using the term 'equality', and the concepts of freedom and justice for that matter, in a rather general and undifferentiated way. In a sense, social goals and basic values of this sort inevitably lack some precision, for they indicate a general direction in which society might move rather than a precise description of the destination and a detailed map of the path that must be followed to get there, with every bend, hazard and milestone clearly marked. But they are important partly because of what they exclude. No one believes that all roads lead to equality, or freedom, or justice. On the other hand, before one begins to move towards equality or another general goal it is helpful and important both to clarify the goal and to work out which is the most appropriate way of moving in that direction.

As soon as we become concerned with application we have to begin to be more specific. For equality means many things. There is diversity and indeed contradiction in the way the word is used. Some understandings of equality are incompatible with others. We need a 'grammar' or 'anatomy' of equality if it is to be useful as more than a signpost to utopia. Application demands clarification. A complex value with many facets and shades of meaning has to generate and justify maxims on which policy may be based; and in the process equality has to accommodate itself to the complexities and ambiguities of life and sort out in some fashion its own internal tensions. Equality, as Douglas Rae shows in his careful exploration of the 'grammar of equality', resolves itself into a whole range of distinct notions. But they *are* related to one another – hence the need for a grammar in which the relationships are spelled out.[30]

Rae's grammar of equality is arranged around five questions or headings: the subject of equality, equality of what, equality of opportunity, the value of equality, absolute and relative equality.

The subject of equality

First, what is the subject of equality? Are egalitarians concerned primarily, or even exclusively, with each person being individually
equal to each other person? This is the kind of equality expressed in
a principle such as 'one person, one vote' – although here children
below voting age as well as some other categories of people in most
democracies are excluded. It is really the equality of adult citizens who
do not have a recognized impediment which debars them from voting.
Often this kind of equality assumes a kind of extreme individualism;
people are understood as beings that have unconditional ownership of
themselves; they are not defined in terms of relationships.[31] Or should
equality concentrate primarily on the relations between classes or
groups of people, for instance, racial equality? It is, of course, quite
possible to advocate that no one should be discriminated against
or treated unequally on account of race without advocating that all
blacks are equal to one another. And, at least in theory, it is possible to
advocate equality between classes, or a classless society, without also
supporting equality between the genders. But it would be ridiculous to
suggest that socially-constructed distinctions such as class and race are
irrelevant to the equal treatment of individuals, or that the egalitarian's
questioning of a particular form of social structure is not based on an
assumption that people are entitled to equality of treatment. I will turn
to the question of equality and difference shortly. Meanwhile, if we
understand human beings as 'by nature political animals' (Aristotle),
beings who cannot be understood except in terms of their relationships,
we need a relational understanding of equality.[32]

Equality of what

Rae's second question has to do with the *kinds of things* that are to be
allocated equally, with equality of what. One may, he writes, distinguish four spheres or domains for possible equality: the political, the
legal, the social, and the economic. Almost everyone is agreed on the
desirability of a kind of formal political equality among citizens. In a
democracy, the power and influence represented by the vote, but not
political power as such, belongs equally to every citizen. This is, of
course, a comparatively recent achievement in most democracies. In

Britain, the first half of the twentieth century saw the gradual extension of the franchise to women on the same basis as men, and the removal of double voting for university graduates and businessmen. In the United States it was a long struggle to get for blacks in many of the southern states the effective right to exercise their votes. Similarly, there is almost universal agreement in theory that there ought to be equality before the law, but in practice this principle is not always uniformly applied. The principle asserts that the law should be blind to the status of the accused, and the verdict and the sentence should relate solely to the gravity of the offence. Practice sometimes differs; and there is a strong argument that sentencing in particular should be sensitive to the particularities of the situation and the individual circumstances of the offender if the judicial process is to be morally and socially constructive. Economic equality is the subject of far more vigorous debate. 'Market liberals' like Milton Friedman and F. A. Hayek resist the application of equality beyond the political and legal domains, and Ralf Dahrendorf argues that in these areas equality may be the foundation of liberty, but if pressed into economic relations it becomes corrosive of freedom.[33] But if there is agreement that the vote and basic civil rights should be equally distributed, why stop there? Is it not true that gross social and economic inequalities subvert equality of citizenship, and indeed equality before the law? It is, for example, far easier for the wealthy than for the poor to defend their interests in court, and there is a strong correlation between economic and political power. 'Political power', as H. J. Laski put it, 'is bound to be the handmaid of economic power.'[34]

If we press the question of equality of what a little further, we find a confusing variety of answers today. For Amartya Sen, the objective is a high degree of capability, 'basic capability equality'; for G. A. Cohen, equal access to advantage; for Ronald Dworkin, equality of resources and treatment as equals; for John Rawls equal liberty and a greater equality in what he calls 'primary goods'. One could go on ... But all are suggested ways of moving from an axiomatic affirmation of human equality to practical policies, ways of implementing equality.

Equality of opportunity

Rae's third area is equality of opportunity. Here he argues that two rather different things are often confused: equal opportunity as equal possibility of achieving the goal, and equality of opportunity as demanding equal means for the achievement of the goal. Equality of opportunity, usually understood in the second sense, is probably the sense of equality which commands the widest support and is the only kind of equality, apart from equality of citizenship rights and equality before the law, which is supported by neo-conservative thinkers. The simplest form of equality of opportunity demands that everyone starts the race from the same place and, as far as possible, with the same resources. This initial equalizing of resources may well involve some kind of handicapping to compensate for inequalities at the starting gate. This is close to what Amartya Sen advocates as 'basic capability equality': steps should be taken to ensure that individuals and groups are equipped with equal capability and resources for achieving their goals.[35] But the race thereafter pays little attention to considerations of equality of distribution, or further continuing arrangements to compensate for disadvantages which individuals or groups may suffer.

Indeed, equality of opportunity as commonly understood accepts the 'race' as something given and immutable; society is inevitably competitive, with the glittering prizes going to winners, while losers go to the wall. Individualism is presupposed; solidarity and fellowship are at a discount; and the best that people can hope for is that they can pull themselves up by their own bootstraps in a society which makes no further concessions to human equality. This is the theory of meritocracy, of talent rising to the top. But in the 'real world' the powerful and the wealthy always have significant advantages at the starting gate and throughout the race as well. And among the 'glittering prizes' are scarce 'positional goods' that cannot be distributed equally. It is, for instance, impossible for everyone to have a ranch-style home with a panoramic view of the Grand Canyon and no neighbours within sight. Nor is it possible for everyone to be a managing director of a company, or President of the United States. But if equality at the start is just, there is surely a case for a degree of equality at the finish, for a wide and fair distribution of prizes, and indeed for the existence of consolation prizes for the unsuccessful. For, as Robert M. Veatch points out, both the Judaeo-Christian tradition and secular thinkers such as Rawls are inclined to see the talents and abilities of individuals as common assets, which should be used unselfishly and for the advantage of the least well off and the benefit of the community as a whole. Even the most talented of individuals do not 'deserve' their success or the advantages of endowment or upbringing which make that success possible.[36]

The value of equality

Fourthly, under the heading of the value of equality, Rae distinguishes 'person-regarding' and 'lot-regarding' equality. This is similar to Plato's distinction between numerical and proportional equality.[37] Numerical equality involves giving identical treatment to everyone; proportional equality 'assigns more to the greater and less to the lesser, adapting its gifts to the real character of either ... It deals proportionately with either party, ever awarding a greater share to those of greater worth.' Rae cites Tawney as advocating person-regarding (or proportional) equality:

> Equality of provision is not identity of provision. It is to be achieved, not by treating different needs in the same way, but by devoting equal care to ensuring that they are met in the different ways most appropriate to them, as is done by a doctor who prescribes different regimens for different constitutions, or a teacher who develops different types of intelligence by different curricula. The more anxiously ... a society endeavours to secure equality of consideration for all its members, the greater will be the differentiation which, when once their common human needs have been met, it accords with the special needs of different groups and individuals among them.[38]

Another example of proportionate equality is offered by Gregory Vlastos: the New York police would not provide equal security by spending an equal sum on the protection of each citizen, or the policing of each block. The man who has received a death threat from the Mafia requires several hundred times more to be spent on his protection than on the protection of the average citizen if he is to have equal security.[39] This is also the justification of positive action and what is called the 'preferential option for the poor'. These are ways of healing inequalities, of restoring an equal balance.

Absolute and relative equality

Rae's fifth and final distinction is between absolute and relative equality. Absolute equality in the distribution of resources is almost inconceivable, although an absolute equality in the more subtle matters of the equal worth of human beings, equal respect for people, and equal regard for people's interests is more possible to envisage. In general, absolute equality belongs in the realm of social ideals and absolute measures; relative equality has more direct 'cash-value' for policy-making. But an understanding of absolute equality gives a criterion which helps us to judge between various relative equalities. Yet absolute equality is not the *only* criterion which requires to be brought into play. We need to bring in other values if we are to explain and justify why a 40:60 allocation between me and my friend is to be preferred to a 50:50 allocation, and why the pursuit of equality should involve more levelling up than levelling down if it is to be morally acceptable.

The simple, formal concept of equality is significant as a social ideal. It indicates a general direction for social reform; it suggests a value which should find expression in a just and decent society; it excludes a positive orientation towards inequality as a social ideal. Before equality can be put to work in policy it is helpful to have its anatomy or grammar laid out for us, as has been done so helpfully by Douglas Rae. But further steps are necessary if equality is to be related to 'life's buzzing complexity', if equality is 'to be made flesh' – two phrases that Rae uses.[40] We need to specify what senses of equality are the more important and why. It is also important to recognize that linking the various sense of equality together are assumptions about human beings and their worth which need to be made explicit, explored and justified. And behind that there is the key question: what is the ground for affirming that equality, in any of its senses or in all, is good, desirable and proper?

Equality and difference

'Human diversity', writes Amartya Sen, 'is no secondary complication
to be ignored , or to be introduced "later on"; it is a fundamental aspect
of our interest in equality.'[41] Modern societies are, almost without
exception, pluralistic, with a rich diversity of religious, cultural and
ethnic groups with varying values, beliefs and commitments, living
together in the one civil society. Although this pluralism is in many
ways an enrichment of the society, it also brings with it tensions and
problems of rivalry, competition and conflict between the various
groups, which are sometimes difficult to handle and resolve. These
social divisions relate in a complex way to class divisions of the traditional sort. The common response to the kind of disparities of wealth,
income and power which are expressed in, and reinforced by, the class
system was in terms of policies seeking a greater equality, mainly
through measures of redistribution.

There is now a vigorous critique emerging mainly from feminist thinkers of the adequacy of egalitarian approaches concentrating
on economic inequalities and relying mainly on redistribution.
Traditional approaches to equality are held to involve ironing out
of differences, a levelling process which is aimed at removing what is
distinctive and particular in favour of a uniform understanding of
human beings and their groups. Traditionally the equality that is
sought involves equal treatment for everyone because they are the
same – except possibly that they have distinct needs depending on their
personal endowments, skills and desert. What is to be recognized and
responded to is the sameness of people.

But this notion of what might be called 'simple equality' tending
towards uniformity and sameness, whether it is imposed by government or freely chosen, is something that many people are increasingly
uneasy with. For a variety of reasons 'the resonance of the ideal of
equality as a shared condition of life is not what it once was'.[42] Instead,
the argument runs, people, and groups, want to be respected and
recognized for what they are, in their difference and distinctiveness.
They do not want to conform to some universal image of 'the US citizen', or the rational human being. They do not wish to set aside as of no
importance their religious beliefs, their personal and family history,
their 'embeddedness' in a particular time, and place, and culture and

community shaped by a particular story. There may be a time and a place for Shylock to assert his common humanity; but there is also a need for Shylock to affirm his Jewishness, where he belongs, his own particular and distinctive heritage and identity. And Shylock is surely entitled in a decent society to have this heritage, this distinctiveness, recognized, valued and affirmed:

> I am a Jew. Hath not a Jew eyes? Hath not a Jew hands, organs, dimensions, senses, affections, passions; fed with the same food, hurt with the same weapons, subject to the same diseases, healed by the same means, warmed and cooled by the same summer and winter as a Christian is? If you prick us, do we not bleed? If you tickle us, do we not laugh? If you poison us, do we not die? And if you wrong us, shall we not revenge?[43]

The argument that it is recognition and difference rather than equality that is at issue is not adequately responded to by the assertion by people like Tawney that the recognition of equal worth does not necessarily lead to identical treatment. This is varying treatment in accordance with need, rather than the recognition of difference as a positive thing. Nor is it enough to assert the value of affirmative action for disadvantaged or needy groups. Few people would wish to reject the usefulness of affirmative action. But it is sometimes seen as a way of assimilating the disadvantaged group into the broader society and eroding or removing what makes them different, particularly the things that give them a distinctive identity. Some differences should surely be respected and valued in a decent society. But other differences need to be disallowed, discouraged, or even suppressed – for instance, anti-Semitism, racism, or child abuse. But despite such clear (and extreme) examples, it is not always easy to distinguish what should be recognized, valued and celebrated and what should be discountenanced or remedied.

The whole discussion of difference versus equality suggests that modern thought on equality has perhaps been over-concerned with economic inequality and how it may be remedied through redistribution – important as this issue is. Other kinds of equality have received rather less attention, and there has been little discussion until recently of the need for differential treatment of people who are different. Elizabeth Wolgast, for instance, suggests that

arguing for women's rights under the banner of equality encourages
women to identify their interests with those of men. What is good
for men, this reasoning requires, must be good for women too … For
women to identify themselves as women – therefore different from
men – changes the logical basis of the reasoning … At bottom of my
argument is the conviction that justice requires men and women to
be treated differently, not in all areas but in some important ones.[44]

She then quotes Mary Midgely's suggestion that trying to right with
the notions of freedom and equality the injustices that women bear 'is
like trying to dig a garden with brush and comb. The tools are totally
unsuitable.'[45]

But why is recognition of difference so important? Charles Taylor
offers an answer:

Nonrecognition or misrecognition … can be a form of oppression,
imprisoning someone in a false, distorted, reduced mode of being.
Beyond simple lack of respect, it can inflict a grievous wound,
saddling people with crippling self-hatred. Due recognition is not
just a courtesy but a vital human need.[46]

Therefore we need what Taylor calls 'the politics of equal dignity'.[47]
The opposition of equality and recognition of difference is ultimately a
false antithesis. We all need to be recognized and our worth affirmed,
and one way of doing this is through egalitarian redistributive
measures. But there is more to recognition than that. There are,
according to Axel Honneth, 'three patterns of recognition – love, rights
and solidarity'.[48] And these, interestingly enough, are also the pillars of
equality.

Nancy Fraser's judgment that both recognition and redistribution
are required is probably a sensible conclusion, provided clear efforts are
made to distinguish needs relating to poverty, health and the like,
which call out for remedy, from differences of culture, gender, religion
and so forth which require recognition and respect. 'Equality or
difference', she writes, 'is a false antithesis … Neither redistribution
alone nor recognition alone can suffice for remedying injustice in
today's world.'[49] We have to have a more complex understanding of
equality, perhaps along the lines suggested by Michael Walzer in his
discussion of 'complex equality',[50] if equality and difference are to

co-exist in harmony. The key issue, to my mind, is this: both social equality and the recognition of difference are about the worth of human beings, and how this equal worth may be implemented. They are complementary rather than opposed to one another. The discussion of recognition and difference has indeed enriched the understanding of what we mean by equality, why it is important, and how we can move towards equality.

The grounds of equality

What is the basis of equality? One might argue, with Isaiah Berlin and others, that the question itself is misconceived; equality is a moral axiom that neither requires nor is capable of defence or justification. Like other human ends, we use it to justify and support certain actions and policies, and we derive second-order moral principles from it; it is the start, not the conclusion of a chain of moral reasoning.[51] This might be a satisfactory resting place if all rational beings were agreed that equality is a good thing, but they clearly are not. Equality has not attracted the same universal approbation as justice or goodness; plenty of rational, if perhaps misguided, people believe equality in many of its senses to be actually *undesirable*. We cannot accept that equality is a moral axiom without a basis. It in fact rests upon more basic convictions about human beings and human society and the reality in which we live. We have to enquire as to the basis of equality.

There is, first of all, the rather imprecise suggestion that people are equal, despite all sorts of empirical inequalities, simply by virtue of being people. This claim is that there is a profound equality among people in the light of which empirically observable differences are superficial and unimportant:

> The rank is but the guinea's stamp,
> The Man's the gowd for a' that

Robert Burns put it.

This conviction that all human beings are equal on the grounds of their common humanity, and the consequence that human equality is of far greater significance than socially imposed distinctions and inequalities was described by Harry Johnson, no advocate of equality, as 'naïve and basically infantile anthropomorphism' arising out of the fact that physically people are more or less alike. Belief in equality erected on such shaky empirical foundations, he argued, is emotional rather than rational, and has disturbing and unhelpful effects when it influences social and economic policy because it disregards, like all moral approaches 'a sophisticated understanding of modern society's economic organization'.[52]

And yet, for many people equality remains a compelling dimension of their moral world-view, and they believe it has a more secure grounding than Johnson believes. Certainly Kierkegaard seems to suggest that human beings are equal by virtue of their common humanity, and that the recognition of this imposes an obligation to treat human beings in a humane way. With a play on Danish words he asks: 'What is humaneness [*Menneskelighet*]? It is human equality [*Menneske-lighet*]. Inequality is inhumaneness.'[53]

Others argue that human equality is rooted in some intrinsic quality or qualities that human beings all share. Thomas Hobbes, for instance, argued that the differences in physical strength between one person and another were such that it was still possible for the weakest person to kill the strongest. This relative equality of strength meant that each person was equally threatened by others, equally insecure, equally vulnerable. It follows for Hobbes that people have an equal need for security, for which they are willing to give up their equality to a sovereign who will protect them and rule over them. Coons and Brennan, in an important recent book, regard equality as 'some characteristic believed to link the individual self to others', and universal among human beings. This 'characteristic' turns out to be the rational capacity to apprehend and conform to an objective moral order; human equality is 'the unique relation that results from people's sharing the sameness of *capacity* for moral self-perfection'.[54] But *do* people in fact have equal capacity for moral behaviour? I think not. Stephen Lukes suggests that 'certain basic human needs and capacities' provide the basis for equality of respect, but he does not spell out as precisely as one might wish what these needs and capacities might be, and why they provide a grounding for equality of respect.[55] One suspects that this is hardly a more precise way of speaking of the ground of equality than talk of 'common humanity'.

That humans are rational beings might seem a good way both of indicating that humans are equal to one another, and excluding animals from the calculation. But are humans in fact *equally* rational? And what about clever animals, compared with human beings of severely limited intelligence? Plato and Aristotle in fact taught that *differences* in rationality and intelligence justified human inequality, explaining why some people should rule and others obey, why some people are natural slaves and others by nature free. H. J. Eysenck and Arthur Jensen related differences in IQ to racial differences, and were vigorously attacked for supporting racism. Whatever the rights and wrongs of this controversy Eysenck and Jensen were arguing that, empirically considered, human beings were not equal. 'Biology', wrote Eysenck, 'sets an absolute barrier to egalitarianism.'[56] Intelligence is not equally distributed, and any theory of equality which rests on the belief that people are equally rational or equally intelligent is built on foundations which can easily be destroyed. But *is* the basis of equality empirical? Surely we must find grounds for affirming the equality of people and of groups whose empirically observable qualities and characteristics are very different indeed.

Others would argue that although equality is not grounded in any empirical quality of people it arises from the transcendental quality of being a free and rational will (Kant). Or that people are in principle moral beings, capable of distinguishing good from evil and making choices. For John Rawls, 'moral personality', the capacity to recognize justice and act upon it, is the quality in human beings which entitles them to equal treatment. He affirms that all human beings are equally moral personalities. But there is, of course, a problem here: are young children, or mental or moral defectives who do not possess a 'moral personality' as Rawls defines it, entitled to equal – that is, fair or just – treatment? Rawls suggests that such people are *potentially* moral personalities, which would appear to be true in some cases, but not in all.[57] It seems more than a little difficult to posit any quality, capacity or need which all human beings share which is adequate to provide a basis for the conviction that human beings are equal and are entitled to equal treatment. Neither observation nor introspection provides adequate ground for a belief in human equality.

If there is nothing intrinsic or observable in human beings which provides a secure ground for the belief in human equality, is it possible that the belief in equality is derived from fundamental religious convictions, and in particular that God ascribes infinite worth to human beings and deals with people in an equal way, so that all inequalities melt before him, and should not be reinstated among the faithful? R. H. Tawney certainly held such a view. For him the ultimate ground for human equality, which is sometimes concealed and sometimes secularized so that all explicit theological reference is removed, goes something like this: God affirms the infinite worth of each person, independently of the individual's qualities and achievements, and God wills and establishes a fellowship which expresses and bears witness to God's equal love for all. Locating equality in the frame of theology gives the concept a distinctive shape and grounding, which I will explore more fully later in this book. Meanwhile, I cannot put the basic conviction better than in G. K. Chesterton's vivid image: people are equal in the same way pennies are equal. Some are bright, others are dull; some are worn smooth, others are sharp and fresh. But all are equal in value for each penny bears the image of the sovereign, each person bears the image of the King of Kings.

2

Convictions, Theories and Theologies

This chapter is concerned with the continuing importance of the religious roots of contemporary social values, such as equality. These roots are not simply of historical interest and importance. They claim, first of all, to provide a grounding for morality in the cosmic or divine order. There are, of course, huge problems at this point in a society in which there is a diversity of religious commitments, and many people sit easy to all religious traditions. But, as I hope to show shortly, there are also problems in suggesting that key social values are grounded in nothing more than the fact that many people in a particular society accept them, in some kind of moral consensus. Most people want to know that their fundamental values are in some sense *true*, not simply based on a show of hands. Ronald Dworkin suggests that such fundamental values 'must be principles we accept because they seem right rather than because they have been captured in some conventional practice. Otherwise political theory will be only a mirror, uselessly reflecting a community's consensus and division back upon itself.'[1] For all the problems of allowing religion a voice in the public forum in a pluralistic modern society, religion does characteristically claim to offer a way of relating the values and the principles of the social order to an objective moral order. And something of this sort is surely necessary if we are to be able to stand at the gates of Auschwitz, or in Rwanda, or in Pol Pot's Kampuchea and say in a totally unqualified way: 'What happened here was radically evil.'

Religion also played, and in many contexts continues to play, a major role in shaping values such as equality, and giving them specific content. It can, I think, be shown that when the connection with the roots is cut, gradually over time the content tends to change. A value such as equality may survive in different form in a radically secular society from that which it possesses within a specific religious tradition.

And finally, religion has a continuing significant role in sustaining fundamental assumptions about morality. The religious formation of new generations includes a major moral dimension. A significant element of any religious tradition that is passed on from generation to generation and which sees itself as having a responsibility for the religious formation of children is the critical appropriation of a specific moral stance. Once again, of course, there are major problems today concerning the transmission and appropriation of a distinctive religious and moral tradition in a plural society. Believers are uncomfortably aware of the difficulty in the contemporary situation of continuing a process of passing on a tradition which was for long almost a matter of routine. But a society requires some process of moral formation, and it is not altogether easy to see how this might be entirely secular.

Traditions of faith and of conviction characteristically crystallize and find expression in theories and in theologies. Theories, that is, can clarify Munuswamy's situation. Some theories – but fewer today than in the past – address the practical problem which we all share of how to respond effectively to him. Modern social theory is on the whole far better at laying out areas of disagreement and clarifying obscurities than in reaching practical conclusions which commend themselves to many people. Theories can also obscure what is actually going on, disguising the real situation. Sometimes theories are consciously manipulated for this purpose; more commonly it is an unconscious process. And theories can be a way of taking flight from the real world and its problems into a rarified forum where such matters as Munuswamy's condition never get onto the agenda. Or some theories give a kind of blanket explanation of the situation which is also its justification, suggesting that that is why Munuswamy is as he is, and there is nothing we can or should do about it.

Theology is, of course, a kind of theory, working around – not just within – a certain tradition of faith. The boundaries between theology and secular theory are not always clear, and even when they appear to be well demarcated, the frontiers are porous. Like some more secular theories, theology can, and sometimes does, light up what is really happening, and issue an insistent call to action. Indeed, much theology is at its heart reflection on action and on active commitment to and solidarity with Munuswamy and his like, the kind of reflection that can reinforce and refine social practice. But much theology, of course, justifies oppression and explains Munuswamy's condition as part of a God-ordained structure of things, most probably part of 'the order of creation'. Even more commonly, theology simply forgets Munuswamy and his kind in order to focus on quite other matters of concern, which are usually narrowly academic or ecclesiastical.

The medieval convergence

In the medieval university, theory, meaning at that time philosophy, and theology, were distinct yet related disciplines, constantly engaged in debate with one another, with common themes weaving in and out of the two disciplines. At times there was real tension between theology and philosophy, especially when philosophy borrowed from classical thought notions about human nature, for instance, which were believed by the theologians to be incompatible with the Christian tradition. Attempts from time to time to suggest that there were two distinct truths, and that it did not matter if theology and philosophy taught contradictory things because these were true only in the respective sphere of one or the other, never found approval for long. Differences had to be resolved either by the rejection of one possibility and the affirmation of the other, or by some form of synthesis.

Natural law was a notable instance of the process of gradual synthesis. The principles of the natural law are believed to be accessible to every rational being, so that it becomes a way of structuring the discussion of a common morality. Most of the roots of natural law thinking are in classical philosophy, although there are some references to natural law in the New Testament, and it has featured in Christian thought from very early times. Philosophy and theology worked together in the Middle Ages to refine the natural law principles of common morality. Medieval schoolmen, particularly Thomas Aquinas, placed natural law in a Christian theological framework which in interesting and important respects modified the way natural law was understood. In particular, the understanding of human nature had now to accommodate the Christian conviction that human beings were fallen, sinful, and that this affected even their reason, which was no longer to be regarded as giving direct and unambiguous access to moral truth and the maxims of the natural law. Sin and selfishness were understood as liable to distort even the operations of the reason.

From Stoic roots natural law thinking brought an understanding of human equality which in some ways was easily compatible with Christian views, but in other respects was sharply divergent. Aristotle's teaching that some people were by nature slaves, whose good was to be used by others as tools for their purposes, for instance, did not fit easily with Christian understandings. Then in the great scholastic debate after the conquest of the Americas as to whether the native Americans were fully human or could be despoiled, enslaved and treated as a kind of inferior subspecies, Aristotle's arguments were resurrected and deployed to suggest the essential sub-humanity of the Indians. The resolution of that debate in favour of the equal humanity of the Indians was an instance of the convergence of theory and theology in the Middle Ages. But divergence also took place.

Secularization of social thought

In the sixteenth and seventeenth centuries a divergence between theology and social philosophy in particular started which still goes on today. The religious fragmentation of Europe caused by the Reformation and the bloody wars of religion that followed raised a huge problem for people of conscience and integrity in Europe. Religion and theology were seen, understandably, as divisive and a source of bitterness, violence and harm to all sorts of people, including the 'Munuswamys' of the time. An initial response, to follow the principles of *cuius regio eius religio,* the ruler's religion is the religion of the people, was intended to separate the contending parties and ideological systems from one another within political boundaries by ensuring that the rulers and people of each state shared a religion, and were discouraged from attempting to impose their faith elsewhere. But this never produced more than a fragile and temporary cessation of conflict.

A more serious and profound response to the fragmentation of Europe and the religious conflicts of the seventeenth century was to search once more for a non-religious grounding for morals, a secular morality, an ethics detached from theological roots. An ethics independent of religion or appealing from the diverse and bitterly conflicting theologies to a very broad and generalized notion of transcendence seemed the only way to protect Europe against moral fragmentation and continuing bitter religious division. The various confessional theologies, for their part, were gradually expected more and more to cease making universal claims and statements. Little by little, religion and theology were expected to withdraw from the general public forum and confine themselves to the various faith communities, and to domestic and family life rather than the public sphere. I am, of course, speaking of a gradual and never completed process. There was no sudden and final parting of the ways between theory and theology, no final divorce; they just gradually drew further apart. And even the most secular of social theories in the modern world, it may be argued, are still haunted by theological ghosts. But the slow separation had major effects on both theology and social theory, each of which carries to this day the wounds of the seventeenth century.

A major early figure in the project to develop a morality independent of specific religious roots, detached from a theological framework, was Hugo Grotius (1583–1645). Public morality, argued Grotius, himself a Christian believer and no mean theologian, should proceed *etsi Deus non daretur*, as if God did not exist. This is not atheism, or even what has more recently been called 'methodological atheism'. It is rather the simple recognition that a common morality is necessary for people to flourish together in community, and this cannot any longer rest on the foundation of Christian theology because of the bitter religious fragmentation of Europe. The religious convictions of individuals and groups could and should now be separated from the standards and values of public morality. Religion because of its divisive and contentious character should be removed from the sphere of social ethics, particularly that dealing with international relations, the so-called *ius gentium*, or law of nations. Even if *cuius regio eius religio* is enforced and becomes effective, there must be guidelines and standards for the relations between such states. In effect Grotius taught that the law of nature was the law of nations, and vice versa. Natural law also bound people as people, not as Lutherans, or Calvinists, or Catholics, and did not depend on the Pope or other religious authorities for its promulgation and enforcement. But natural law continued, according to Grotius, to rest on the existence of an objective cosmic moral order.

This natural law was now detached from the specific Christian theological framework within which it had been located throughout the

Middle Ages. This linkage to theology had involved for centuries an ongoing dialogue between the fundamentals of Christian belief and the morality of natural law, initially largely derived from classical philosophy, so that the natural law taught up to the seventeenth century was deeply penetrated by distinctively Christian notions of, for example, human nature. Aquinas and the other scholastic theologians had done far more than cobble together ideas of natural law borrowed from classical philosophy and Christian doctrine. Fundamentals of their account of natural law had been reshaped by Christian convictions.

The new morality initially represented by such as Grotius was in some important ways more simple, less complex and ambiguous than earlier understandings of natural law and social morality. It depended on a relatively unnuanced account of human nature. The Christian emphasis of such as Pascal on both the *grandeur* and the *misère* of the human condition, the stress that human beings are both sinners and a little lower than the angels, that in reality we are constantly pulled in opposite directions, tended now to be replaced by a more uniform understanding of human beings as rational self-interested individuals. Because categories central to the Christian tradition such as sin, guilt and forgiveness no longer featured prominently, the new morality was not very good at dealing with moral ambiguities, with situations where there is no available choice between good, and bad, or where one has to act without moral certainty. The new secular morality had difficulty in understanding Paul's profound dilemma, which is close to the heart of Christian morality:

> I can will what is right, but I cannot do it. For I do not do the good I want, but the evil I do not want is what I do. Now if I do what I do not want, it is no longer I that do it, but sin that dwells within me. So I find it to be a law that when I want to do what is good, evil lies close at hand. For I delight in the law of God in my inmost self, but I see in my members another law at war with the law of my mind, making me captive to the law of sin that dwells in my members. Wretched man that I am! Who will rescue me from this body of death? Thanks be to God through Jesus Christ our Lord![2]

An example from the tradition of just war thinking may illustrate my point. In the Middle Ages, just war thinking was located squarely in a framework of Christian theological assumptions, central among which was the conviction that violence was inherently and unavoidably sinful and evil, if sometimes, in a fallen world, inevitable and even necessary. Thus the invasion of England in 1066 by William the Conqueror was declared a 'just war' by the Pope. But the knights and soldiers who fought on the Norman side at the Battle of Hastings had none the less to do penance after the battle for the shedding of human blood. They had done something that was believed to be necessary and in that limited sense right, but none the less their actions in shedding human blood were sinful; they were victors, but guilty victors who required pardon.

The secularization of just war thinking (which is, of course, part of natural law thought) from the seventeenth century onwards simplified the whole matter. Now the tendency was to suggest that war, or other acts of violence, were either just or unjust, and that was the end of the matter. One made careful and responsible calculations in accordance with the criteria offered by the just war tradition, and following this informed choice one's actions should leave one with a good conscience, and certainly no need for penance.

But in actual situations of war and military conflict, such an approach is inadequate to the moral complexities and ambiguities involved. For example, I remember the case of a British general, a professional military man and a committed Christian, who spoke on a BBC television programme on ethics in warfare. In the final stages of the Second World War, he said, he had been responsible for the safe crossing of the Rhine by a large contingent of allied troops. He was advised that the only way to guarantee the security of his men was to ask the RAF to 'take out' the historic city of Cleves. He knew Cleves to be crowded with refugee civilians as well as German troops and command centres. He agonized as long as he was able, and finally ordered the destruction of Cleves. Cleves was flattened by blanket bombing; the crossing of the Rhine was uneventful, but certainly made a contribution to shortening the war, and therefore saved many lives. Yet, the general said, he still feels distress, guilt would perhaps be a better term, for the 'taking out' of Cleves. He believes it was necessary; just, according to the criteria of *ius in bello*. But it cannot be called *good*; rather it was something sinful but necessary, for which penance should be done. Because of his Christian faith, the general was operating instinctively with a theory of the just war which was still within a theological frame which recognized guilt and spoke also of forgiveness and reconciliation. An adequate ethic must be able to cope with the ambiguities of the 'real world', and respond not only to decisions but also to their aftermath.

If there is anything in the suggestion that secularization of morals brought with it in relation to the ethics of war a narrowing and simplification which made modern just war ethics less capable of coping with some of the complexities and ambiguities of the real choices and decisions that have to be made, it is worth asking whether something similar may have happened with the discourse of equality.

Perhaps three things have happened. In the first place the complex Christian view of human nature has been replaced with more monochrome ideas: the assumption is now that either human beings are natural altruists, capable of generosity and instinctive builders of community, or they are essentially self-interested, selfish beings. They cannot be both, and policy builds upon one or the other understanding of human nature. Either we happily recognize and endorse our shared equality, and generously are willing to sacrifice our interests for its fuller realization, or egalitarian measures have to rest on appeals to the self-interest of the majority, or on threats of coercion. But politicians, and indeed all of us, have to 'wrestle with both the angel and the serpent which is in each of us', to quote Frank Field.[3] So perhaps a full-blooded theological ethic has still rich resources to cope with the complexities and ambiguities of the 'real world'.

Secondly, there seems today to be a pervasive unwillingness to talk about the basis or grounding of a commitment to human equality. It is as if this were something we just don't talk about these days, having realized that such fundamental values cannot be rationally demonstrated, that there are significant problems in endorsing any particular religious basis for human equality, and that consensus is not enough.

And, finally, there has been for a long time in some quarters an obsession with economic equality and redistribution, as if that were the whole of the matter. Is this because money and economic redistribution are in a way the easiest parts of the subject to handle, in the absence of any overarching theory or system of shared belief?

Enlightenment self-evidence

The Enlightenment was in a way a delayed and considered response to the problem of religious plurality and religious conflict. It is perfectly understandable how following the Wars of Religion the Enlightenment project sought a secular and a universal ethics. That project has made a huge contribution to human flourishing, and should not be denigrated or despised. Much of the Enlightenment was sympathetic and supportive to religion and of theology.[4] At the time in Scotland, England, Germany and America at least, theologians and intelligent believers embraced the Enlightenment with enthusiasm. As religious sceptics, David Hume and the French *philosophes* were exceptions to this general rule.

The Enlightenment project was a sustained effort to develop a universal theory, applicable always and everywhere, and governing all rational human beings. While it claimed to detach itself for the most part from particular narratives – whether the parable of the Good Samaritan, or the story of Munuswamy – theological assumptions still lurked like ghosts in Enlightenment thought. Enlightenment thought tended, at least formally, to affirm human equality. 'We hold these truths to be self-evident', sonorously proclaimed the American Declaration of Independence of 1776, 'that all men are created equal, and that they are endowed by their Creator with certain inalienable rights, that among these are Life, Liberty and the pursuit of Happiness.' Here we have a classic Enlightenment document.

But what does it mean to say that a value such as equality is self-evident? At its simplest it involves the suggestion that there is no need for supportive argumentation, that any rational person can see that all 'men' are equal and have equal rights. It follows that failure to recognize human equality must be either an infirmity of the mind or of the moral sense. All rational and moral beings have access to this truth; it is as it were part of the structure of things that anyone who can think straight and see clearly must recognize. Equality, in other words, is regarded as a fundamental moral axiom so clear and distinct as to require no justification; one need not, and perhaps cannot, go behind it to something more basic still. It is the starting point rather than the conclusion of social, moral and political reasoning. Its self-evidence makes it a remarkably secure foundation for moral reasoning. Common sense confirms that equality is a good thing, and the ordinary person, not just the scholar, can see clearly that equality is desirable. Equality needs no justification, it is a self-evident truth or value.

And the Declaration is at this point saturated with theological language. We have been *created* equal. We have not become equal through education or civilization. We have not simply been born equal; we have been created equal by the Creator God who has also endowed us with rights. If the theological language were removed, the argument of the Declaration at this crucial point would fall apart. The ultimate and only ground for human equality, the American Declaration of Independence suggests, lies in the will of the Creator God.

If one side of Enlightenment thought declares equality to be self-evident, the other suggests that *in*equality is an anomaly which calls for explanation and legitimation or removal. The very term *in*equality suggests a deprivation of something that is good in itself, a lack of something that people want and deserve. Equality is self-evidently a good thing; inequality is wrong and evil. It is not without significance that the original draft of the American Declaration of Independence spoke of 'these truths' as 'sacred and undeniable'. This was later altered, probably by Benjamin Franklin, to the less theologically charged 'self-evident'.[5] There was thus some toning down of the explicitly theological references. The wording was mildly secularized, but that did not mean that equality and the other rights were no longer to be regarded as holy, given by the hand of God, and to be reverenced as such.

It is necessary to remember, of course, that the framers of the Declaration actually meant males when they wrote 'men'; and not only males, but white, free males. It did not appear to have occurred to them that what they were drafting might have a bearing on the place of women, or be incompatible with slavery, any more than the ancient Greeks saw nothing strange in excluding women, slaves and aliens – the large majority of the population – from the rights of equal citizenship. But the language, as in so many Enlightenment documents, is both theological and universal; it has meaning that its original framers did not recognize. A theological ghost has got into the machine. And it is to this, as well as directly to the Bible, that Martin Luther King appealed successfully nearly two centuries later in the course of the civil rights movement.

A couple of concluding comments on the Enlightenment before we move on: The adequacy of its universalism is today questioned by postmodernists and by feminists who accuse it of imposing a rigid and unreal structure on morality which disallows difference. And in another respect perhaps in a way we have come full circle, as the horrors of the twentieth century – the Holocaust, the Rwandan genocide, the Gulag, Pol Pot, and many another – are for the most part based on secular ideologies, or blatant, unabashed vindictiveness or ethnic hatred, just as the wars of the seventeenth century were fought largely about religion. Could it be that today even in plural societies religious belief might once again give reconciling shape and justification to morality?

The liberal dilemma

Modern liberalism faces a dilemma. On the one hand there are liberal thinkers, most notably Bruce Ackerman, who teach that the state must be strictly neutral on moral issues, on all matters concerning the good. And on the other hand, there are those like Ronald Dworkin who suggest that liberal societies should have 'a positive commitment to an egalitarian morality'.[6] Ackerman argues that it cannot be demonstrated that any particular conception of the good is better than another: 'while everybody has an opinion about the good life, none can be known to be superior to any other'.[7] The state, for Ackerman, has to police moral discussion in the society, acting as a kind of referee. Rather optimistically he continues: 'While ... neutral dialogue begins with the affirmation of a right to equal shares, subsequent conversational moves will define a liberal conception of equality that is compatible with a social order rich in diversity of talents, personal ideals and forms of community.' This he calls 'undominated equality'.[8] Religion and theology are given harsher treatment by Ackerman than are moral commitments. He clearly himself believes that religion is a matter of irrational prejudice. But nevertheless in a liberal society, 'any group of like-minded citizens have the right to worship God in any way they see fit. All such spiritual communions, however, must be founded on a *voluntary* decision by each communicant, affirming the value of his particular church's form of divine dialogue.'[9]

Dworkin argues that what Ackerman supports is 'liberalism based on neutrality', which can support only such egalitarian measures as result from that principle. It is not easy to see how this could take us very far, or indeed how a government could operate on the principle of strict neutrality in a whole series of policy areas in which decisions have to be made. Dworkin himself supports 'liberalism based on equality' and requires moral neutrality 'only to the degree that equality requires it'. The state, he argues, should have a steady commitment to an egalitarian morality which challenges privilege and concentrations of power and wealth. It is not the role of government to impose personal morality. But people should for the pursuit of their individual life plans have 'no more than an equal share of the resources available for all'.[10] Government, for its part, 'must impose no sacrifice or constraint on any citizen in virtue of an argument that the citizen could not accept without abandoning his sense of his equal worth'.[11] But what the *foundations* of Dworkin's 'liberalism based on equality' might be is not altogether clear.

Both Ackerman and Dworkin, and indeed most liberal thinkers, support to some considerable extent the idea that the liberal state has to be neutral on matters of values and morality. Both are also anxious that the state should express and support some egalitarian form of 'liberal values', and that these should command the passionate allegiance of the citizens.[12] But characteristically they have little to say about the grounding of the 'liberal values' they advocate. They operate within the 'givenness' of liberalism, just as Christian dogmatics in theology operates within the structure of Christian belief. There is no way of commending their conclusions outside an acceptance of liberalism. They reflect the contemporary collapse of confidence in the possibility of a rational and universal base for a common morality in a plural and global society. And, again reflecting common views, they are particularly suspicious of the possibility that religion might have something positive to offer to the debate about social values and their grounding. Like so much of contemporary social theory, there is here great clarity in laying out the argument and defining concepts, but difficulties in going beyond that, either in the direction of specific policy prescriptions or of commending liberalism to others.

The American political philosopher, John Rawls, is probably the most significant liberal egalitarian writing today.[13] The development of his thought shows the changing strengths and problems of liberal egalitarianism. When his magisterial *A Theory of Justice* was first published in 1972 it was generally read as a Kantian style Enlightenment theory, claiming some kind of universal or general truthfulness and applicability. It rested on what appeared to be a series of axioms or assumptions about human beings and how they would behave when asked to select the principles of a just society behind what Rawls calls a 'veil of ignorance'. Rational human beings, it is suggested, behave in more or less the same way in all ages and cultures. And justice will be the same, always and everywhere.

The second reading of Rawls is rather different, but it is the one that he has increasingly firmly endorsed as the correct interpretation of his intentions. Here the principles of justice are distilled from the 'considered convictions' of most people in a typical modern liberal democracy. There is now no appeal to an objective and rational moral order, or even to the idea that human nature is the same always and everywhere. The principles of justice, through a process of reflective equilibrium, are to match the considered convictions of the majority of reasonable people in a liberal democracy. Justice and equality rest on a consensus which results from a kind of open and tolerant conversation about justice and equality – the sort of public discourse which is necessary for a healthy democracy to flourish.

Why does Rawls so emphatically prefer the second reading of his theory? The answer is fairly obvious. Modern liberal democracies are plural societies, in which a wide range of philosophical and religious positions may flourish. Accordingly, 'in a constitutional democracy the public conception of justice should be, as far as possible, independent of controversial philosophical and religious doctrines'.[14] Rawls's theory of justice apparently makes no claim to 'truth' or universality; it is rather a co-ordination of, and an engagement with, the considered convictions of people in the specific historical and political circumstances of liberal democracy.

But in a liberal democracy there remain within a general acceptance that liberal democracy is a good thing, a wide diversity of what Rawls calls 'reasonable comprehensive world views'. There is substantial disagreement among them. A liberal democracy needs, Rawls argues, a generally accepted account of justice; but no one 'comprehensive world view' – even liberalism, if it is such a view – is capable by itself of generating such an account of justice. Particularly in his second major book, *Political Liberalism*, Rawls develops the idea of an 'overlapping consensus' between the various reasonable comprehensive world-views.[15] Rawls's account of justice depends on consensual agreement on what is right in politics and economics, but can co-exist with a wide diversity of views of ultimate truth and goodness located in the various comprehensive world-views. The overlap, where the reasonable comprehensive world-views agree, is the place where public debate about justice and equality may take place, and where these views, including religious views, may make their contribution to public debate.

At first sight, Rawls's theory of the overlapping consensus seems quite hospitable to religious views and religious arguments. But closer inspection reveals problems. Rawls is benignly confident that that part of the various reasonable comprehensive doctrines which lies within the overlap will endorse his account of justice and the associated notions of equality. Indeed this appears to be the principle according to which the boundary between the overlap and the remainder of the rational comprehensive doctrines is to be drawn. But what if a specific reasonable comprehensive doctrine contains in the part of its teaching which lies outside the overlap significant themes which it feels are important contributions to public debate, and might challenge certain aspects of the consensus? Are they to be excluded? Is there not a danger that the most distinctive and perhaps challenging and constructive contributions of a particular system are to be disregarded because they do not fit neatly into today's consensus?

It has been argued that Rawls initially, like many other liberal theorists, was deeply suspicious of religion and regarded it as divisive and arbitrary, and thus to be excluded as far as possible from the public forum and relegated to the private realm. More recently, it is suggested, he has moved to a slightly more positive attitude towards religious arguments. These, he suggests, can be admitted to public debate provided they meet the commonly accepted criteria of public reason and can be expressed in secular, non-religious terms. And religion Rawls now recognizes, is a part of civil society that may strengthen the civic virtues and encourage attachment to liberal democracy. This limited acknowledgement of the significance of religious discourse in the public sphere has been recently further developed in an essay on 'The Idea of Public Reason Revisited', to which I now turn.[16]

A democratic society, Rawls argues, is characterized by 'reasonable pluralism', in the sense that we should expect to find 'a plurality of conflicting reasonable comprehensive doctrines' which attract the allegiance of citizens.[17] The term 'reasonable' here is a little perplexing. It might be a way of excluding from the discussion over-confident religious or ideological systems which wish to reshape the whole society autocratically according to some revealed or intellectually developed overall plan; a liberal democracy, in short, does not operate like a communist autocracy or a fundamentalist Islamic society. But it is, of course, tendentious to suggest that such positions are necessarily *unreasonable*. Sometimes, perhaps, they are only too reasonable and intellectually coherent. The next stage in Rawls's argument is the suggestion that arguments drawn from the heart of a comprehensive system should not be offered as they stand to public debate. They must first be translated into the generally accepted terms of public reason. A story such as that of the Good Samaritan may only be introduced into public debate to support a conclusion reached on independent rational grounds. The common religious 'zeal to embody the whole truth in politics is incompatible with an idea of public reason that belongs with democratic citizenship'.[18] Unqualifiedly religious discourse may have its place in what Rawls call, 'the background culture', but must not intrude into the mainstream of public reason, which is the appropriate idiom of judges, public officials, legislators and candidates for office. Official Roman Catholic social teaching, which is, as we have seen, expressed in terms of natural law believed to be accessible to all rational beings, seems to be relegated to operating mainly or entirely in the background culture, and thence it feeds in rather different terms into public political discourse.[19] A little later, and rather strangely, Rawls declared that Roman Catholic views on the common good and solidarity may be admitted, provided they are presented in terms of political values, which presumably means separated from their natural law framework.

How, Rawls inquires, is it possible for people of faith to be whole-hearted citizens in a democratic society? Things have come full circle since the days when those who differed from the established faith were constantly suspected of sedition, and it was commonly assumed that an

atheist could not be moral! Now in the Rawlsian scenario, believers
may only be admitted to full citizenship on certain conditions. They
may not, for instance, use the political process for religious purposes:
'While no one is expected to put his or her religious or non-religious
doctrine in danger, we must each give up for ever the hope of changing
the constitution so as to establish our religion's hegemony, or of qualifying our obligations so as to ensure its influence and success.'[20]
Religious views can only be introduced with secular supportive arguments. In an astonishing aside, Rawls suggests that 'the principles of
political justice do not apply to the internal life of the church, nor is it
desirable or consistent with liberty of conscience or freedom of association that they should'.[21] Nor does justice as fairness apply to the
family – to my mind a quite extraordinary statement in itself, and one
that completely neglects the need to have formation for citizenship,
inculcating the values of equality and justice, in the family and in the
school.

In this essay, as in *Political Liberalism*, Rawls has been wrestling
with 'a torturing question in the contemporary world, namely: Can
democracy and comprehensive doctrines, religious or non-religious, be
compatible? And if so, how?'[22] His answer seems to me to be grudging
and to suggest a very narrow and unreal understanding of the public
forum in a democratic society. From that forum, it would appear, most
of the kinds of arguments that were contributed by Martin Luther
King, or more recently by Desmond Tutu in the South African Truth
and Reconciliation Commission would be disallowed, or replaced with
arguments which, whether or not they convince the intellect, do not
touch the heart, or the springs of human motivation. The same is true
of the two remarkable Pastoral Letters of the US Catholic Bishops
on War and Peace, and on the Economy. These made a significant
contribution to public debate in the United States. While they were
primarily addressed to American citizens who were Catholics as they
framed their consciences in relation to issues of the day and their
public responsibilities as citizens, they also sought and received a far
broader hearing. While the Pastoral Letters made some use of natural
law thinking, a great deal of the argumentation was biblical or
specifically theological. As a whole, they represented the kind of public
discourse that Rawls would disallow.[23] But they were widely welcomed
as making a major, and fresh, contribution to the way these issues were

debated in the American public square. This illustrates that we need a far more open, dynamic, and hospitable understanding of the democratic public forum if democracy is to survive and flourish, and win the enthusiastic allegiance of democratic peoples.

A 'third way' to equality?

Attempts in recent times to rehabilitate equality as a central social value have tended to make two particularly contentious assertions: firstly, that a society can move towards equality with determination and speed without any sector of society's interests being negatively affected, that is, without redistribution from the rich to the poor; and, secondly, that equality for all practical purposes means no more than equality of opportunity.

Both these points featured largely in the Report of the Independent Commission on Social Justice which was established in 1992 by the former Leader of the Labour Party, John Smith, and which was presided over by Sir Gordon Borrie. It reported in 1994. The Commission was set up partly because of deep internal ideological problems in the British Labour Party, but also with a recognition that Britain as a whole had lost its sense of direction.[24] With the collapse of the old commanding ideologies of the left and the right, a fundamental reconsideration of the kind of society that is desired, of the values that should be expressed in society, and an associated programme of national renewal were the rather grandiloquently stated objectives for the Commission. It was also, of course, intended to give the Labour Party in particular a sense of direction, some key principles and values and the beginnings of a programme that would enable the party once again to win elections. It was hoped that here there might be a kind of second Beveridge Report, which would have something of the same fundamental and continuing impact on British society. Great expectations were thus invested in the Commission's Report.

The initiative was as timely as it was imaginative. For Britain, like most western countries, was – and is – in a state of considerable ideological confusion. Some people still look back nostalgically to the welfare consensus that was dominant for two decades and more after 1945. This had been in general accepted by both main parties. They vied with one another about how best to fine-tune heaven, rather than being divided by any fundamental disagreements about the kind of society Britain aspired to be. This consensus disintegrated under the impact of the collapse of a general acceptance of Keynesian economics, a rather unexpected frontal assault from a newly confident New Right ideology, and above all, the rapid disintegration of the East European state socialist regimes. 1989 had seemed to many to signify that the old-style socialism as well as Marxist communism was dead. The Commission's task was to develop a compelling social vision around which a new consensus could crystallize, and which would be in some kind of continuity with the tradition of the Labour Party. Accordingly its remit was to develop or refurbish an account of social justice, and it was assumed that it would give attention to issues of equality, as a major emphasis in the Labour Party heritage.

The Report speaks quite emphatically of its task as being 'to set a vision for the future'.[25] 'We need to be clear about our values, understand the forces shaping change, create our own vision for the future – and then set out to achieve it.'[26] An alternative vision is required, which is realistic in the sense that it arises out of a careful discernment of the present situation. Without such a vision, we remain ensnared in a situation where, in Matthew Arnold's words, we are, 'wandering between two worlds, one dead, The other powerless to be born'.[27] This vision is a broad-gauge orientation towards a society and its future. One hopes that it is something that elicits enthusiasm, commitment and sacrifice. A social vision is often capable of constraining selfishness, individual and group, for the sake of a higher end, and encouraging altruistic behaviour. A good social vision is grounded in conviction – that history is on our side, or that the vision corresponds in some way to a coming reality. The Thatcherite vision claimed to be rooted in reality, and it was expressed in conviction politics – the belief that the vision must be followed and implemented, whether or not it was popular at the time, that pragmatism is not enough, that we must in politics do what is right, and the vision defines the right and the good. Conviction politics is, of course, an ambiguous phenomenon. Under Thatcher it led to an amazing disregard for the facts if they appeared to cut across the path of the vision, and a blindness to the effects on real people of the policies which were adopted to implement the Thatcherite vision. But we certainly need conviction politics in the sense of a politics in which politicians seek to do what is right whether or not it is immediately electorally or economically advantageous. A lively and well-grounded vision is a great support to pertinacity and integrity in politics.

The Borrie Report frequently assumes, without anywhere demonstrating, that a more just and equal society will be more economically successful. Often this may be true. But social justice and equality are surely to be pursued even if they do not in the short term lead to economic success, even when they cannot ride a wave of economic growth.

The Report is also much – perhaps too much – concerned to suggest policies that would be popular with the British electorate. A good vision can attract the support of a majority at the polls. 'Electoral success', writes Gerry Cohen, 'is to a large extent a by-product of commitment to something other than electoral success.'[28] He is right. The vision that swept Labour into power in 1945 had emerged out of the grim experiences of the Depression and the Second World War, and had roots far further back. Long before it commanded mass support it had been developed and nourished in a variety of groups, most of them rather remote from the power centres, operating at the margin of things, dreaming dreams of the future. The vision was grounded in experience and in suffering, in understandings of human beings and society, of the historical process, and in a surprisingly large number of cases, beliefs about God and God's Reign. The vision, initially articulated by William Beveridge, Clement Attlee, William Temple and many other people, was translated into a manifesto, Labour gained power, and the welfare consensus emerged.

The Thatcherite vision had a not dissimilar trajectory. In the 1940s and 1950s few people took Hayek's jeremiad about the 'road to serfdom' seriously. The Thatcherite vision had arisen primarily out of the dreadful assaults on freedom and human dignity of the two great totalitarian systems of the twentieth century, although like the 1945 vision, it had intellectual and experiential roots going back a long way. This vision was nurtured and refined in the wilderness, far from the places where economic and political decisions were made, in study groups, and little think-tanks often dismissed as quaint oddities by those in the mainstream of political, intellectual and economic life. Both these visions – of the welfare state, and of Thatcherism – were embraced with enthusiasm and conviction by small groups long before they could command an electoral majority, let alone gather around them consensual support.

One of my concerns with the vision of social justice and equality presented in the Borrie Report is this: unlike the other two visions I have mentioned, each of which claimed in some sense to be *true*, to be right, to be grounded in reality, then gradually gathered wide support, and finally provided the ideological heart for a consensus, this vision claims to be based on no more than what most people in Britain already believe. Belief in social justice and equality reflects 'the common sense of the vast majority of people', a preparatory publication of the Commission affirms. In seeking to present a conceptual structure for thinking about justice 'we have attempted to articulate some widely-held feelings about the character of our society'.[29] The Report, accordingly, does not so much claim to create or shape a consensus as mirror an existing one.

One of the reasons for this is that the Report is very much indebted to the thought of John Rawls, who, as we have seen, presents his theory of justice and equality as based not on any ontology, meta-physics or religious convictions, but on the 'considered convictions' of most people in a modern liberal democratic society. It is not hard to see why Rawls is attractive at this point. In most modern societies there is no belief system which commands general assent; but perhaps there may be a moral consensus about the just and the decent to which appeal can be made. Does such a consensus exist in Britain today? The Commission felt that it does, and frequently makes reference to 'most people's sense of right' as a kind of criterion for public policy. But if the opinion polls consistently suggest that there is a widespread view that the unemployed should be properly provided for and that the National Health Service is a good thing, the election statistics also suggest that this exiguous moral consensus is not strong enough to constrain people's selfishness in the privacy of the polling booth, behind a real rather than Rawlsian veil of ignorance. Rawls believes that people are basically self-interested, his consensus is a co-ordination of convictions which are at their heart selfish; and accordingly it is impotent when the need is to take collective selfishness head-on.

Furthermore, the moral consensus to which the Report appeals can easily and imperceptibly slide into becoming simply a central concern for a majority at the next election. The vision then becomes not so much a series of convictions about what is true and right around which a consensus and an electoral majority may in the course of time crystallize, as an orientation of policy dominated by the need to win a majority at the polls. But a vision is more than a series of pragmatic adjustments within a generally accepted social order, of a sort which find wide acceptance in the society. It must have something of the flavour of the new Jerusalem if it is to arouse the passion and the commitment that are necessary to enable serious moves towards justice and equality. To quote the Latin American theologian, Rubem Alves, 'When utopias are not imagined, ethics is reduced to solving problems within the established system.' The Commission appeals to a consensus around a series of piecemeal measures rather than around a vision of the new society that the Report seems to advocate. Whether such a consensus has the capacity to arouse and sustain enthusiasm and commitment remains to be seen. What we need, in Gerry Cohen's words, is 'the strength of conviction that depends on depth of convictions, and depth comes from theory that is too fundamental to be practicable in the direct sense'.[30]

Not surprisingly, the Report claimed to put equality – 'the equal worth of all citizens' – at the heart of its work. Equality was intended to be the co-ordinating normative principle of its proposals. But equality of worth was quickly translated into equality of opportunity, and equality of outcome was largely disregarded.[31] This was a more serious and controversial step than the Commission seemed to realize at the time. As Adrian Sinfield points out, the inequalities at the starting post and at the finish are so serious, and getting more so, that real equality of opportunity is impossible without addressing issues of redistribution. But the Commission was notably coy about even discussing redistribution, except something they called 'redistribution of opportunity', perhaps because redistribution is commonly believed today to be an electoral liability. There is some mention of social exclusion as being caused by inequality, but this idea is undeveloped and plays a peripheral role compared to the place it has occupied in more recent days.

To sum up: The Report of the Social Justice Commission suggests that equality should be a guiding principle for social and economic policy, but it is quite clear that it is equality of opportunity rather than any sort of radical moves of redistribution or educational reform which is in view. Equality so conceived is proclaimed as an economic necessity: 'We believe that under more imaginative policies it [the UK] can be both fairer and more successful; indeed that it must be both fairer and more successful if it is to be either … It is a constant theme of this report that there is not an opposition between these two aims. On the contrary, each demands the other'.[32] The structure of the argument is basically Rawlsian, but the report hesitates to agree with Rawls that all inequalities require to be justified, and that the basic allowable justification of an inequality is that it benefits the least well off. As with Rawls, the whole theory rests on nothing more stable than a consensus, or rather a series of assumptions about what people in Britain like and find acceptable – and presumably might vote for. 'We are confident', the Commission writes, 'that at least in our belief that there is such a thing as "social justice", we reflect the common sense of the vast majority of people.'[33] Even controversial judgments appeal to the arbitration of 'what many people believe', and most people's sense of what is right. For example:

> What the various arguments about entitlement and desert suggest seems to be something close to what many people believe: that there is basic justice in people having differential reward for their productive activities, but they have no right to any given differential of their reward over others. It is not simply self-interest, or again scepticism about government spending programmes … that makes people resist the idea that everyone's income is in principle a resource for redistribution; that idea also goes against their sense of what is right … [In our attempts to present a conceptual structure for thinking about justice] we have attempted to articulate some widely-held feelings about the character of our society.[34]

The Report of the Commission on Social Justice demonstrates very clearly some of the problems and issues that arise not infrequently with secular understandings of equality. First of all, there is the problem of the grounds of equality. Not only is it felt that no references to the Judaeo-Christian tradition may appropriately be made, but more neutral suggestions that human equality is part of an objective moral order to which natural law gives us access are also excluded. The only grounding that is acceptable is in terms of a consensus. Whether such a consensus exists or not is debatable, but what seems clear is that for many people talk of consensus is really a way of talking about electoral majorities. In practice expectations of what 'the people' will support or tolerate are allowed to control the content of the equality that is to be transposed into policy. So volatile a grounding for equality makes vision and commitment almost impossible and allows calculations of electoral advantage to dominate the theory and the strategy of equality.

The new struggle for 'true equality'

At the Labour Party Conference of 1997, Prime Minister Tony Blair declared, 'The class war is over; the struggle for true equality is just begun.' The year before, Gordon Brown had delivered a John Smith Memorial Lecture in which he suggested the 'the missing link' in discussions about the future was serious engagement with issues of equality. Equality of outcome, he suggested, invoking support from the grave of John Smith, was a blind alley; instead we should be seeking 'a far more vigorous definition of equality of opportunity'. Equality of opportunity was important both for achieving social justice and for economic efficiency. Thus the issue of equality, with a strong slant towards equality of opportunity, was put squarely on the agenda of what quickly became known as 'the Third Way'.[35]

This emphasis on equality was picked up and developed particularly by Professor Anthony Giddens in two books, seeking to define what might be meant by the phrase 'the Third Way', and to provide the new social democracy with solid theoretical underpinning.[36] Giddens sees an emphasis on equality as distinguishing the Left from the Right in politics, but he treats equality virtually entirely as equality of opportunity, which has, of course, usually been applauded in modern times by right-wing movements as well. Social democrats, Giddens suggests, must revise their understanding of equality in the wake of the collapse of socialism. Now equality must 'co-exist with pluralism and life-style diversity'. And it was now necessary to recognize that two of the great traditional agents of equality – the state and the welfare system – are now also part of the problem.[37] Michael Walzer is enlisted to criticize the 'egalitarianism at all costs' which was believed to be characteristic of the Left:

Simple equality of that sort is the bad utopianism of the old left ...
[P]olitical conflict and the competition for leadership always make
for power inequalities and entrepreneurial activity always makes for
economic inequalities ... None of this can be prevented without
endless tyrannical interventions in ordinary life. It was an historical
mistake of large proportions, for which we [on the left] have paid
heavily.[38]

Gerry Cohen distinguishes this kind of 'left-liberal' equality of
opportunity which 'corrects for social disadvantage, but not for native,
or *inborn*, disadvantage' from what he calls 'socialist' equality of opportunity. This latter seeks to correct for all unchosen disadvantages, that
is, for which the agent cannot reasonably be held responsible, whether
they be disadvantages that reflect social misfortune or disadvantages
that reflect natural misfortune.[39] This socialist equality of opportunity
is also concerned with reducing inequalities of outcome. But it is not
equality of opportunity to get more than others; rather it is equality of
opportunity 'to live as one wants'.

In many ways a more clear presentation than that of Giddens of the
Third Way's approach to equality was given by Patricia Hewitt of the
Institute for Public Policy Research, a member of the Borrie Commission, and now a government minister. The old Left, she suggests,
demanded that a choice be made between social justice and economic
efficiency. The Third Way realizes that this is a false choice; social
justice and economic efficiency are interdependent: 'the policies that
are required in the interests of social justice are precisely the same as
the policies needed for a successful modern economy'. In the 1980s,
discussions of equality had become 'hopelessly bogged down' in
issues of equality of outcome, and the Labour Party's commitment to
equality was seen as an attitude of resentment against the rich. At that
stage, left-of-centre thinkers began to talk in semi-Rawlsian terms, of
fairness rather than equality, and neglected Rawls's own central concerns with equality, and the difficulty in justifying inequalities. As we
have seen when discussing the Borrie Commission, there was a rather
vague distinction, which was however central to the Report's argument, between 'justified' and 'unjustified' inequalities. But even
'justified inequalities' 'represent a challenge to any government committed to reducing inequality, tackling social exclusion, and creating an

egalitarian culture of equal respect'. For Patricia Hewitt, the Third Way is in fact about more than simply equality of opportunity. It is about establishing 'an egalitarian culture of equal respect', in which everyone 'should have the greatest possible opportunity to find and fulfill our potential'. This directly involves a reduction, probably a very gradual reduction in the more blatant 'unjustifiable inequalities', by way of what she calls 'redistribution through wealth creation'. Redistribution through the taxation and welfare systems does not find favour, direct attacks on poverty should be replaced with 'the best anti-poverty programme ... steady growth and high employment'.

Equality, as Patricia Hewitt understands it, is compatible with difference: 'Egalitarianism and equal respect do not mean equal outcomes. They cannot. Nor do they mean identical treatment.'[40] But surely equal respect must go beyond respecting differences and giving 'each of us ... the greatest possible opportunity to find and fulfil our potential'. It is necessarily tied in to questions of remuneration. And even when people are encouraged to fulfil their potential there has to be an acknowledgement that some people – say those with severe learning difficulties - have not a great deal of potential, or rather, quite different potential from those not so constrained. How is their equal worth to be respected and recognized? Patricia Hewitt seems to endorse a broader understanding of equality than equality of opportunity. She recognizes the need for positive action to increase personal autonomy and equal respect:

If the equal respect we want for ourselves and for each other implies personal autonomy and social connection, then how we get our money matters, too, not just how much we get. Higher social security benefits do not change the conditions that lock people in poverty and social exclusion. They do not enable the 21 year old who cannot read the instructions on a medicine bottle to get a job. They do not help a parent and her children to learn to read. They do little to improve the self-esteem of the young mother who was neglected or abused by her own parents. They enable a family to spend more but they don't increase its chances of earning and saving in future.

The latest research suggests an extraordinarily close connection between inequality and ill-health. But inequality of power – power over one's own life – turns out to matter as well as inequality of money. More money, wherever it comes from, improves people's health. But lasting improvements lie in tackling the lack of self-esteem and sense of powerlessness that underlie teenage pregnancy. Drug and alcohol abuse, vulnerability to heart disease, and so on.[41]

The centre-left in Britain, and indeed in a number of other countries as well, has a profound ambivalence about equality. On the one hand, it wants equality to be the keystone in a new value structure to replace the old socialist ideologies. On the other hand, it is extremely nervous about much of the traditional content of the concept of equality, and through a strong emphasis on equality of opportunity it wants to water down the notion of equality. This translates into policies of welfare to work and an emphasis on education in an effort to improve people's position at the start of the race, or at the bottom of the ladder. Equal worth and equality of opportunity are affirmed, but there is virtually no unease discernable at widening gaps between top and bottom incomes, and indeed the new rhetoric of social inclusion (of which more later) tends to dilute the concern for equality.

What service might theology render?

To whom or what might theology render a service today? If we put the Munuswamys of this world at the centre, it is in the first place to them that theology should seek to render service. Only thereafter, and as a consequence of serving Munuswamy, theology needs to address the policymakers, and the citizenry, and the church with a message that is often disturbing and challenging. Theology has a responsibility to represent Munuswamy to the intellectual and political 'powers', to speak for him in situations where his voice is not heard, where he cannot as yet speak for himself. Munuswamy should haunt these powers as he haunts me. This kind of theology is rooted in the real world and its issues and its suffering. It is intended to arouse conviction and lead to action. It cares for people more than for intellectual coherence, or literary elegance, or academic respectability.

Christian theology, unlike philosophy and social science, has in the church a large and varied constituency to which it is responsible and for which it often speaks. By this I do not mean that theology defends the institutional interests of the church, although sadly it sometimes does just that. Rather I mean that even in secularized liberal democracies the church has in its membership some of the weakest and poorest in the land, and some of the most powerful and wealthy. In as far as the church is really trying to be the church it encourages serious dialogue among its diverse membership around themes that really matter. When that happens, influential people are enabled to understand the human reality of social problems, and challenged to relate their faith to these issues. And, at least on occasion, the church can speak for the voiceless, can represent the poor and the disabled and the weak. This is in fact an important public function of the church that it should not shirk.

And the church is an ecumenical, world-wide fellowship. That is why this book wrestles with the question of our responsibility to and for Munuswamy. He belongs to another nation and political system. He is an alien, far away. But Christians feel a sense of responsibility for him and to him, and seek to give this sense a reality in what they say and do about the world economic system, about development, and so forth. Within the *oikumene* Christians have an increasingly real sense of accountability to and responsibility for others – not just for their fellow believers – around the world.

Christian theology is also concerned with investigating, criticizing and renewing a great tradition of thought about God and the world, about human beings and human community, about morals and politics, about the purpose and end of it all. Western secular thought has largely emerged out of this tradition, and, as Jeremy Waldron suggests, 'in a number of ways the Christian conceptions out of which modern liberalism originated remain richer and deeper than their secular offspring'.[42] The responsible theologian who recognizes this must seek to offer and commend this tradition in public debate. For the riches and continuing relevance of the tradition have not been fully assimilated into secular social thought. Christian theology continues to be the guardian of insights into the shape and grounding of human equality which are of continuing public significance. To withdraw them from public debate would result in its serious impoverishment. Waldron presents a kind of challenge to contemporary theology: 'We might reasonably expect to find further clues to a rich and adequate conception of persons, equality, justice, and rights in what is currently being made of the Christ-centred tradition by those who remain centred in Christ.'[43] And a similar challenge comes from Robert Veatch in his fine book, *The Foundations of Justice: Why the Retarded and the Rest of Us have Claims to Equality*,[44] where he suggests that secular thought just does not have the resources to deal with fundamental questions such as the moral claims and status of those with severe and uncorrectable physical or mental handicaps. In such situations, Veatch suggests, practice calls out for help and support from Christian theology.

It is in the hope that Christian theology may shed some light on the nature and grounds of equality among human beings and in human communities and thus help with the practice of equality that this book is written. We turn now therefore to consider the roots of the Christian theology of equality.

Part Two:
The Christian Shape of Equality

3

Biblical Roots

The Bible no more determines the analysis of human equality than it resolves the debate about the origins of the universe. Yet the foundational texts of Western religion have offered those of an egalitarian disposition material to bolster their convictions. The text of Genesis is, in fact, the beginning of the thread favouring equality that binds the earliest legends of creation together with Lincoln's reformulation of the Declaration of Independence. The foundations of equality emerge in the book of Genesis; they are restated in a secular idiom by Kant; and they come into modern political discourse as an unquestioned assumption of the liberal pursuit of justice.[1]

The Bible: canon and diversity

The Bible is the foundational and authoritative text for the Christian faith and life in all their various expressions. But it is more than that: it has had a pivotal place in Western culture and society as they have developed down the centuries. Alasdair MacIntyre suggests that every great civilization has at its roots a canonical text which is essentially narrative. From this come the varied resources for moral enquiry, for philosophy, for criticizing practice, and for affirming and celebrating goodness and virtue. The canon presents models of virtue and of vice, and complex, many-layered stories which represent and stimulate reflection on what is good and true, and on how our existence and activity may relate to larger structures of meaning. This canonical narrative – for Graeco-Roman civilization, Homer, and for Christians and Jews the Hebrew Scriptures, with or without the New Testament – is discussed, examined, sung, recited, modified and passed on to each new generation. Although it has a saga-like narrative at its heart, the canon offers much else. Any rich and lively canon includes diversity, disagreement, argument, development, even outright contradiction. It sets flexible parameters within which debate may take place, and provides the major elements which may be deployed in that ongoing discussion.

In the past people in the West understood their individual and group narratives in relation primarily to the biblical grand narrative; the Bible provided them with the main resources for developing a sense of identity. Thus, when the Anglo-Saxon kings of England were converted to Christianity they were alarmed to discover that their official genealogies traced their descent back, generation after generation, to the old Norse Gods – Odin, Wotan, Thor and so on. Genealogies at that time were not simply condensations of the family history, but related it to a broader purpose, and were statements about identity and status. The kings responded to the embarrassment involved in Christian princes claiming descent from pagan gods by adding a prologue to their old genealogies, now tracing their descent back through Thor and Woden and the other Norse gods, back through the Old Testament patriarchs to Adam. Now their official table of descent grafted their own old story into the biblical grand narrative. And lest we think that this kind of grafting together of stories was finally disposed of centuries ago, it might be worth mentioning now what I will discuss in rather more detail in the next chapter – that the crucial late seventeenth century debate about government by consent as against absolute power was conducted by John Locke, the father of modern liberalism, almost entirely in terms of biblical exegesis. Locke's principal antagonist, Filmer, argued for the absolute power of kings on the grounds that Adam had been given supreme patriarchal power which had descended to the kings of the seventeenth century. Locke responded with impressively rigorous exegetical argument. Both Filmer and Locke were arguing about a political theory relevant to their times in terms of the proper interpretation of a particular part of the Judaeo-Christian grand narrative. This kind of fundamental biblical debate about equality may still be relevant today.

In pre-modern days the general effort was to locate specific studies, and questions about practice and the social order within a biblical grand narrative;[2] in modern times the Bible, religion, the Christian faith, theology and ethics are commonly seen as to be fitted into the project of an 'encyclopaedia', ordering all knowledge in terms of some more or less secular principle. Alasdair MacIntyre argues that the ninth edition of the *Encyclopaedia Britannica* (1873–) pointed towards a time when '[t]he Encyclopaedia would have displaced the Bible as the canonical book, or set of books of the culture'.[3] Accordingly, the Bible (and all thinking rooted in the Bible), MacIntyre suggests, 'is judged by the standards of ... modernity in a way which effectively prevents it from standing in judgement upon that modernity'.[4] Is this perhaps a main reason why there is such an awkward silence about religion and the Bible in most modern, and postmodern, discussion of equality?[5]

Modern *opponents* of equality have not been so slow to recognize the biblical, and indeed Christian roots of equality. 'Equality of all men is the biggest lie ever told', proclaimed Nietzsche, and then went on to lay the blame for this lie squarely on Christianity. This 'Christian dynamite' has been responsible, he claimed, for the 'brutalizing of man into a pygmy with equal rights and claims'. Equality, for Nietzsche, is a prime instance of the 'slave morality' inculcated by Christianity which has, he believed, subverted Western society and culture, and threatens all heroic impulses.[6] Other modern detractors of equality have recognized the biblical roots of the notion,[7] but it is more fashionable for those who are antagonistic to equality to declare it a modern prejudice without roots in the past and certainly without connections, historical or other, with the Christian faith.[8]

There are, of course, probably insuperable obstacles in the way of a return to a pre-modern way of understanding the Bible, and relating our practices, social forms and behaviour to it in the way that was common before the Enlightenment. Even Karl Barth's sustained effort to re-enter what he called 'the strange world of the Bible' was not a simple return to an age of innocence. Instead he found in the Bible unexpectedly rich resources for grappling with the issues and questions of the twentieth century. Although powerful ideas such as human equality do not spring out of nothing, and some understanding of their origins and development is helpful for proper comprehension, I am not primarily interested in history or exegesis. I am searching in the Christian tradition for insights which might guide practice and understanding in relation to equality, at a time when there is much uncertainty about the nature and grounding, the shape and justification of human equality. I intend to argue that the Judaeo-Christian tradition, and more precisely the Christian Faith, is the major (but not the only) source of the modern worldwide emphasis on equality; and also that it has decisively shaped the way in which equality is understood, initially in 'Christendom', and now around the globe.

I argue that Christianity engendered egalitarian ideas, shaped them, persistently implanted them in the soil of Christendom, and continues to sustain a commitment to equality as a central part of its ethical expression. In this chapter I will examine briefly the biblical roots and shaping of the value of equality. I do not have space for more than a quick and necessarily superficial survey of an important theme which has suffered quite extraordinary neglect at the hands of theologians and historians of ideas alike.[9] The Judaeo-Christian tradition has decisively influenced the shape of modern egalitarian thought in the West. And it still has relevant resources to offer.

The Bible, the foundational document of the Judaeo-Christian tradition, is, to be honest, a vast, sprawling collection of ancient documents, full of diversity, conflicts and downright contradictions. Much of it seems totally remote from the modern world and its concerns. It does not present a unified and carefully worked out view on equality – or on almost anything else, for that matter. On many of our pressing concerns it has nothing direct to say; and large sections seem confined in a remote and very different ancient world, quite inaccessible to us moderns. It is not easy to apply biblical insights on many matters to today's world. And yet there is coherence in the Bible, particularly around the movement from the beginning to the culmination of all things, from creation to the New Jerusalem, to the full realization at the end of God's Reign. Debates and conflicts in the Bible are often ones that we moderns can enter into and find there resources, help and encouragement.

Scholars such as Walter Brueggemann,[10] Norman Gottwald[11] and George Pixley have helpfully suggested that there are 'trajectories' in the Bible. Brueggemann distinguishes the royal and the liberation trajectories. The royal trajectory, he says, uses myths of unity, and stresses creation and the continuity of royal institutions. It tends to be socially conservative, stressing stability, the glory and holiness of God, and institutions and practices which stress that holiness. It appears to have been particularly cherished among the more prosperous people in the towns. By contrast, the liberation trajectory has at its heart concrete stories of liberation, such as the narrative of the exodus. It speaks of conflict and discontinuity; it tends to be socially revolutionary with a stress on transformation, and an emphasis on the righteousness and justice of God, rather than God's holiness.[12]

The two trajectories weave in and out of one another and interact with one another; they are not self-contained and isolated bodies of text. Issues of equality arise in rather different form in each, as we shall see shortly in rather more detail. For instance, many of the roots of Christian equality are to be found in the creation narratives, and inequality is often seen as something that threatens the stability of community life. The holiness and transcendence of God are sometimes treated as qualities which make human inequalities trivial, irrelevant or offensive. In some ways the liberation trajectory provides the more congenial home for egalitarian thought, with its emphasis on communities of equals challenging or escaping from systems of inequality, dominance and oppression.

So Norman Gottwald in his magisterial study reminds us that the Hebrew tribes wandering in the desert after the exodus had no king but Yahweh. They were egalitarian groups without hereditary rulers, until they settled in the Promised Land and either chose, or had imposed on them, the Davidic kingship. A vigorous debate goes on in the Hebrew Scriptures, and continues in altered form in the New Testament, about whether the monarchy is God-given, and the king a representative of God; or alternatively a recognition and a remedy for the faithlessness and rebellion of God's people. Gottwald finds in the prophetic and liberative strain in the Hebrew Bible resources for liberative practice today. Similarly, Pixley discerns 'a significant liberating tradition within sacred texts'.[13] This is not the *only* thing that is to be found in the Bible; indeed, there is, he says, much that is oppressive, and obscures the stress on liberation. He rightly says that God's Reign is a key theme in both testaments. The coming of the Kingdom is the heart of Jesus' message, which can only be understood in the light of the Hebrew Bible. This Reign calls into being a community of justice, love and equality. In the Bible, Pixley argues, God's Reign is always presented in terms of some embodiment or 'historical project'. He suggests that some of these are oppressive, others are liberative, and others again are manifest failures. The attempt to express God's Reign in the Davidic kingship, or in the centralized worship dominated by priests in the Jerusalem temple, he sees as oppressive. But other projects such as the pilgrim people in the desert, or the strategy of Jesus and the first disciples, were highly liberative. Jesus and his disciples expressed in their life together the egalitarian principles of God's Reign, and culminating in his death, Jesus engaged with the forces of oppression. Pixley believes that this kind of biblical material, responsibly appropriated, can be a major resource for faithful and constructive living, and for challenging the forces of oppression of today.

There is a very central, and persistent, egalitarian thrust in the Bible, alongside much that pulls in a different direction. It is demanding, distinctive, and often seditious. It contrasts strikingly with the dominant hierarchical and authoritarian emphases in many other holy books, particularly in the Hindu tradition. In this chapter I will explore some of the features of this powerful egalitarian 'trajectory' in the Bible, not as an exercise in biblical scholarship but rather to seek in the Bible for resources to help us to heal the relationship with Munuswamy and deal with the structures which keep us apart and obstruct love and justice. I hope this material will provide challenges and resources for faithful action and social change.

Creation and the image of God

The narrative framework of the Bible suggests that equality is the original, the final, and the proper condition for human beings. This is expressed in the narratives of creation and fall at the beginning, by the eschatological images which poetically point to the culmination of God's purposes, and by the anticipations of the coming Reign of God, particularly in the Jesus-event, and the company that gathered around Jesus. The myths of creation and fall in the first three chapters of Genesis, like many myths, have a function of providing an explanation of why things are as they are, especially things that are regarded as in some way manifestly incongruous or anomalous. In this they are aetiological myths, like Kipling's children's stories explaining 'How the elephant got its trunk', and so forth, providing some kind of explanation, but not necessarily a justification, of something that is markedly odd. But myths commonly have normative content as well: suggesting that this is how things ought to be, or this is the kind of behaviour that is required because it was the way people behaved in the days of innocence, and will behave again at the end of time. The creation narratives in Genesis are affirming, among other things, that the original condition of humankind was one of equality, and addressing the question of how humankind was deprived of its primal equality, and how inequality, and discord, came on stage.

In the Yahwist narrative of Genesis 2, Adam cannot find the kind of fellowship he needs for his flourishing, 'a helper as his partner'. However benign and peaceful the relationship with the animals might be, the animals cannot provide the quality of fellowship that Adam needs; their difference is such as to make this impossible. Adam names the animals, but he needs an equal with whom he can be bound in loving co-operation. God then provides in Eve one who is 'bone of my bones and flesh of my flesh'.[14] The stress is on the incompleteness of Adam and of Eve without the other; they belong together in relationship; they need one another and they are basically equal to one another; the fact that Adam was created first and Eve was taken from Adam's rib does not significantly qualify their equality; they need one another and belong together as equals.

With the Fall, as depicted in Genesis 3, inequality and subordination enter in as one consequence of sin and disobedience; equal relationships are disturbed, and Eve is told that her husband will rule over her.[15] Inequality is a *punishment*. Now the primitive condition of equality remains not only as a dream-memory but also as an expression of God's will in its purity, which stands in judgment on the compromising inequalities of the present age; the recovery of equality and innocence continues as a messianic hope.

In the alternative, Priestly, creation narrative in Genesis 1, God creates humankind after the animals, as a kind of culmination of the process of creation. And God creates them together in God's 'image and likeness':

> Then God said, 'Let us make humankind in our image, according to our likeness; and let them have dominion over the fish of the sea, and over the birds of the air, and over the cattle, and over all the wild animals of the earth, and over every creeping thing that creeps upon the earth.'
> So God created humankind in his image, in the image of God he created them; male and female he created them.[16]

Notice two points in particular. First, *all* human beings are created in the image of God, they all share equally in this crucial, definitive characteristic. There is no question of some being more and others less involved in the *imago Dei* as far as the created order is concerned. And, secondly, the juxtaposition of creation in God's image and creation as male and female has led some exegetes and theologians to stress that the *imago Dei* can only be predicated of people in relationship, not of an isolated individual. Relationship is of the essence of the image of God.[17] The *imago Dei* is not some abstract quality that each human being possesses, but relates to the capacity for relationship. Human beings are essentially relational, made for loving. It is in human relationships of love, solidarity and equality that the image of God is manifest.

The *imago Dei* speaks both of the importance of equal relationships and of the need to give equal respect, treatment and indeed *reverence* to all, for all bear the image even if now only in partial and broken form. Equality is ascribed by God in the work of creation; it is not a human achievement or an empirical characteristic of human beings. Equality before God and with one another is the original and proper human condition, and is an aspect of the promised culmination of all things. Meanwhile it must find real, if partial, expression among faithful people and in godly societies, indeed wherever the dignity and worth of human beings should be affirmed and celebrated. The image of God is thus a way of affirming and interpreting human dignity.[18]

The idea of the image of God is used in three ways in the New Testament. It provides a way of explaining the relationship between Christ and the Father; Christ is perfectly the image of God, and equal to the Father. It continues to be used as a way to speak of our co-humanity, and in a general way of human equality, and it is used to describe the transformation that believers enter into through faith in Jesus Christ.[19] In Christ, that is, true humanity is restored, the image of God is manifested in its fullness. According to John's Gospel, Jesus is accused of having 'made himself equal to God',[20] while in Philippians 2 it is declared that although Christ was in the image of God, he did not regard equality with God as something to be exploited or grasped.[21]

It may appear that in emphasizing that the Bible stresses that people are created equal, making its point in terms of powerful and evocative myths and symbols, and drawing from this a range of ethical conse-quences, I have been labouring something rather obvious. 'Religion always asserts the equality of all men', wrote Lord Eustace Percy, 'In a sense that is what religion is for.'[22] It is easily said; but it is not true. In popular Christianity it was no accident that in a wonderful Victorian hymn celebrating the glories of creation there occurred the now embarrassing verse:

The rich man in his castle,
The poor man at the gate,
God made them high and lowly,
And ordered their estate.

That might be a minority voice in the Judaeo-Christian tradition. But in the ancient *Rigveda*, and in many other places in the vast corpus of Hindu religious writings, we find an account of creation in which the various *Varnas* (roughly translatable as castes) emanate from the parts of *Purusha*, the primeval man. The Brahmans come from the head or the mouth, and therefore represent rational control; the *Kshatriyas* are warriors – they come from the arms; the *Vaisyas*, or traders, emanate from the belly or the loins; while the *Sudras*, the labourers, come from the feet.[23] And always there are the lowest of the low, the so-called Untouchables, who are below the whole hierarchical ordering of society, suspended between the human and the animal. Hierarchical ordering, these myths tell us, has been there from the beginning. By birth one is pure or polluted. And the corresponding ethic is one of conformity to the functions of one's caste in the hope that faithfulness in this will enable one's next birth to be into a caste of higher status. Inequality here is part of the primordial, created, and therefore proper, state of things.

Thus for the *Rigveda* humans are not created equal, in solidarity with one another, as human beings *simpliciter* before social distinctions enter in. Human beings can only be understood as belonging from the beginning to a caste, and it is the system of castes, the hierarchical social order as a whole, which reflects the being of God, which manifests the *imago Dei* (to use alien but not inappropriate language): 'the Brahman was his mouth, the Rajanya was made from his arms; the being called Vaisya, he was his thighs; the Sudra sprang from his feet'.[24] A hierarchical ordering of society has been there from the very beginning, the *Rigveda* teaches, and it bears a permanent divine sanction.

Thus for a principal Hindu tradition caste is represented as one of the fundamental orders of creation. But the Bible presents a stark, almost insurmountable obstacle to this style of entrenched inegalitarian thinking. As the Talmud put it: 'One man alone was brought forth at the time of Creation in order that thereafter none should have the right to say to another, "My father was greater than your father."'[25] The Hebrew and Christian Scriptures declare emphatically that there is one common origin for human beings, that all bear the same image, and that hierarchical rankings are defects which enter in later, and lack the same ultimacy as human equality.

The equality of the family[26]

Equality is thus rooted in the order of creation. But more: equal relationships are also commended in the Hebrew Scriptures either on the basis of God's special concern for the poor and the oppressed, shown most dramatically in the deliverance of Israel from bondage in Egypt (to which I will shortly turn), or as the equality expressed in the created order which should be reflected in family-style relationships among human beings: 'Have we not all one father? Has not one God created us? Why then are we faithless to one another, profaning the covenant of our ancestors?'[27] The ancient family, in Israel and elsewhere, was, of course, normally patriarchal; in recent times feminist theologians have helped us to affirm non-patriarchal understandings of the family, and suggested models of the family in the Bible, and particularly in the New Testament, were not universally patriarchal.[28] The stress may be not so much on the authority of the father as on the family gathered around the meal table to share food and much else with one another. In a family there are, of course, always inequalities of need, power and responsibility, but within the family unit the equal worth of each is affirmed. Patriarchy in the ancient world was often seen as part of the natural order; the husband's superiority rested on the supposed intellectual inferiority of women.[29] In the Bible the stress is rather upon the need for men and women to fulfil the complementary roles that have been given them by God. Job bases his magnificent ethic of fellowship on the equality of birth; God has made everyone and is therefore father of the whole human family. Thus less than equal treatment is derogatory to the majesty of God the Father of all:

If I have rejected the cause of my male or female slaves,
when they brought a complaint against me;
what then shall I do when God rises up?
When he makes inquiry, what shall I answer him?
Did not he who made me in the womb make them?
And did not one fashion us in the womb?

If I have withheld anything that the poor desired, or have caused the
    eyes of the widow to fail,
or have eaten my morsel alone,
and the orphan has not eaten from it—
for from my youth I reared the orphan like a father
and from my mother's womb I guided the widow—
if I have seen anyone perish for lack of clothing,
or a poor person without covering,
whose loins have not blessed me,
and who was not warmed with the fleece of my sheep;
if I have raised my hand against the orphan,
because I saw I had supporters at the gate;
then let my shoulder blade fall from my shoulder,
and let my arm be broken from its socket.
For I was in terror of calamity from God,
and I could not have faced his majesty.

If I have made gold my trust,
or called fine gold my confidence;
if I have rejoiced because my wealth was great,
or because my hand had acquired much …
this also would be an iniquity to be punished by the judges,
for I should have been false to God above.[30]

The philosopher Gregory Vlastos uses this image of a loving family
to defend his egalitarianism. A visiting Alien asks for an explanation of
why we believe in human equality. Vlastos replies, 'Because the human
worth of all persons is equal, however unequal may be their merit.' The
moral community is like a family, not 'a club from which members may
be dropped for delinquency'. He continues:

Our morality does not provide for moral outcasts or half-castes. It does provide for punishment. But this takes place within the moral community and under its rules. It is for this reason that, for example, one has no right to be cruel to a cruel person. His offence against the moral law has not put him outside the law ... He is still protected by its prohibition of cruelty – as much as are kind persons ... Here, then, as in the single-status political community, we acknowledge personal rights which are not proportioned to merit and could not be justified by merit.

The law books of the Hebrew Bible, and particularly Deuteronomy, are based on the presupposition that Israel as a whole is to be a kind of family, and the rules and procedures proposed are to be appropriate to this understanding. Under God's sovereignty there is to be a serious approach to a family style of equality among his people. Since ultimately God owns the land and intends it for the delight and for the welfare of his children, there is something thoroughly anomalous in a few amassing great wealth while others are in poverty. In delivering his people from bondage in Egypt, God has shown that he does not intend them for slavery. Again and again God is presented as one who has a special care for the poor, the oppressed, the widow and the stranger.

There were, of course, rich and poor, weak and powerful, slave and free within Israel. Indeed we read, 'there will never cease to be some in need on the earth'.[31] But this is not presented as a reality to which we should be resigned. The statement that there will always be poor people around is immediately followed by the command: 'Open your hand to the poor and needy neighbour in your land.' Such differences were seen not as the inscrutable will of God, or a given of the created order, but as social defects that a faithful people must seek to remedy. Laws constantly enjoined special consideration for the poor and weak, reflecting God's partiality and compassion for them. Legislation relating to the Year of Release,[32] and the Year of Jubilee[33] provide for the release of Hebrew slaves, the cancelling of debts, and the redemption of land – all involving a recognition that inequalities are subversive of the kind of fellowship God wills for his people. And although at some points a sharp distinction was drawn between the Israelite and the Gentile, so that the outsider was not entitled to the benefits available to full members of the fraternity, there was, even in the law books, a strand which sees the stranger as entitled to equal treatment with the Jew: 'When an alien resides with you in your land, you shall not oppress the alien. The alien who resides with you shall be to you as the citizen among you; you shall love the alien as yourself, for you were aliens in the land of Egypt: I am the LORD your God.'[34]

The prophets

The prophets' repeated calls for justice suggest not only that God has a special care for the weak and helpless, but also that there is an integral connection between justice and equality, two sides of the one coin, together being an expression of the will of God. The prophets typically seek not a *reversal* of the present structures of injustice, so that the rich become poor and the poor rich, and the old victims become the new oppressors, but a new – or rather restored – structure of equality and justice, because this is the clear will of God. The true service of God involves just and equal treatment of one's fellows. Worship which is detached from this passionate commitment to the needs of the neighbour becomes blasphemy:

> I hate, I despise your festivals,
> and I take no delight in your solemn assemblies….
>
> Take away from me the noise of your songs;
> I will not listen to the melody of your harps.
> But let justice roll down like waters,
> and righteousness like an ever-flowing stream.[35]

The election of Israel, it is true, does create a fundamental difference between God's chosen people and 'the nations'. Israel is again and again called to be separate, and her election is occasionally interpreted in terms of dominance or superiority over the nations. But the more general emphasis is on the responsibilities entailed by God's choosing of his people. Israel may be enjoined to preserve her purity from Gentile contagion, but her vocation to be 'a royal priesthood, a holy nation' is not for her own sake, but for all humankind. God's reiterated promise to Abraham is that 'in you all the families of the earth shall be blessed'.[36] Israel's role is increasingly clearly seen as being universal. She is to be a 'light to lighten the Gentiles', and the servant suffering for all humankind. The universality of God's purposes and his equal care for all human beings does not conflict with the election of the Jews; they have special responsibilities within God's plan, but the weight is on responsibility rather than privilege, dominance or superiority.

There is an ongoing and never totally resolved debate within the Hebrew Scriptures about political equality, in particular about the question whether a people which recognizes the sovereignty of Yahweh might also have another king, an earthly superior, as well. What is abundantly clear, even in the most 'royalist' strands of the tradition, is that kings have a special responsibility for defending the poor and the oppressed:

> Give the king your justice, O God,
> and your righteousness to a king's son.
> May he judge your people with righteousness,
> and your poor with justice…
>
> May he defend the cause of the poor of the people,
> give deliverance to the needy,
> and crush the oppressor.[37]

Kings are as much subject to the law of God as any of their subjects. The prophet Nathan confronts King David directly with his adultery and his murder of Uriah the Hittite,[38] and Elijah taxes Ahab with his theft of Naboth's vineyard and his doing away with Naboth.[39] All are equal before the law of God.[40] Within Israel there are, it is true, social gradations, but before the law, as before the Giver of the law, these fade away: 'You shall not revile the deaf or put a stumbling block before the blind; you shall fear your God; I am the LORD. You shall not render an unjust judgment; you shall not be partial to the poor or defer to the great: with justice you shall judge your neighbour.'[41]

Lest we take equality before the law for granted, as an axiom so obvious that every rational being must believe in it, consider this, from the Indian *Code of Manu*, in which crimes and penalties are related to the caste of the parties involved:

A Kshatriya, having defamed a Brahmana, shall be fined one hundred [panas]; a Vaisya, one hundred and fifty or two hundred; a Sudra shall suffer corporal punishment. A Brahmana shall be fined fifty [panas] for defaming a Kshatriya; in [the case of] a Vaisya the fine shall be twenty-five [panas]; in the case of a Sudra twelve. A once-born man [a Sudra] who insults a twice-born man with gross invective, shall have his tongue cut out; for he is of low origin. If he mentions the names and the castes of the [twice-born] with contumely, an iron nail, ten fingers long, shall be thrust red-hot into his mouth.[42]

In the Hebrew Scriptures there is also a recognition that there is, perhaps inevitably and unavoidably, a tension between the egalitarian will of God and the way actual societies, even Israel, operate and structure themselves. But the ideal and the expectation of equality and justice always stands in tension with the compromises of political and social life, challenging any attempt to base society on other values, or become complacent about the inequalities and injustices of the present.

The one great exception to this is the place of women. Feminist theologians and exegetes have made it impossible to deny that the Hebrew Scriptures are profoundly patriarchal, and that they assume, despite the creation narratives, with some consistency that women are inferior to men and ought to be subordinate to men. This is not to forget that there are remarkable and influential women in the narrative – Sarah, Rebecca, Deborah, Ruth, Hannah and Jael, for instance. But that cannot conceal or excuse the pervasive assumption that women are chattels and essentially inferior to men.

Apocalyptic and eschatology

When we turn to the New Testament we find ourselves dealing with documents produced in a very different social context. The New Testament books were written in and for churches which were small, almost totally without secular power or influence, and expecting an imminent end of the present order. There was, of course, diversity between and within the churches, and development over time, particularly in eschatology. Some churches were poorer than others; some were bitterly divided by theological disagreements; there was change and development in the shape of the eschatological expectation. As a consequence there was little uniformity in the way in which certain ethical issues, particularly those relating primarily to 'the world' rather than to individual behaviour or the life of the church, were regarded. Yet, even in the most apocalyptic strands of the material in which it is believed that the whole social and political order of the world bears the mark of the Beast and is destined for imminent destruction, both the behaviour of Christians and the organization of the church are regarded as matters of eternal significance. Indeed, apocalyptic literature suggested with great force that the church was a sort of counter-culture. Apocalyptic was deeply embedded in the early Christian world-view, and in many ways continued the prophetic witness of the Hebrew Bible.[43]

Among the functions of apocalyptic, three are of particular importance for our purposes. First, it claimed to reveal, to unveil, the inner reality of what was happening in the world. The powers of evil that presented themselves as angels of light were unmasked, and believers were enabled to discern what was happening in history.

Secondly, apocalyptic persistently denied the finality and acceptability of the existing order of things. The pretensions of rulers and authorities were relativized, and cut down to size. Apocalyptic declared that their days were numbered, and that they were not a final manifestation of God's purposes. An alternative order, in which the poor and the oppressed had a place of honour in an egalitarian community, was not only possible but it was promised. With this in view, Dietrich Bonhoeffer called on the church of today to be 'a community which hears the Apocalypse ... to testify to its alien nature and to resist the false principle of inner-worldliness' in order to serve those who suffer and to 'take to itself all the sufferers, the forsaken in every party and status. "Open your mouth for the dumb."'[44]

In the third place, apocalyptic nourished a confident hope not only that things could be different, but that they would be different, that God was bringing out of the injustice and oppression of the present a Reign which would be characterized by peace, justice and equality. Indeed, the reality of that Reign was clearly manifest in the life, teaching and praxis of Jesus and could already be glimpsed and tasted in the fellowship of disciples gathered around Jesus. In the church was to be found an earnest, a down-payment [*arrabon*] of the joys of the Reign which would come in its completeness at the end.

Despite the obvious differences, there are clear lines of continuity and development between the New Testament and the Hebrew Scriptures. The New Testament may not be concerned, as was the Old, with the life and structuring of a nation under God. But it was not solely concerned with the individual; the church was commonly regarded as a 'royal priesthood and a holy nation' in continuity with the old Israel, and looking forward to the coming Reign of God that had been inaugurated by Jesus. God's Reign was envisaged as 'the city' or the New Jerusalem; it was a structured political community in which God's sovereign, loving will would be fully expressed. And there was a serious concern with the 'nations', that were brought to account for their treatment of the weak, the poor, the captives, and the hungry in the story of the sheep and the goats in Matthew 25. The nations too had a mandate to prefigure God's Reign and deal gently, justly and lovingly with the poor and weak; they too came under judgment for their failures in this regard.

The universalistic emphasis which is to be found in the Hebrew Scriptures, particularly in the later prophetic writings, now becomes more explicit and central. The ethnic election of Israel expands to become the openness of God's Reign to all believers. God is the universal Father of all, and enjoins that not only fellow believers but everyone should be treated with equal love and reverence by virtue of their humanity – such is the teaching of the parable of the Good Samaritan and many another passage.

The equality of the incarnation

The famous hymn in the second chapter of the Letter to the Philippians expounds the incarnation as Jesus Christ letting go, 'emptying himself', of his equality with God in order to humble himself and enter the human condition alongside human beings as their equal. Christ takes 'the form of a slave' in order to be with the weakest, the poorest and the most despised, and love them. He finally enters into the ultimate despair and desolation of death, the path for him and those who are found in him, to exaltation:

Let the same mind be in you that was in Christ Jesus,
who, though he was in the form of God,
did not regard equality with God
as something to be exploited,
but emptied himself,
taking the form of a slave,
being born in human likeness.
And being found in human form,
he humbled himself
and became obedient to the point of death –
even death on a cross.
Therefore God also highly exalted him
and gave him the name that is above every name,
so that at the name of Jesus
every knee should bend,
in heaven and on earth and under the earth,
that every tongue should confess that Jesus Christ is Lord,
to the glory of God the Father.[45]

This emphasis on God in Jesus Christ making himself equal with humankind and identifying particularly with the lowest, the poorest and the most oppressed is so central to the teaching of the New Testament that it appears again and again in various forms. Christ's humiliation of himself, his self-emptying (*kenosis*), his abandoning of his status, is absolutely crucial to the understanding of the work of Christ, and is exemplary for disciples:

Jesus … said, 'You know that the rulers of the Gentiles lord it over them, and their great ones are tyrants over them. It will not be so among you; but whoever wishes to be great among you must be your servant, and whoever wishes to be first among you must be your slave; just as the Son of Man came not to be served but to serve, and to give his life a ransom for many.[46]

In John's Gospel this crucial saying which links Christ's identification with the weak, the poor and the oppressed, is acted out. On the night of his betrayal, Jesus takes a towel and performs the role of the humblest servant in washing his disciples' feet. He embraces degradation in order to love and dignify the degraded. 'I am among you', he says in Luke's Gospel, 'as one who serves.'[47] He identifies with us even in the equality of our sinfulness 'so that in him we might become the righteousness of God'.[48] Jesus is moved with compassion at human hunger, human lostness and human suffering. The compassion of Jesus is not patronizing; it points to a strange ability to identify affectively with others, to feel their emotions as his own, and in this profound sense to become equal to them. Such chosen equality is the condition for love and for helping.

Jesus broke through the barriers of status, and purity, of rank and power, of race and gender which keep people apart. In Ephesians he is said to have broken down the dividing wall of hostility and suspicion which separate people.[49] In the Gospels this is exemplified particularly vividly in the fact that Jesus caused scandal by welcoming to his table women of the streets, publicans, quislings and all sorts of unsavoury characters. 'This man welcomes sinners and eats with them' they said in horror and amazement.[50] And in this table fellowship we see the kind of community of equals that Jesus sought to establish, prefiguring God's Reign which he was inaugurating. In Acts and the Epistles there is a major concern with the need for Gentiles and Jews to eat together, at the Lord's Table as at the common table, as an expression of the overcoming in Christ of the old barriers of purity and pollution, ethnic suspicion, and economic inequality.[51]

Discipleship of equals

The sayings about the Son of Man being a servant or slave come as rebukes to the disciples who are arguing about which of them is to have the highest status, and highlights the contrast between the humble equality proper to disciples and the arrogance engendered by status and rank in the world.[52] Disciples are expected to embrace the active, loving equality demonstrated to them by the Lord. There is a transposition of worldly values so that 'All who exalt themselves will be humbled, and all who humble themselves will be exalted.'[53] Gerd Theissen sees renunciation of status as one of the two basic values of early Christianity, the other being neighbour love.[54] Sharp differences of status obstruct the love of neighbour which is enjoined; they must be relativized or overcome, either by the superior renouncing status following the pattern of the incarnation, or the elevation of the inferior. 'Humiliation and exaltation go together.'[55] The humiliation of the powerful and the exalted is for the exaltation of the weak. In contrast with the classical tradition, humility becomes a key social virtue through a major 'transvaluation of values'. Thus, in Theissen's words, 'Exaltation and humiliation are images of hope for the great eschatological turning-point which begins in the midst of time.'[56]

A similar theme resonates throughout the Magnificat, so redolent with Old Testament echoes that we are reminded at every point that the God who is acting in the incarnation of Jesus Christ is the God of Abraham, Isaac and Jacob:

> He has shown strength with his arm;
> he has scattered the proud in the thoughts of their hearts.
> He has brought down the powerful from their thrones, and lifted up
>   the lowly;
> he has filled the hungry with good things,
> and sent the rich away empty.[57]

In the 'fellowship of equals' that gathered around Jesus, women had a strikingly prominent place, as has been emphasized by Elisabeth Schüssler Fiorenza.[58] Women thronged around Jesus, and although none were of the inner circle, 'the Twelve', they had a prominent role in the broader circle of disciples, and were the first witnesses of the resurrection. The earliest church was, according to Elisabeth Schüssler Fiorenza an egalitarian *koinonia* in which women and other people marginalized by the surrounding culture found a place, and dignity, and were widely welcomed into leadership roles. She does not argue that early Christianity was a uniform and placid egalitarian movement in which the dignity of women was assured and unquestioned. From the beginning there were tensions and conflicts between the egalitarian thrust and patriarchal and hierarchical trends, which became dominant, but never totally unchallenged, in later Christian history. But she demonstrates that the equality of women had its roots in the earliest period of the church and was an enduring, if often hidden, element in the tradition. In worship women found and experienced equality in Christ. But this was not something that was to be flaunted, according the Paul, for the church still had to exist in the context of a radically unequal social order.

Agape and equality

The New Testament constantly moves between doctrinal or narrative accounts of the significance of Jesus Christ, and the ethical implications of the Christ event for believers. The Philippians hymn immediately follows injunctions to follow in the path of Christ: 'Do nothing from selfish ambition or conceit, but in humility regard others as better than yourselves. Let each of you look not to your own interests, but to the interests of others.' God's loving generosity, or *agape*, comes equally to all, independent of their deserts or achievement – such is the lesson of the parable of the workers waiting for hire in the market-place. They are given exactly the same pay, independently of their desert, or ability, but in relation to their equal need.[59] This is what might be called the equality of grace.

Love is central in the New Testament understanding of God, and in its account of Christian ethics alike. 'Love concerns above all the relationship between the insider group and the outsider group. Primitive Christian love seeks to cross this boundary', writes Theissen.[60] The basis for this crossing of boundaries is the belief that God pours forth his love upon the world; the quality and the costliness of that love is shown in the life and death of Jesus Christ; and for disciples the command to love the neighbour as oneself is tied inseparably to the injunction to love God without reserve and without condition.[61] This, of course, demands putting oneself on a level with one's neighbour. The neighbour is anyone who has need of one's care, concern or fellowship. One cannot love God without loving one's neighbour, and the neighbour is the one in need, with whom Christ continues to identify himself, so that in loving or rejecting them, we are loving or rejecting him.[62] As Kierkegaard put it very aptly:

The neighbour is the absolutely true expression for human equality. In case everyone were in truth to love his neighbour as himself, complete human equality would be attained. Everyone who loves his neighbour in truth, expresses unconditionally human equality.

Everyone who, like me, admits that his effort is weak and imperfect, yet is aware that the task is to love one's neighbour, is also aware of what human equality is.[63]

The preference for the poor which pervades the Gospels is both an expression of God's love and a move to restore the equality without which neighbour love is not really possible. In Luke's Gospel, Jesus starts his public ministry with what has been called 'The Nazareth Manifesto':

> The Spirit of the Lord is upon me,
> because he has anointed me
> to bring good news to the poor.
> He has sent me to proclaim release to the captives
> and recovery of sight to the blind,
> to let the oppressed go free,
> to proclaim the year of the Lord's favour.[64]

The rich man in the parable was given Lazarus, the beggar at his gate, to love as himself. The rich man neglected to establish a neighbourly equality in this life, their roles were reversed in heaven, the rich man being in torment, and Lazarus in Abraham's bosom.[65] Neighbourliness on the basis of a recognition of human equality was what the situation called for, the overcoming of barriers of inequality so that love and justice might be possible (see Epilogue: Dr Dives and Poor Lazarus, pp. 249–56 below).

The egalitarian emphasis is continued in Acts and in the Pauline epistles. In Christ everyone is equal, and old distinctions of status, suspicion, competition and hostility are overcome: 'There is no longer Jew or Greek, there is no longer slave or free, there is no longer male and female, for all of you are one in Christ Jesus.'[66] This is founded on the work of Christ on the cross,[67] and should be reflected in the relations among believers and in the structures and activities of the church. Peter is led in the course of his encounter with the Gentile centurion, Cornelius, to recognize that he 'should not call anyone profane or unclean',[68] and Paul in his Areopagus speech asserts that God has made all nations from one stock and, quoting from a Stoic poet, affirms that all have equal access to God.[69] The distinctions of the world have already been made superfluous in principle; they must not be resuscitated within the church; and the eschatological expectation is of the messianic banquet when 'people will come from east and west, from north and south, and will eat in the kingdom of God'.[70]

The Body of Christ

In his powerful development of the image of the church as the Body of Christ,[71] Paul takes an idea common in the culture of his day and reshapes it radically to make it serve a new purpose. The common use of the metaphor was to suggest, as Paul does, that within the community 'we are members one of another',[72] that society involves diversity, difference and interdependence. But the image was commonly used also to suggest that some parts were superior to others, that some were made to rule and others to obey. In addition, in the Hellenistic version of the Body, the 'members' were commonly not individuals but classes.[73] Paul gives the metaphor of the Body a strongly egalitarian slant. Within the Body there is diversity of function depending on the diversity of the gifts which God has given through the Spirit, but *all* the gifts are for the good of the whole. Believers enter the Body through baptism and repudiate their earlier hierarchical differentiations as being no longer significant or desirable in the light of the new common status as members of the Body of Christ, members of one another, and participants in the work of Christ, which is to establish unity and peace. The old differences of status fall away as irrelevant in face of the new equality which God has established: 'God has so arranged the Body, giving greater honour to the inferior member, that there may be no dissension in the Body, but the members may have the same care for one another. If one member suffers, all suffer together with it; if one member is honoured, all rejoice together with it.'[74] Diversity of gifts and functions does not lead to diversity of worth, esteem or status. The work of Christ has established an equality which must be clearly expressed in the life of the church. Without equality, oneness and peace true Christian fellowship is impossible.

Instances of the Greek term *isotes* (= equality) and its cognates are rare in the New Testament. But none the less, it is a significant term. Paul urges the more prosperous Gentile churches to contribute generously for the poor Jerusalem church that the necessary equality may be established on which fellowship (*koinonia*) must rest; equality is the aim for the sake of loving fellowship.[75] The collection is to demonstrate the koinonia between the Gentile churches and the Jerusalem church, in which there was already a high degree of equality.[76] And it is also to establish equality, so that one does not have a superabundance, while another is in need. The collection thus demonstrates a general principle.[77] Similarly, in discussing the Lord's Supper, the regular weekly manifestation of what it is to be church, Paul sees divisions of status and wealth as causing arrogance and dissension which divide the Body and corrode and destroy the equal fellowship which is to be expressed in and through the Supper. The flaunting of the resources of the rich involved a contempt for the church and a degradation of the poor which has so deeply corrupted the Body that Paul says, 'When you meet together, it is not the Lord's Supper that you eat.'[78]

Luke gives in Acts a picture of what is sometimes, and rather misleadingly, called 'apostolic communism'. In the Jerusalem church the fellowship of the gospel was expressed in the sharing of property:

> Now the whole group of those who believed were of one heart and soul, and no one claimed private ownership of any possessions, but everything they owned was held in common … There was not a needy person among them, for as many as owned lands or houses sold them and brought the proceeds of what was sold. They laid it at the apostles' feet, and it was distributed to each as any had need.[79]

Complex problems in the interpretation of the accounts need not detain us. Many scholars believe that Luke's depiction of the Jerusalem church is highly idealized. For our purposes what is important to note is that certain groups at least in the early church believed that participation in the Christian fellowship involved far more than occasional almsgiving for the needs of the poor. These people saw the ideal for Christians and for the church as including economic equality, and they believed that true *koinonia* is impossible without radical sharing, without giving and receiving generously. This conviction continued, although usually as a minority opinion, so that as late as two centuries after Tertullian could assert that 'among us everything is common except our wives'.[80]

Christian worship in the New Testament is regarded as a central encounter with the God who 'shows no partiality'[81] At the simplest level, this means that believers must not be impressed or intimidated by the worldly status that has in principle been abolished by Christ. Above all, they must not allow it to corrupt the egalitarian inner life of the church. So the Letter of James writes:

> My brothers and sisters, do you with your acts of favouritism really believe in our glorious Lord Jesus Christ? For if a person with gold rings and in fine clothes comes into your assembly, and if a poor person in dirty clothes also comes in, and you take notice of the one wearing the fine clothes and say, 'Have a seat here, please', while to the one who is poor you say, 'Stand there', or, 'Sit at my feet', have you not made distinctions among yourselves, and become judges with evil thoughts? Listen, my beloved brothers and sisters. Has not God chosen the poor in the world to be rich in faith and to be heirs of the kingdom that he has promised to those who love him? But you have dishonoured the poor.[82]

The issue was not simply that the distinction between rich and poor had to be transcended or forgotten if Christian worship and fellowship were to be possible. The two sacraments of baptism and the Lord's supper provided the principal arena in which the dispute about the proper relationship of Jew and Gentile, that ancient distinction which was seen as being of such importance that it was paradigmatic of all other distinctions among people, was fought out. The matters at issue were no trivial concerns. It was not merely a matter affecting the realm of ritual, but on its resolution depended the understanding of the church as a community that reflected and continued the reconciling work of Jesus Christ, and the universal availability of the gospel of God's grace on an equal basis to all. In what appeared to be miniscule controversies about whether circumcision and the observance of the Old Testament law would be required of Gentile converts, and whether Jewish and Gentile Christians might refrain from social and eucharistic sharing or 'commensalism', the real underlying issues involved the universality of the gospel and the equality of human beings. And the resolution of these controversies not only moulded Christian worship but decisively shaped Western society and culture.[83]

Inequality in the early church

It is true, however, that Christian equality was not always seen as having immediate or total applicability to the social and political order. Indeed, in the New Testament, and particularly in the epistles, non-egalitarian values are also recognized and these sometimes seem to balance, if not cancel out, the affirmations of equality, or perhaps to suggest in some cases that there are spheres in which Christian equality has no place, or no place yet. The need for order, respect and hierarchy in the state and in the family or household is stressed in the epistles. Slavery is given at least a qualified recognition, and it is clear that the early church did not see its task as the direct questioning or rejecting of the inequalities of the surrounding society; indeed some of them were to be accepted as necessary and even desirable in the present age. Yet the Hebrew Bible often stresses that it is undesirable for an Israelite to become, or to be treated as, as slave. Israel has been brought out of slavery by God's deliverance, and it is inappropriate for any of God's people to return to slavery. Yet, even in the New Testament, slavery is a delicate issue with which the church had to come to terms, for it was an established social institution which could not be destroyed by a Christian minority, even if they could subvert its rationale.[84]

Paul famously argues in Romans 13 that 'the powers that be' should be obeyed and reverenced by believers, for they receive their authority from God. The ruler, whether he recognizes it or not, is God's servant, and should be treated as such. And this injunction is backed up by numerous calls elsewhere in the epistles to respect and pray for rulers and those in authority. Even when the state appears as 'the Beast', all his blasphemies and oppressions are not a justification for believers to revolt and establish an egalitarian kingdom of the saints. Judgment belongs to God.[85]

In relation to the social order, Paul's cautiously conservative call that everybody should remain in the condition in which they were called or converted,[86] makes it abundantly clear that Paul did not expect conversion necessarily to make people discontented with their secular lot. Indeed, Paul spells out in relation to slavery and family life the theory that Christians should be more conscientious in the fulfilment of the duties of their station, regarding this as in some way God's calling to them. It seems that from early times the only occupations which

Christians were expected to eschew were those that were blatantly immoral, such as prostitution or robbery, or those that involved idolatry, particularly emperor worship, demanded of soldiers in the imperial army. Here it seems it was idolatry rather than any feeling that Christians should not participate in an inegalitarian social order that caused the scruples. But it is also good to remember that the early Christians were for the most part in menial and lowly occupations, and for them the problem of compulsory emperor worship seldom arose.

The so-called 'household tables' in the epistles enjoin a very traditional pattern of family relationships.[87] The headship of the father, and indeed the superiority of men over women, are virtually taken for granted. Parents are entitled to expect obedience and respect from their children, but are not to 'provoke them to wrath'. And Christian slaves have an added religious sanction for obedience to their owners:

> Slaves, obey your earthly masters with fear and trembling, in singleness of heart, as you obey Christ; not only while being watched, and in order to please them, but as slaves of Christ, doing the will of God from the heart. Render service with enthusiasm, as to the Lord and not to men and women, knowing that whatever good we do, we will receive the same again from the Lord, whether we are slaves or free. And, masters, do the same to them. Stop threatening them, for you know that both of you have the same Master in heaven, and with him there is no partiality.[88]

There seems to be little or no disturbance to the established order of things involved here. Is it, perhaps, that these countervailing values were able to erase or neutralize the strong egalitarian thrust that we have discerned in the New Testament, so that Christians would realize that they were not to be taken seriously in the present age? Were egalitarian values believed to have no saliency outside a narrowly defined spiritual realm? Was the talk of there being 'no longer Jew or Greek, there is no longer slave or free, there is no longer male and female, for all of you are one in Christ Jesus'[89] only valid in a spiritual realm, or in the coming age?

The answer to these questions lies in part in a rather closer scrutiny of New Testament attitudes to slavery. It is true that Paul tolerated slavery, that he never denounced the institution as such, that he called on Christian slaves to be obedient to their masters in wholehearted fashion, as part of their Christian commitment, and that he returned Onesimus, the runaway slave, to his master. But Paul returns Onesimus as a brother rather than a slave, and bids Philemon accept him as he would receive Paul himself.[90] Paul obeys the law, but in returning the runaway slave he does not confirm the institution of slavery but subtly relativizes it and suggests its incompatibility with the gospel. Worldly distinctions between the slave and the free man dissolve to nothing in the presence of God, and among believers they should be transformed if not abolished. They are relativized in the light of the gospel. There is a sense in which it seems ultimately not to matter for Paul whether one is a slave or free, because this condition is temporary, and worldly distinctions are of little importance when compared with the equality which we have in Christ and before God. Thus, immediately after enjoining everyone to remain in the state in which they were called, Paul continues:

> Were you a slave when called? Do not be concerned about it. Even if you can gain your freedom, make use of your present condition now more than ever. For whoever was called in the Lord as a slave is a freed person belonging to the Lord, just as whoever was free when called is a slave of Christ. You were bought with a price; do not become slaves of human masters. In whatever condition you were called, brothers and sisters, there remain with God.[91]

The contrast with Aristotle on the treatment of slavery is marked. Aristotle was presenting the conventional wisdom of the ancient world on the matter when he declared that by nature some people are free and others slaves, and for those who are by nature slaves, slavery is both right and expedient, for their defective reason makes them people who should receive and obey rather than give orders.[92] For Paul, on the other hand, everyone, slave and free, male and female, Jew and Greek bore the divine image and accordingly was of infinite worth.

To sum up this part of the discussion: the early church in New Testament times did not press for organic social reform or any kind of revolutionary change in institutions such as slavery, the state, or the family. Indeed the detailed ethical injunctions in the later epistles have a cautious and conservative character which seems to contrast quite sharply with the radicalism of the love-ethic of the New Testament, especially in the Gospels. Even when we allow for the fact that a small and powerless church could have done little or nothing to influence the state or modify the institution of slavery and would have been suppressed with great savagery had it appeared as a revolutionary political movement, we are left with the fact that the conservatism extended to the family and some other aspects of the inner life of the Christian community. Nevertheless the equality of the practice and teaching of Jesus was subversive of received notions of order, and was not easily or quickly assimilated within the church. Nor did the early church embark on an egalitarian crusade or seek to reshape public institutions on an egalitarian basis. Rudolph Bultmann was right to say that 'The negation of worldly differentiations does not mean a sociological program within this world.'[93]

But the questioning of these differentiations, the denial of their finality, the affirmation that they dissolve before God and must be transcended in the Household of Faith, and that even in the world they are temporary and the result of sin, added up to an orientation which was quietly seditious. Gradually it undercut the acceptability of structures of inequality by forcing them again and again to justify themselves, for they had been uncovered as anomalies that require explanation and justification if they are to be tolerated. In Christ, inequality has no place. That does not mean that equality is confined to the individual's inwardness, or in some narrowly defined spiritual realm. For to be in Christ is to be in his Body, and here distinctions of status must fade away. Thus even when it sponsors no social or political programme, the church is to be understood as showing in its life, fellowship and worship an egalitarian alternative to the 'way of the world'. An assertion of Christian equality was not seen as an immediate attack on an unequal social order; indeed, as we have seen, it often happily endorsed the existing inequalities in society.

Yet the radical implications of the universalistic and egalitarian position were all the time there, even if sometimes below the surface, and worked like the seed growing secretly. Wrote Ernst Troeltsch:

The message of Jesus is not a programme of social reform. It is rather the summons to prepare for the coming of the Kingdom of God; this preparation, however, takes place quietly within the framework of the present world-order, in a purely religious fellowship of love, with an earnest endeavour to conquer self and cultivate the Christian virtues.[94]

This fellowship was both a kind of imperfect working model and an anticipation of the coming Reign of God, to which people can look for clues as to God's purposes for all humankind.

Biblical ideas of human equality, nurtured and to some extent expressed in the life of that fellowship, developed and flourished, constantly raising question marks against existing structures of inequality. And through teaching, preaching, worship, Bible reading and egalitarian Christian communities of various sorts, biblical egalitarianism gradually became deeply implanted in the soil of lands where the gospel was taken seriously. There it acted as an irritant and a disturbance, hierarchical structures and practices being deconstructed and made again and again to serve an egalitarian purpose. The implantation of this disturbing egalitarian memory and expectation is the theme to which I next turn.

4

Shoots of Christian Equality

Men and women who acknowledge each other's equality, claim the rights of free speech, and practice the virtues of tolerance and mutual respect, don't leap from the philosopher's mind like Athena from the head of Zeus. They are creatures of history; they have been worked on, so to speak, for many generations; and they inhabit a society that 'fits' their qualities and so supports, reinforces, and reproduces people very like themselves.[1]

A resilient tradition

Values and convictions as to what is true, right and good are passed on within a tradition in part through a conscious process of education and formation. Thus Dag Hammerskjöld was aware that he had received from his parents and forebears as part of his Christian faith a belief in human equality which was inseparable from that faith. The process of handing on a tradition is commonly a less conscious activity than that. As a by-product of nurture, teaching, preaching, liturgy, theological reflection and dispute certain beliefs and values come increasingly to be taken for granted as obviously true or right, as matters beyond serious question. Thus, for example, drawing largely unconsciously on their Christian heritage the compilers of the American Declaration of Independence (1776) declared, 'We hold these truths to be self-evident, that all men are created equal…'. In saying this, they suggested that human equality was so obviously true that it required no rational or argumentative support; any normal rational being must assent to it. Equality is a moral axiom that needs no justification; it is a self-evident moral truth that needs no justification. One need not, and perhaps cannot, go behind it to something more basic still. It is the starting-point rather than the conclusion of a train of argument.

One side of the coin declares equality self-evident; the other that inequality is an anomaly that calls for explanation and justification or removal. The very term *in*equality suggests a deprivation of something that is good in itself, a lack of something that people want and deserve. Inequality, in other words, is a problem which individuals and societies have to face; it is not a solution or a resting place. It is a question, but not an answer. Explanation after explanation, justification after justification have been produced for inequality, from the myth of 'man's first disobedience and the fruit of that forbidden tree' whereby the primal equality was lost, to the studies of modern sociologists. As Ralf Dahrendorf argues, the problem of inequality is the foundation issue for modern sociology and the key to the history of sociology.[2]

But inequality is often regarded as more than an intellectual problem; it is something which is held to be repugnant and unacceptable unless allowed for the most compelling reasons. This is presumably because the culture is strongly orientated towards equality (even if this orientation sometimes serves to hide the existence of inequality, and is commonly not a little vague about what equality means) and regards it as self-evident, as a fundamental moral axiom. And this certainly is related to the deep penetration of Western culture by the Christian faith over many centuries, so that some of the distinctive values of that tradition are now assumed to be self-evident.

It is, of course, the case that not everyone would accept it as a self-evident truth that all people are created equal to one another. Extreme instances such as Nietzsche or Nazism remind us that there have always been dissenters from the mainstream who view equality as harmful and indeed immoral, and pour scorn on the idea of its self-evidence as nothing but a pretentious way of saying that a lot of poor, weak and ineffectual people seek to better their lot through the efforts of others. But such thinkers in the West in a sense prove the rule that in the modern world most people share a vague belief that equality is a good thing, and inequality suspect. And it is significant that those who attack equality with the greatest vehemence are often also people who expend a great deal of energy in denouncing Christianity, because they recognize the connection.

And if one goes to other cultures and other ages one finds that equality has by no means always and everywhere been regarded as a good thing. Indeed the opposite has often been the case, especially when one is far removed from the influence of the Judaeo-Christian tradition. Louis Dumont, the French anthropologist, in his classic

study of the caste system, *Homo Hierarchicus*,[3] describes Hindu society
as based on hierarchical principles, and tending to regard inequality as
axiomatic. Dumont provides a useful reminder that the self-evidence
of equality cannot be taken for granted. In a different culture and under
the influence of another religious system, hierarchy and inequality may
have a clear priority. 'It is not surprising', wrote Irving Kristol, 'that all
the golden ages, all the utopias, and all the paradises created by the
human imagination are egalitarian.'[4] He is wrong, of course: Valhalla is
not a very egalitarian paradise, and Plato's utopia was divided rigidly
into classes. But this remark does remind us of the role of a religion to
implant and sustain basic value orientations in a society, a task which in
some situations means legitimating whatever values are politically
approved of, but in other contexts may mean a prophetic challenge to
the prevailing values of the society, the nurturing within the community of faith of alternative values.

In a Christian or post-Christian society the issue of equality is
unavoidable. It is not that everyone sees equality as a good thing; it
often falls far short of appearing self-evident. But inequality is always a
problem, an anomaly, something that calls for explanation and probably for remedy. The ideal of equality haunts any culture that has been
shaped or influenced by Christianity, because that moulding has given
it an orientation towards equality. Equality as an ideal and as a presupposition 'lies embedded in the very foundations of European civilisation', writes David Thomson.[5] That said, I will in the rest of this
chapter examine the persistence of 'Christian equality' in the Western
tradition, and some of the various forms it has taken as the result of a
steady process of the implantation of egalitarian values derived from
the Judaeo-Christian tradition.

Other sources of equality

Like so much else in the Western heritage, equality has a dual source;
it has roots both in the Graeco-Roman and in the Judaeo-Christian
traditions. I have already given some attention to questions of equality
in the Hebrew and Christian Scriptures. Now I turn to the classical
heritage. To unravel these two strands, each composed of diverse
threads, would be a task of unbelievable complexity for which this is

not the place. From early times the two understandings have interacted and influenced one another. In some ways they were so similar that it should cause no surprise that Paul, preaching to the philosophers on Mars' Hill, should argue in a way which he knew to be congenial and familiar to them, that one God had created everyone, and then proceed to quote a Stoic poet to back up his case for human equality under the fatherhood of God: 'In him we live and move and have our being'; as even some of your own poets have said, 'For we too are his offspring.'[6] But it would be a mistake to conclude that there were not significant differences between the classical, mainly Stoic, and the Christian views of human equality.[7]

For the Stoics the fact that people were rational beings was the foundation of their belief in human equality. For Plato and Aristotle, inequalities in rational endowment were so important that they made these differences the basis for structures of inequality, the more rational ruling and guiding the less. But for the Stoics, these differences disappeared from view when faced with the great gulf between human beings and irrational creatures. Jews and Christians, on the other hand, simply set aside this whole discussion. For them, the starting-point was the creation of people on a par with one another because they were created in the image of God. Some people might be more rational than others, but it made no acceptable sense to speak of some people as being more in the image of God than others.

Other differences arose from the contrasting views of human nature. The Stoics understood human beings primarily as separate individuals; the ideal was the maintenance of as much aloofness and independence as possible from one's fellows. Because relationships did not provide a primary frame of reference, the Stoic view of equality was largely unconcerned with matters of social status or equality of opportunity. The wise man, they taught, should be indifferent to such things, and strive to cultivate inwardness in the confidence that all men (and it usually meant men) were his equals. Artificial differences of status were of no ultimate significance and should be disregarded. Superficially Seneca or Cicero, speaking of slavery, sound similar to St Paul. 'It is a mistake', writes Seneca, 'for anyone to believe that the condition of slavery penetrates into the whole being of a man. The better part of him is exempt.'[8] The Stoic strove for detachment from earthly conditions; he hoped to rise above them in spirit, and demonstrate how unimpor-

tant they are in practice. He saw the slave as an equal in the abstract, but
not a brother in fact. The Christian tradition, on the other hand, found
it hard to avoid a struggle about the bearing of the faith on matters of
status and social equality. Detachment from such matters was not an
option on offer. The worldly order might be seen as doomed to destruction, but the inequalities of that world were part of its evil, which would
not be found in the new Jerusalem. Christians understood people as
persons in solidarity and fellowship; their understanding of equality
was inevitably relational. The Stoics, according to John Plamenatz,
believed that the human being

> must be as independent as he can of other men; he must be his own
> master, and master also of his circumstances, or else indifferent to
> them, if he is to have peace of mind ... The Stoic preached the
> simple life that he might be less dependent on other men.[9]

The Christians, on the other hand, not only believed that fellowship
was essential for human flourishing but understood solidarity as
based on love and demanding compassion, the ability to be involved
affectively with others, to share feelings as well as things. We are tied to
our neighbours, they taught, by mutual responsibility and accountability. And social structures which separate one from one's neighbours – for the Stoics, the defences of one's inner tranquillity – were for
the Christians barriers which had been broken down in Christ in order
for them to enter a broader community.

Omnes homines, iure naturali, aequales sunt, all men are, by the law of
nature, equal, – such was the teaching of the Stoics which passed into
an axiom of Roman law. But, as Sir Henry Maine argued:

> The jurisconsults who thus expressed themselves most certainly
> never intended to censure the social arrangements under which
> civil law fell somewhat short of its speculative type; nor did they
> apparently believe that the world would ever see human society
> completely assimilated to the economy of nature.[10]

It was not until the eighteenth century, Maine suggested, that the legal
indicative became a practical imperative that the notional equality of
people should be translated into more than equality before the law. But

Maine neglects the crucial fact that for Christians equality was other than a legal notion; it was seen as a condition for the loving, compassionate fellowship which was God's will and which already found preliminary expression in the life of the church. Christian baptism from the beginning was an affirmation of equality. Christian concern for equality, therefore, was more than a wistful longing for an unrecoverable past, more than something to be hoped for at the final consummation of all things – it was a belief that steadily questioned existing social structures and sought expression, however partial and incomplete, in the present age.

Early Christian equality: continuity and compromise

I have already explored key egalitarian themes in the complex network of material that is the Bible, particularly the creation of women and men as equal bearers of the image of God, the expectation that equality will be restored at the end, the egalitarian movement around Jesus with its deep suspicion of earthly status and its celebration of God's self-humbling in Christ, the significance of the love of neighbour, and the stress on the privilege of the poor. I also tried to show that, both in the Hebrew Bible and in the New Testament, egalitarian emphases were often subversive of more hierarchical teachings and approaches in the same documents. Even in the Christian community, equality was sometimes seen as properly confined to the private, spiritual and churchly spheres. Beyond that there was the hope of the new heaven and the new earth in which the fraternity now only glimpsed in the church would be fully expressed for everyone. But egalitarian ideas could not be easily domesticated, because from the beginning the universal claims of Christianity made it impossible for the church to live in tranquillity in a ghetto. Because the gospel was for everyone and for all nations, it could not be withdrawn from the public arena, simply to provide solace for a small deviant sect. Furthermore, as the expectation of an imminent cataclysmic end waned, the church had to construct an ethics not simply for a short period before the End arrived and the present order was swept away, but for the guidance of Christians' attitudes and behaviour in what seemed likely to be a long period of waiting. It now became necessary to have a Christian assessment of the significance of the present social and political orders in God's providential ordering.

Furthermore, as the church gradually grew in numbers and influence, individual Christians and the church as an institution had to face problems to which the scriptures sometimes gave little guidance. A new social ethics had to be formulated, wider in scope and in more detail than anything that had been required hitherto, and this ethics could seldom be read directly off the Scriptures. Early church leaders and theologians – the Fathers, as they are called – accordingly turned for help to extraneous ethical and philosophical systems, and in the process of formulating a new Christian social ethics these systems – particularly Stoicism, which I have already mentioned, and Neo-Platonism, a fundamentally hierarchical system – deeply influenced Christian thinking.

It is particularly notable that even as the church grew in power, influence and wealth and 'Christendom' gradually emerged, the Fathers of the first five centuries continued to teach the need for equality, sometimes in words which do little more than repeat the teaching of the New Testament, or sometimes in ways that showed clearly that their thought had also been influenced by Stoic or other philosophical systems. For the Fathers, human equality is based on the conviction that all people are created equal and in the image of God, on the constant equality of God's dealing with humankind, and God's special care for the poor, on notions of *koinonia* founded on equality, and sometimes on ideas borrowed from philosophy, such as a stress on the common rationality of human beings as the basis for equality.

Clement of Alexandria (c.150–216), who developed a kind of synthesis of classical (mainly Stoic) wisdom and Christian truth, sees equality as a quality of God, who provided the necessities of life for all. These gifts of God should accordingly be shared in an equal way if fellowship of a kind pleasing to God is to be sustained. Christians are called to become like little children and that, Clement argues, means becoming equal to other people. Private property and private wealth can only be justified if used for the sake of fellowship, and shared with those in need: 'Goods are called goods because they do good, and they have been provided by God for the good of humanity', he writes.[11] And elsewhere:

It is God himself who has brought our race to a *koinonia* by sharing himself, first of all, and by sending his Word (Logos) to all alike, and by making all things for all. Therefore, everything is common, and the rich should not grasp a greater share.[12]

A similar point was made more strongly by Basil the Great (330–97):

> The bread which you keep, belongs to the hungry; the coat which you preserve in your wardrobe, to the naked; those shoes which are rotting in your possession, to the shoeless; the gold which you have hidden in the ground, to the needy. Wherefore, as often as you were able to help others, and refused, so often did you do them wrong.[13]

Gregory of Nazianzus (329–89) speaks of an 'original equality' which is still shown in God's equal provision of rain, air, sun and the other basic necessities of living. Christians should strive to restore something of this primal equality by sharing with their needy fellows. John Chrysostom (c.347–407) argues in similar vein that within God's household there should be equality:

> Is this not evil for some one person to have what is the Master's, for some individual to enjoy what is common property? Or is not 'the earth God's and the fullness thereof'? If what is ours belongs to the common Master, it belongs to our fellow-slaves; for the Master's property is common property. Or don't we see that matters are arranged thus in great houses? Thus a quantity of bread is given to all equally, for it comes from the Master's treasures. The Master's house is open to all. Similarly all imperial property is common property: cities, markets, arcades are common for all; we all share equally. Now see God's world: He made some things to be held in common in order to put the human race to shame, such as air, sun, water, earth, sky, sea, light, stars; he distributed them to all equally as to brothers. He made eyes the same for all, body the same, soul the same, a like frame among all, from one man all humanity, in the same house all humanity. But none of these put us to shame. And he made other things common, such as baths, cities, markets, arcades. See how there is no conflict over common property, but everything is peaceful. But when some one ventures to seize something and make

it his own, then jealousy enters in, as if nature herself were dis-
pleased, because although God gathers us together from everywhere, we compete in separating and detaching ourselves when we
make things our own and say Mine and thine – that frigid expression. Then comes conflict, then disgust.[14]

Ambrose of Milan (c.334–97) sees almsgiving as a kind of restitution, a
move towards the original equality:

> Not from your own do you bestow upon the poor man, but you make
> return for what is his. For what has been given as common for the
> use of all, you appropriate to yourself alone. The earth belongs to all,
> not to the rich ... Therefore you are paying a debt, you are not
> bestowing what is not due.[15]

One could go on for a long time detailing the strength and persistence of the patristic affirmation of equality. Sometimes it took a strongly biblical shape, sometimes, as with Lactantius or Minucius Felix,
there was clearly much Stoic influence at work; and the most radical of
all, Epiphanes, was a kind of Gnostic Pythagorean whom later generations have decreed to be just outside the bounds of orthodoxy.[16]

The whole was aptly summed up by Gregory the Great: *Doctrina
inaequalitas surget ex fonte superbia*, belief in inequality arises from
the spring of pride.[17] Sometimes the church's advocacy of equality
sounded more Stoic than Christian, and often attempts were made to
spiritualize the notion of equality so that it was in danger of losing its
cutting edge in the church and in society alike. Often the practice of
Christians and the institutional structures of the church denied an
egalitarian gospel. But the church could not escape from the issue of
equality without rejecting its foundational document. The ideal of
equality continued to haunt the church even when theologians and
church leaders regarded it as little more than an irritant. Yet the seditious memory and the entrancing hope of equality would not go away.

Christian equality: the Middle Ages

Turning to the later history of the church, it is easy to demonstrate that Christianity in all its main branches tolerated and indeed sanctioned and justified inequality, sometimes glaringly oppressive forms of inequality. The church early on adopted for itself a hierarchical structure which might seem to conflict blatantly with Paul's image of the Body in which there was diversity of function but equality of status, and with Jesus' example and teaching on authority and rank. As early as the First Epistle of Clement, Paul's image of the Body is given a strongly hierarchical skew, which brings it closer to pagan uses of the metaphor than to Paul's own understanding.[18] Ignatius and particularly Cyprian stress the indispensability of a hierarchical ordering of the church, which owes a great deal to secular parallels.

Hierarchical thinking in Christianity was strongly reinforced by the amazingly pervasive and prolonged influence of Neoplatonism. This philosophy saw the universe as a vast cosmic hierarchy, a kind of pyramid, or 'Great Chain of Being' in which the lower derived its being from the higher, and all nature demonstrated unchangeable gradations of status, significance and worth. According to the 'Principle of Plenitude' everything existed that should exist, and everything had been put in its proper ranking and place in a vast cosmos of interdependence and pervasive inequality. Plotinus, who can fairly be regarded as one of the founding fathers of Neoplatonism, enquired, 'Is it by the mere will of the Being who meted out to all their several lots that inequalities exist among them?' To which he answered: 'By no means; it was necessary according to the nature of things that it should be so.'[19] In this 'best of all possible worlds' (Leibniz and Voltaire's *Candide* were merely reiterating Neoplatonic commonplaces) any assertion of equality was subversive, not simply to the social and political order, but to the whole cosmic system of which human society was but a part, incorporating the fundamental principles which pervaded the whole system. Neoplatonism powerfully affirmed that each created being had a place in the vast cosmic pyramid which was necessary, right and proper; and the whole depended on everyone keeping to their place and performing the duties of their stations. Thus Neoplatonic influence in Christianity formed a powerful dissuasive to egalitarian movements and to social unrest.

Whereas Stoicism had reinforced as well as modifying Christian commitment to equality, Neoplatonism, wherever it became influential in theology and the life of the church provided a convenient way of forgetting about equality and offered a quasi-Christian way for the legitimation of hierarchy, ranking and all kinds of distinctions of status both in society and in the church. Perhaps it was only a version of Christianity that was deeply influenced by Neoplatonism that could play the role of a civil religion, concerned among other things with social control and the legitimation of authority after the conversion of Constantine. Under Constantine theologians, most notably Eusebius, taught that the Emperor's rule reflects or anticipates the rule of God, and the Emperor in his person represents God himself. The same is true of the whole political order: the earthly hierarchy is both a copy of the heavenly hierarchy, and it participates in the rule of God. Thus to question the structure of things on earth is not only seditious, but vicious and heretical. Things as they are, and that includes existing inequalities, are as they ought to be, and should not be challenged but accepted as from the hand of God by all believers.

Yet significant elements of the primitive, more egalitarian, tradition continued, both in teaching and in practice. In the first place – and it is hardly possible to exaggerate the significance of this – throughout Christendom the whole community, rich and poor, serf and noble, gathered in one church around one altar to celebrate the eucharist and join in ritual commensalism. The eucharist or mass never ceased entirely to be a rite in which the equality of all was proclaimed and an egalitarian norm affirmed over against the inequalities of daily life. And every celebration was redolent, too, of the disturbingly egalitarian table fellowship of Jesus, who ate with the poor and the outcast and sinners, and reminded people of a God who is no respecter of persons.

Secondly, recruitment to the priesthood or the religious life, and promotion in the church's own hierarchy were to a significant degree open and equal. Even when the church accepted without question and indeed provided elaborate theological justifications for the structures of inequality in society it never totally forgot that in the service of God, and before him, all are equal. Both the monasteries and holy orders were open even to slaves.[20] Wolsey as cardinal was despised by some because he was the son of a butcher; but his career reminds us that the church remained, to some extent at least, an avenue of mobility open to all.

In the third place, the monastic movement created a kind of counter-culture that rejected many of the compromises which the church as a whole made with 'the world', and attempted to structure life in accord-ance with the gospel. It is not surprising that this meant witnessing, among other things, to equality as a Christian value in situations where this had been all but forgotten. While all forms of monasticism have egalitarian elements in their structure, this stress was particularly marked in a succession of reforming religious orders, most notably the various orders of friars and especially the 'Spiritual Franciscans'.

Finally, and perhaps most significant of all for the implantation of egalitarian values was the reading and expounding of the Bible. The Bible, as we have seen, is full of disturbing and challenging egalitarian ideas which did not fit neatly into the Neoplatonic, or even the Thomist, synthesis. The Bible ensured that a longing for equality was nourished and sustained within the church among ordinary people even when the institutional church scorned equality. This subversive strain in the tradition never totally disappeared, although the dominant emphasis in preaching and in teaching was that 'The social ranks and their respective duties, ordained by God for humanity, were intended to remain fixed and immutable. Like the limbs of the Body, they cannot properly exchange either their place or function.'[21]

Popular egalitarian movements

In medieval society, popular egalitarian notions could be contained and made more or less innocuous in three main ways. First, equality could find an expression within a recognized religious order which was controlled by the hierarchy and consciously distinct from 'the world'. Problems arose with the establishment of orders which were not enclosed but moved about among the people, the poor among Christ's poor, and preaching a simple evangelical and radical message which often had clear egalitarian implications. Secondly, the use of Latin ensured that the common people did not normally have direct access to the foundational documents of Christianity, and had serious difficulty in understanding the significance of the mass, obscured by so much linguistic and ritual mystification. Thirdly, Christian worship with its strong egalitarian thrust could, and sometimes did, become a confirmation of a rigidly stratified society by providing regulated, partial, and temporary ritual suspensions of the social hierarchy. Carnival is the most obvious instance of this, when servant and masters exchanged roles and boy bishops parodied the Christian cultus for a day. But other rituals and even the eucharist could perform the function of confirming the social order by periodically enacting its opposite.[22]

Such forms of control over egalitarian ideas could not always be sustained indefinitely. Groups such as the Spiritual Franciscans took the teaching of Jesus and the precepts of St Francis with a seriousness which was quite unacceptable to the church authorities because the friars taught that the gospel injunctions were applicable immediately and to everyone. The resultant criticisms of the structures of the church and the inequalities of the social order were infected with the millenarian expectations of Joachim of Fiore, and regarded as seditious by church and state alike. Later on, Wyclif, Hus and their followers bridged the gulf between the universities and the common people and preached ideas which were simple, evangelical, populist and egalitarian. The church's endeavours to integrate and effectively neutralize egalitarian thinking and practice could not be sustained indefinitely. The church was not uneasy if it was taken for granted that the original and final states were conditions of equality, as long as this did not become the basis for criticizing or opposing the existing state of things in church or society. Popular statements such as this, from the *Roman de la Rose*, could safely be tolerated:

> Naked and impotent are all,
> Rich-born and peasant, great and small,
> That human nature is throughout
> The whole world equal, none can doubt.[23]

But the use of biblical and theological arguments to support attempts to realize greater equality here and now was another matter altogether.

It was precisely this that was characteristic of the great European peasant revolts of the fourteenth and fifteenth centuries, and of almost all egalitarian movements up to the time of the Enlightenment and the French Revolution. The proliferation of egalitarian popular movements owed much to the Christian soil in which they flourished. Despite all the efforts to tame or eradicate it, Christianity persistently held up human equality as a memory, a hope and an ideal, an ideology likely to nourish dissatisfaction and constantly available for use as a weapon by the oppressed. These movements often take a millenarian or chiliastic form, and frequently appeal to the Bible and the primitive church. The experiment in community of property recounted in the Book of Acts, the Epistle of James, the Apocalypse, Daniel, and the Creation narratives in particular provided material which was used in support of egalitarian protests.

The English Peasants' Revolt of 1381, for instance, took as its slogan the proverb:

> When Adam delved and Eve span,
> Who was then the gentleman?

This was also used, according to Walsingham's account, as a text for a sermon by the leader of the Revolt, a priest, by name John Ball. Ball argued that all men had been created free and equal; serfdom, oppression, poverty and the luxury of the rich have been introduced by wicked men and are all against the declared will of God. Froissart gives what purports to be a sermon of Ball's, and probably offers a fairly accurate idea of his thinking:

> And if we are all descended from one father and one mother, Adam and Eve, how can the lords say or prove that they are more lords than we are – save that they make us dig and till the ground so that they can squander what we produce? They are clad in velvet and satin, set off with squirrel fur, while we are dressed in poor cloth. They have wines and spices and fine bread, and we have only rye and spoilt flour and straw, and only water to drink. They have beautiful residences and manors, while we have the trouble and work, always in the fields under rain and snow. But it is from us and our labour that everything comes with which they maintain their pomp ... Good folks, things cannot go well in England nor ever shall until all things are in common and there is neither villein nor noble, but all of us are of one condition.[24]

Walsingham's account of what appears to be the same occasion adds a little detail:

> And to corrupt more people with his doctrine, at Blackheath, where two hundred thousand of the commons were gathered together, he began a sermon in this fashion:
>
> 'When Adam dalf and Eve span,
> Who was thanne a gentilman?'
>
> And continuing his sermon, he tried to prove by the words of the proverb that he had taken for his text, that, from the beginning all men were created equal by nature, and that servitude had been introduced by the unjust and evil oppression of men, against the will of God, who, if it had pleased Him to create serfs, surely at the beginning of the world would have appointed who should be a serf and who a lord.[25]

Similar types of theological and biblical egalitarian propaganda were used in other medieval protest movements. The causes of these movements lie primarily in the economic and social conditions of the times, but Christian thinking certainly contributed to the awakening of a sense of injustice and a feeling that something should be done, and Christian homiletic rhetoric and imagery provided the most appropriate, as well as the most readily available, ideological weapon.[26]

The Reformation and Christian equality

Wyclif, Hus and their followers were initially concerned primarily with the purification and reform of the church, an endeavour which was often understood as involving a restoration of the so-called 'communism' of the Book of Acts. Wyclif's doctrine of the dominion of grace applied to society as a whole:

> Firstly, that all good things of God ought to be in common. The proof of this is as follows: Every man ought to be in a state of grace; if he is in a state of grace he is lord of the world and all that it contains; therefore every man ought to be lord of the whole world.

But, because of the multitudes of men, this will not happen unless
they all hold all things in common; therefore all things ought to be in
common.[27]

Norman Cohn suggests that Wyclif uttered sentiments like this in
Latin, and with careful qualifications appended to make it clear that he
did not intend to subvert the established order in society; his primary
and immediate concern was the reform of the church. But Lollard and
Hussite preachers, moving around the country among the peasants and
the urban masses, disseminated such ideas widely beyond the walls of
the academy, and in the vernacular, where they had truly potent effects.

The Reformation as a whole cannot be regarded as an egalitarian
movement, although it often brought to the forefront of discussion the
possibility of a more equal ordering in both church and society. Luther
denounced in typically vehement terms both the hierarchical structure
of the church and the distinction between the spiritual and the temporal estates. But when the Swabian peasants enquired why, if they too
belonged to the spiritual estate, their 'brothers in Christ' held them in
serfdom, Luther responded that Christian equality has no place in 'the
world', but only applies among 'true Christians'. Social distinctions
may be human inventions and not part of the divine ordering, but
nevertheless, 'A worldly kingdom cannot stand unless there is in it
inequality of persons, so that some are free, some imprisoned, some
lords, some subjects.'[28]

Calvin's ambivalence about equality was of a different kind from
Luther's. For Calvin there is an equality in sin – all are equally
depraved – and this gives a reason for equality of treatment; no one has
earned by good works or otherwise high status. Calvinism also provides
early roots for political democracy. Joshua Mitchell argues that democracy's 'pedigree can be traced to the Christian notion of the equality of
all under God', and is to be linked specifically to Protestant thought on
equality.[29] For Calvinist political thinkers the sinfulness of the individual or group may best be restrained by a system of 'checks and
balances', or 'dykes against sin'. Undemocratic systems, on the other
hand, tend to allow free rein to the pride and sinfulness of one man or
group. In terms of church structure, of 'ecclesiastical polity', Calvinist
churches from the beginning were markedly more democratic in their
operation, and provided in the life of the congregation and the broader

church a kind of school of democracy. Calvin's strong stress on pre-destination may temper the egalitarian strain in his thought: although all are created equal and bear the image of God, God does not in fact treat people on an equal basis.

Egalitarian motifs were stressed by the movements that are together classified as the Radical Reformation. Thomas Müntzer appears to have believed that the law of God recognized and sanctioned no differences of status and of wealth, although this emphasis was some-times overshadowed by his vivid and bloodthirsty apocalyptic out-bursts.[30] John of Leyden's Anabaptist utopia in Munster had as one of its objectives the abolition of privately owned money.[31] Other sects, such as the Hutterites and the Mennonites, believed in and practised community of property, but their quietism made them less of a threat to the established order than many of the other, more militant, millenarian-egalitarian groups. Sects that believed in equality only before God, or that equality was only possible among perfect Christians, posed little challenge. But groups such as the English Levellers and Diggers moved quickly from a belief that all Christians should be free and equal to the assertion, first, that all Englishmen, and then everyone, should be free and equal.[32] The equality they sought extended into the social, economic and political spheres, as the Leveller arguments presented at the Putney Debates of 1647 make clear. Their leader, Colonel Rainsborough, put it in famous words:

For really I think that the poorest he that is in England hath a life to live, as the greatest he; and therefore truly, sir, I think it's clear, that every man that is to live under a government ought first by his own consent to put himself under that government.[33]

On the scaffold about to be executed for taking part in the abortive rebellion by Monmouth in 1685, the elderly Leveller leader, Richard Rumbold, summed up their egalitarianism in memorable words: 'I am sure there was no man born, marked of God above another; for no man comes into the world with a saddle on his back, neither any booted and spurred to ride him.'[34]

The seventeenth century

It has sometimes been suggested that the modern idea of equality can be traced back only as far as the eighteenth century, and was radically different from anything that went before. I would hesitate to accept such a verdict. Great and influential ideas do not suddenly spring from nowhere; they have their histories and their pedigrees which are not only interesting in themselves but provide a necessary element for the proper understanding of these ideas. But nonetheless the eighteenth century was a major turning point in the history of equality. The idea of equality, hitherto regarded as primarily a religious notion was secularized in a gradual, haphazard and often incomplete way. Classical and mainly Stoic views were rediscovered and led to substantial reformulation of the concept of equality. And, most important of all, the conviction that the shaping of society lay in human hands rather than God's meant that in some quarters equality changed from being a focus of hope, nostalgia or protest into being a fundamental value underlying projects of social revolution or reform, in which old beliefs in the 'givenness' of the social order were replaced by a determination to take human destiny and the moulding of the life of the community into human hands.

Secularization of egalitarian thought had been taking place earlier as well. Thomas Hobbes, for instance, writing in the mid seventeenth century, produced a political philosophy in which he claimed to follow closely the methods and procedures of modern science and mathematics. But this political philosophy developed, according to its author, *more geometrico*, can be shown both in general and in detail to be a kind of secular transcript of Calvinist theology. In Hobbes's state of nature human beings are equal, but human nature is so self-centred and aggressive (Calvin would have said 'depraved') that each person's hand is against the neighbour. Total equality means total insecurity; the state of nature is a state of war in which each person's life is 'solitary, poor, nasty, brutish and short'. Natural equality – meaning essentially the physical equality which enables even a frail individual to threaten the life of the neighbour – is at the heart of the human predicament. Hobbes writes:

Nature hath made men so equall ... that, though there be found one man sometimes manifestly stronger in body ... than another, yet when all is reckoned together the difference between man and man is not so considerable ... For as to the strength of body, the weakest has strength enough to kill the strongest.[35]

The only solution which promises security and a civilized life is for each to abandon equality and hand over all rights to an absolute sovereign, who reflects at the human level something rather like the Calvinist understanding of the sovereignty of God. Equality, for Hobbes, is natural, but in a fallen world dangerous and destructive; it must be abandoned if true social life is to be possible. But it would be a mistake to interpret Hobbes as simply a secularizer of religious and theological notions, transposing them into a non-religious mode. After all, two large parts of Hobbes's *Leviathan* (the parts that students rarely read!) are basically theological: 'Of a Christian Commonwealth' and 'Of the Kingdom of Darkness'. It would be a serious distortion to read Hobbes as a secular thinker of the style of the twentieth century. Theology and theological disputes pervade his political writings, and he does not follow the anti-theological path trodden before by Machiavelli.[36]

The same is true of another of the great founding figures of modern liberal thought, John Locke. Locke developed an immensely influential account of equality that was firmly located in a theological framework, but which is now often read as if it were the conclusion of a process of secular reasoning, with the theology no more than an ornamental top-coating. But, according to one of his most perceptive modern interpreters, John Dunn, any faithful account of Locke's thought must take account of the fact that 'The entire framework of his thinking was "theocentric" and the key commitment of his intellectual life as a whole was the epistemological vindication of this framework.'[37] Jeremy Waldron, in his Carlyle Lectures on 'Christian Equality in the Political Thought of John Locke' goes further than Dunn, and argues very convincingly that the shape and grounding of Locke's view of human equality are to be found in Christian faith and specifically in the Bible. He quotes a remark by Alasdair MacIntyre to the effect that in Locke's *Two Treatises of Civil Government* 'the arguments ... concerning basic equality and individual rights were so imbued with religious content that they were not fit, constitutionally, to be taught in the public schools of the United States of America'! And, Waldron continues, maybe he is right: a Constitution interpreted in a way that prohibits the 'Our Father…' at the beginning of classes (or even a non-sectarian blessing by a Rabbi at the beginning of a High School graduation) is certainly in no position to instruct students in a doctrine of equality or equal protection that takes as its premise that we are 'all the workmanship of one omnipotent, and infinitely wise maker; all the servants of one sovereign master, sent into the world by his order and about his business; [all] his property, whose workmanship [we] are, made to last during his, not one another's pleasure: and [that] being furnished with like faculties, sharing all in one community of nature, there cannot be supposed any such subordination among us, that may authorize us to destroy one another, as if we were made for one another's uses …'[38]

Waldron concludes his lectures by reminding us that although in the modern West we assume that we can have a purely secular idea of equality, all the hard work on the shape, grounding and justification of equality has been done in the past on a religious basis. Whether and how it may survive and flourish when detached from that basis is an open question:

Equality cannot do its work unless it is accepted among those whom it consecrates as equals. Locke believed this general acceptance was impossible apart from the principle's foundation in religious teaching. We believe otherwise. Locke, I suspect, would have thought we were taking a risk. And it is not entirely clear – given our experience of a world and a century in which politics and public reason cut loose from these foundations – that his cautions and suspicions were unjustified.[39]

Other thinkers share the conviction of Hobbes and Locke that human beings are equal, but often interpreted the primordial equality in a different way and drew different conclusions from it, in general seeking ways in which political order might be made compatible with the maintenance of the maximum possible equality. In various places the language was transposed from theology to a more secular mode. Few seemed to enquire about the axioms from which the argumentation flowed; it was enough to declare them clear and distinct ideas, or rational and necessary notions, or self-evident truths. But all this took place in a context which was still deeply permeated by Christian assumptions.

Implantation of values is not exclusively or primarily a matter for the philosophers and theologians. Its primary loci are the family, the school and the congregation. And we have some fascinating material on how this took place in the seventeenth century. The Puritan pastor, Richard Baxter, produced among many other works a *Christian Directory, or Body of Practical Divinity*, written in 1664 and 1665, and first published in 1673.[40] This was an example of Protestant casuistry and spiritual direction, giving guidance for practice and behaviour in economic, political and domestic affairs, and endeavouring to shape the conscience by Christian principles. Baxter was no revolutionary, but in many ways his teaching was profoundly subversive. To take a pivotal example, in addressing masters about 'The duty of Masters to Slaves in the Plantations', he does not directly attack slavery as an institution, but his injunctions if taken seriously would profoundly disturb existing practices and structures. Slaves must not be regarded or treated as animals; they are in fact in the ways that really matter, equal to their masters:

> Remember that they are of as good a kind as you; that is, They are reasonable Creatures as well as you; and born to as much natural liberty ... Nature made them your equals. Remember that they have immortal souls, and are equally capable of salvation with your selves.[41]

Slaves must not be worked so hard that they cannot fulfil their duties to God. Slave owners are reminded that they have no absolute ownership of their slaves:

> Remember that God is their absolute Owner, and that you have none but a *derived* and *limited Propriety* in them ... Remember that *they* and *you* are equally under the Government and Laws of God. Remember that God is their Reconciled tender Father, and if they be as good, doth Love them as well as you. And therefore you must use the meanest of them no otherwise, than beseemeth the Beloved of God to be used; and no otherwise than may stand with the due

signification of your Love to God by Loving those that are his. Remember that they are the Redeemed ones of Christ; and that he hath not sold you his title to them.[42]

This is followed by a direct address to 'any of our Natives in Barbado's or other Islands or Plantations' (that is, slave owners) who are roundly denounced for their 'heinous sin', and the cruelty which brings the Christian name into disrepute. The institution of slavery is not absolutely rejected by Baxter, but his injunctions, based on the conviction of the Christian equality of slave and slave owner would transform the institution into something totally different. Thus faithful pastors implanted Christian values and challenged oppressive and unloving institutions.

Enlightenment and the secularization of equality

A rediscovery of the classical tradition was as characteristic of the Enlightenment as its amazing confidence in the human reason. Classical motifs in art and architecture were dominant in both the American and the French revolutionary periods. And in intellectual life the awakening from the 'dogmatic slumbers' of the immediate past involved a new interest in, and a desire to emulate, classical secular philosophy, sometimes as a kind of antidote to Christian theology. Equality was often understood more in a Stoic than a Christian way. With the gradual emergence of the idea that human beings were masters of their own destiny, equality became a concrete aim, linked inseparably with freedom and fraternity, as in the American and French Revolutions. The new order that was to be shaped would be radically egalitarian. But theology continued to haunt egalitarian thinking, especially in America.

Rousseau seemed largely to lack Locke's sense of religious conviction, but he continued to be deeply concerned with the social and political function of religion. He represents someone who attempted with some success to detach political thought from its embeddedness within the biblical narrative, and place it in a more universal and less Christian frame. In this sense, he is a major figure in the secularization of political thought. His radical view of the sovereignty of the people, which underlies so much modern democratic thought, contains very thinly disguised the theological notions that all are equal under one sovereign, and that 'the power of each citizen is made perfect in weakness'.[43] In accordance with the spirit of the age *and* the Christian heritage, Rousseau accepted as axiomatic that equality was the original, natural and proper condition for human beings. In his prize essay, *A Dissertation on the Origin and Foundation of the Inequality of Mankind* (1754), he set out to provide an explanation, but not a justification, of the anomaly of inequality. He distinguished two kinds of inequality, only the second of which was deeply problematic:

> One, which I call natural or physical, because it is established by nature, and consists in a difference of age, health, bodily strength, and the qualities of the mind or of the soul: and another, which may be called moral or political inequality, because it depends on a kind of convention, and is established, or at least authorised, by the consent of men. This latter consists of the different privileges which some men enjoy to the prejudice of others; such as that of being more rich, more honoured, more powerful, or even in a position to exact obedience.[44]

In the state of nature, human beings are both free and equal, in the most total sense; but in political society people are 'everywhere in chains' and equality has been displaced. The problem – and here Rousseau shows himself to be a social reformer rather than merely a theorist – is to find a form of political association in which the maximum possible freedom and equality is assured. Liberty and equality belong together; the one cannot survive without the other. Rousseau is thus no naïve utopian seeking in civil society absolute equality of the sort that had characterized the state of nature. The relative equality that is desirable in a politically ordered society means

> Not that the degree of power and riches are to be absolutely identical for everybody; but that power shall never be great enough for violence, and shall always be exercised by virtue of rank and law; and that in respect of riches, no citizen shall ever be wealthy enough to buy another, and none poor enough to be forced to sell himself: which implies, on the part of the great, moderation in goods and

position, and, on the side of the common sort, moderation in avarice and covetousness.[45]

In proposing such a relative political and economic equality as the best that can be hoped for in civil society while affirming that the original and in a sense proper position for human beings is one of thoroughgoing equality, Rousseau is a typical Enlightenment thinker, drawing on the Judaeo-Christian heritage, and attempting to transpose it into secular terms. Extreme inequalities, he teaches, must be protested against and if possible remedied; any inequality requires a justification; but a condition of absolute equality is quite unthinkable because incompatible with organized social life.

Emmanuel Kant, in many ways the epitome of the Enlightenment thinker, has been called 'the philosophical apostle of human equality'.[46] He spoke of human inequality as a 'rich source of much that is evil, but also of everything that is good'.[47] He adopts in his ethics egalitarian positions which look very like secularized versions of a Christian understanding of equality. Other people are always to be treated as ends and never as means, for example, and maxims are to be universalized since only that act on my part is moral if the situation would be improved if everyone acted in the same way. At least as moral agents, everyone is equal and all are entitled to equal treatment. As Bernard Williams puts it:

> The respect owed equally to each man as a member of the Kingdom of Ends is not owed to him in respect of any empirical characteristics that he may possess, but solely in respect of the transcendental characteristic of being a free and rational will. The ground of the respect owed to each man thus emerges in the Kantian theory as a kind of secular analogue of the Christian conception of the respect owed to all men as equally children of God. Though secular, it is equally metaphysical: in neither is it anything empirical *about* men that constitutes the ground of equal respect.[48]

There is an interesting change of emphasis in Kant's political writings. Here the concern is with civil or political equality which is inextricably involved with liberty. But for Kant it is only independent adult males who are politically equal citizens. Women and those who are dependent on others, such as poor people who live off charity, are not equal citizens. Nor is Kant at all interested in economic equality.

For reasons such as these it has been suggested that thinkers of the eighteenth century such as Rousseau and Kant in many ways represent more a revival of Stoic and Roman ideas of equality than a secular version of 'the Christian shape of equality'. The situation is, however, more complex than a choice between two self-contained systems. Although in some respects much eighteenth-century thought on equality seems to be close to Stoic models, it also shows clearly the influence of the Christian tradition of thought on equality. For thinkers such as Rousseau and Kant, assertions about human equality are not abstract propositions about human nature, without implications for behaviour or society. Human beings are not seen as isolated individuals. For Kant, they are members of the Kingdom of Ends; for Rousseau, the state of nature in which human beings do not depend on others cannot be sustained and must be replaced by an organized political society in which the essential values of the state of nature, prominent among which is equality, are as far as possible protected. 'It is precisely because the force of circumstances tends always to destroy equality,' wrote Rousseau, 'that the force of legislation ought always to tend to maintain it.'[49] Neither thinker is satisfied with the adequacy of equality before the law. A belief in human equality – or, rather, the rational conviction that all people are equal – must issue in attitudes, behaviour and forms of social organization which express this conviction more or less well.

The French Revolution is only the best known of many instances in which equality and fraternity are found together as necessary partners – Siamese twins, that cannot be separated without the destruction of both. The American Revolution used a deist rhetoric much influenced by Calvinism and did not have the anti-clerical and anti-Christian thrust of the French Revolution. But here, too, equality was linked with liberty as the necessary foundations of a fraternal and just society. Some people may have been reticent about the specifically Christian roots of a commitment to equality, but the roots were there, and the shape of the equality advocated betrayed the fact that it had been shaped by the Christian faith.

The nineteenth century and after

The nineteenth century was a time of competing and incompatible understandings of equality. Equality of opportunity – Napoleon's *carrière ouverte aux talents* – seemed almost an essential ingredient of developing industrial capitalism as well as a great aid to efficient government. The American ideal of a mobile society in which one could move 'from log cabin to White House' seemed to offer an attractive combination of equality, liberty and competition. But it soon became clear that equality of opportunity, while it might corrode the old styles of patriarchal stratification, led to new kinds of inequality which were no longer mollified by paternalistic links between the ranks of a traditional society. Those who had won their way to the top by their own efforts felt that they had no responsibility to the unsuccessful competitors they had passed on their way up.

Utilitarian thought rested on what appeared to be an egalitarian axiom, that 'each is to count for one and no one for more than one'. For the stricter Benthamites the happiness or misery of the duke or the dustman had exactly the same value in the calculus of pains and pleasures against which the morality of behaviour was to be measured. 'The greatest good of the greatest number' provided a criterion for social reform which ensured that there would be a steady move in social policy towards equality of treatment, and probably towards greater economic equality as well. Everyone, whatever their class or condition, had an equal right to happiness. This was at the time pretty revolutionary teaching, which issued in a multitude of efforts at social reform intended to ensure equality of happiness, or at least equal opportunity of achieving happiness, throughout the population. The concept of equality had narrowed and perhaps sharpened, making it an effective instrument for the reshaping of society. The underlying understanding of human nature had also narrowed, becoming sometimes quite banal. And few utilitarians before John Stuart Mill cared to examine very critically their presuppositions about human nature and society, or ask where the predisposition in favour of human equality had come from, or how it could be sustained.

Alexis de Tocqueville studied the United States as a kind of laboratory of equality. During his time in America, he reported, 'nothing struck me more forcibly than the general equality of conditions'.[50] This

was for him the great new fact of the age. Never before had there
been such great equality of condition in any nation in the world. This
equality, he believed, was rapidly spreading into every dimension of
American life, and de Tocqueville saw it as destined to spread by a kind
of providential process to every other civilized nation. De Tocqueville
himself made a sober and balanced assessment of the equality he found
in America. He felt, for instance, that enthusiasm for equality could
lead to a neglect of liberty and a descent into despotism. He believed
that equality, unless shaped by religion, might become materialistic.
He saw American equality as arising directly out of Christian faith:
'Christianity, which has declared all men equal in the sight of God,
cannot hesitate to acknowledge all citizens equal before the law.'[51] His
deep conviction that a modern egalitarian ordering of things was
coming meant that lessons of general relevance were to be learned from
the American experience. He ends his great study of democracy in
America by concluding that 'The nations of the world cannot prevent
the conditions of men from becoming equal; but it depends upon·them-
selves whether the principle of equality is to lead them to servitude
or to freedom, to knowledge or to barbarism, to prosperity or to
wretchedness.'[52]

'A nation', in Lincoln's words, 'conceived in liberty, and dedicated
to the proposition that all men are created equal', wrote equality into
its foundation documents as a fundamental truth. Commonly the
Christian roots of equality were recognized, as by Tocqueville, who
laid down as a general principle 'every religion has some political principles linked to it by affinity'.[53] Sometimes the American egalitarian
commitment was reduced to little more than rhetoric; sometimes it was
declared compatible with slavery and the subordination of women; and
often it was reduced to equality of opportunity as if this made palatable
the widest disparities of wealth and status. Lincoln himself sought to
define with care the significance of the Declaration of Independence's
commitment to equality:

> I think the authors of that notable instrument intended to include *all*
> men, but they did not intend to declare all men equal *in all respects* ...
> They defined with tolerable distinctness in what respects they did
> not consider all men created equal – equal with 'certain inalienable
> rights among which are life, liberty, and the pursuit of happiness.'

This they said, and this they meant. They did not mean to assert the obvious untruths that all were then actually enjoying that equality, nor yet that they were about to confer it immediately upon them. In fact they had no power to confer such a boon. They meant simply to declare the rights, so that the enforcement of it might follow as fast as circumstances should permit.[54]

This foundational national commitment to the equality of people, rooted in the Christian faith and enshrined in the Declaration of Independence and the Constitution stands as a plumb-line against which the actualities of society can be measured. It is constantly appealed to by underprivileged groups, and used as a potent weapon in struggles for greater justice and equality. Thus Martin Luther King declared a century after Lincoln's Gettysburg address that he had a dream

> that one day this nation will rise up and live out the true meaning of its creed – *we hold these truths to be self-evident, that all men are created equal.* I have a dream that one day on the red hills of Georgia, sons of former slaves and sons of former slave-owners will be able to sit down together at the table of brotherhood.[55]

This American constitutional commitment to equality has been plagiarized time and again in the constitutions of other countries, notably India, where it stands as an irrevocable undertaking to move towards the establishment of a more equal order of society. It is reflected in the wording of the Universal Declaration of Human Rights of 1948, which declares in its Preamble that recognition of the inherent dignity and of the equality and inalienable rights of all members of the human family is the foundation of freedom, justice and peace in the world. Article I of the Universal Declaration proclaims that 'All human beings are born free and equal, in dignity and in rights.'

Such commitments to equality as a social goal were recognized by rather few of their proponents, but by their more acute adversaries such as Nietzsche, as being Christian in origin and Christian in shape. Even in a plural or post-Christian context, the Christian origins and shape of equality lay a continuing responsibility on Christians for the sustaining and support of human equality wherever it is challenged or threatened by other opposing goals or values.

5

Modern Theologies of Equality

In his remarkable and important book on justice, Robert M. Veatch argues that discussions of justice are one place where 'theology may make a difference' today. He then goes on to suggest in a compelling fashion that theology and theology alone can really give an adequate account of the nature and grounding of justice, because Judaeo-Christian faith has decisively shaped the concept of justice down the centuries. The key working assumptions of secular theorists, argues Veatch, are borrowed from the religious tradition, usually without acknowledgement; secular theorists, as much as any theologian, in fact make 'faith moves', although they seldom acknowledge them as such. Philosophers and theologians are, on the whole, agreed on a range of ethical principles such as beneficence, autonomy, truth-telling and promise-keeping. But it is, says Veatch, in relation to equality that differences appear most clearly: 'those working out of religious ethics have, for the most part, made egalitarian assumptions while those working in secular philosophy are split'.[1] The basic assumptions of egalitarian philosophers are, Veatch argues, in fact Judaeo-Christian assumptions, whereas the anti-egalitarians make 'faith moves' derived from sources outside the mainstream Judaeo-Christian tradition.[2]

Perhaps today Christian theology can suggest a theological vindication of human equality which might be helpful at this particular juncture. It is the hope that this book will make some small contribution to 'making a difference' in debates about equality, particularly in its theological sections. For these are concerned with the shape of equality, how we understand equality, why we should be committed to equality, and how equality might shape social policy.

In this chapter, in dialogue with a number of modern theologians and Christian social thinkers, I want to explore these issues, examining how they engage with the Bible and the tradition, and how their thought on equality interacts with practice. The thinkers with whom I will be particularly engaged are the economic historian and Christian moralist, R. H. Tawney, the Danish nineteenth-century existentialist theologian, Søren Kierkegaard, and some recent liberation theology and Roman Catholic official social teaching.

These represent rather different ways of tackling the question of equality theologically. R. H. Tawney was an economic and social historian, best known perhaps for his work on Puritanism and the origins of capitalism. He was a layman, without formal theological training, although he was a close friend of several prominent theologians, and was certainly himself no theological ignoramus. He was influenced particularly strongly by his Christian socialist friends, notably Charles Gore and William Temple, and he was very active in Anglican and ecumenical social ethics, as well as in the labour movement and the Workers' Educational Association. In his major writings, even *Equality*, there is little that is overtly theological, but it is not hard to see from his articles and journals that he was a thoughtful Christian thinker. Christian assumptions and positions were the foundation of his thought, and lie just below the surface in most of his major writings. His primary concern was with the *practice* of equality, and he was impatient with any theology which seemed to be pure speculation without implications for behaviour and for policy. He taught that equality was the necessary basis for fellowship. He goes into considerable detail in developing a 'strategy of equality', outlining how egalitarian ideas might be implemented.

Søren Kierkegaard was a maverick figure in Danish church and public life in the first half of the nineteenth century, who has had immense influence on modern theology and philosophy. Like Tawney, he was not an academic theologian. Tawney never developed a systematic theological position and Kierkegaard explicitly rejected system-building as dangerous and unreal as an approach to Christian truth. Instead, Kierkegaard adopted a critical Socratic approach to theology which provoked and stimulated a great deal of fresh theological reflection. He had some pithy things to say about professors of theology, and the persistent tendency to distance reflection from practice and accord high status to the academic:

What does 'professor' signify? That religion is a question for the erudite; the professor is the greatest satire on 'the apostle'. To be professor – in what? In something a few fishermen have put into the world; oh, splendid epigram! That Christianity should succeed in conquering the world; yes, that is something the founder himself forecast, and the 'fishermen' believed it. But the trophy, that Christianity should triumph to the point of there being professors of theology – that is something the founder did not predict, unless it is where it is said that 'the apostasy' will set in.[3]

Like Tawney, but in a different mode, Kierkegaard is passionate that Christian equality should be embodied, expressed in life and practice, in 'acts of love'. Tawney is primarily concerned with the egalitarian reframing of society; Kierkegaard with equality as the condition for the loving behaviour of individuals. Kierkegaard has some important cautionary remarks to make about the ways Christian equality may be expressed. And his Christian grounding of equality is interestingly divergent from that of Tawney.

Liberation theology is a profoundly challenging egalitarian movement which initially emerged in Latin America in the 1960s and is now a global reality addressing a wide variety of issues of oppression and exploitation, stressing the 'preferential option for the poor' as the way to an egalitarian society. It has been one of the major factors in encouraging Roman Catholic official social teaching to move significantly towards an affirmation of human equality as integral to Christian faith.

'In order to believe in human equality it is necessary to believe in God'[4]

Richard Tawney's (1880–1962) striking statement at the masthead of this section may come as a surprise or even an offence to some. After all, one may read Tawney's major published works, including *Equality*, his passionate tract for the times first published in 1931, and never find his Christian view put so sharply, uncompromisingly and clearly. But the vision, structure and motive for his work on equality are powerfully Christian and theological. Tawney does not often wear his heart on his sleeve, or talk a great deal in public about his faith commitment. It has been argued that his Christian belief, with its realism about sin and human nature, which saved him from becoming a utopian.[5] Certainly Christianity was the single greatest influence on the life and thought of this, 'the towering figure of ethical socialism in the twentieth century'.[6]

The foundations of equality

In his Inaugural Lecture at the London School of Economics Tawney described his vocation as an historian thus: 'If the historian visits the cellars it is not for love of the dust but to estimate the stability of the edifice.'[7] His conclusion when he first visited, early on in his career, the cellar marked 'equality' was that the foundations were shaky and needed to be restored. Much of his life was devoted to this endeavour. He did not believe that absolute equality was attainable, or even desirable; what mattered was that it should be consistently aimed at.[8] 'A just society', writes Ronald Preston expounding Tawney, 'will have a built-in tendency towards equality.'[9]

The quotation at the head of this section comes from Tawney's private *Commonplace Book*,[10] and although this may not originally have been meant for publication to a wider audience, it seems not only a reliable clue to the well-spring of Tawney's social and political attitudes, but also a general statement that he believed to be true (and held for the rest of his life): belief in God is the prerequisite for belief in human equality. Without such belief, a commitment to equality is uncertain and fragile, cut off from its sustaining roots. It might have been easier for us if Tawney had here been making an historical statement about the *origins* of the understanding of equality, and the way the Christian faith has shaped as well as supported the idea of equality down the centuries – the kind of issues with which we have been concerned in earlier chapters of this book.

But Tawney is quite explicit about two things: we are here dealing with *beliefs* or *convictions* about the nature of God and the worth of human beings, and, secondly, there is a kind of sustaining umbilical cord which it is very hazardous to cut between Christian belief and convictions about equality. The conviction that human beings are equal is not the end result of a line of reasoning, it is not the conclusion of empirical study, nor is it a self-evident truth, or an arbitrary assumption. It is a matter of faith, and it coheres with the rest of Christian faith. It reaches below appearances and finds its transcendental grounding in the reality of God. It cannot be simply an arbitrary hunch, and it is certainly not the uniform conclusion of public discussion, the 'considered conviction' of most or all reasonable and thoughtful people in a modern liberal democracy.

Equality is thus, for Tawney, a matter of faith. It is not a free-floating assumption, but it relates integrally to the structure of Christian belief, and in particular to the Christian understanding of God. Tawney is not, I think, denying that many people who have no religious belief in fact operate on the assumption of human equality; or that many Christian believers do not really believe in, or recognize, human equality. What he is, I think, suggesting is that one cannot probe the concept of human equality very deeply without discovering that it rests on explicitly Christian theistic grounds, and therefore those who are serious about equality should also take God seriously. And he is likewise suggesting that Christian believers should be encouraged, provoked and helped to see that their Christian commitment leads, or should lead, directly to a commitment to human equality. This offers us one way of understanding Tawney's central intellectual project. And in its more modest way this is the kind of thing this book is also attempting to do.

Tawney does not simply leave us with a stirring slogan, a superb one-liner: 'In order to believe in human equality it is necessary to believe in God.' He expounds it in an interesting way, he unpacks the notion, and elsewhere in his writings he addresses the question of the public responsibilities of the Christian community and of the state in relation to equality. I will turn to the second later in this book. Meanwhile, here is how Tawney develops his argument in the *Commonplace Book*:

In order to believe in human equality it is necessary to believe in God. It is only when one contemplates the infinitely great that human differences appear so infinitely small as to be negligeable [*sic*]. To put it [an]other way, the striking thing about man is that he is only a *little* lower than the angels themselves. When one realises this it is absurd to emphasise the fact that one man is, even so, lower than another. One can't look a gift cherub in the mouth. What is wrong with the modern world is that having ceased to believe in the greatness of God, and therefore the infinite smallness (or greatness –

the same thing!) of *man*, it has to invent distinctions between *men*. It does not say, 'I have said, "Ye are gods!"' Nor does it say, 'All flesh is grass'. It can neither rise to the heights nor descend to the depths …What it does say is that *some* men are gods, and that some flesh is grass, and that the former should live on the latter (combined with *paté de foi gras* and champagne) and this is false. For what elevates or depresses, what makes man regarded from one point of view an angel and from another an ape, is not something peculiar to individuals, but characteristic of the species, which cannot distinguish between men, precisely because it is inherent in man[11]

Tawney is arguing here that in face of God's greatness all human distinctions seem trivial and unimportant. That does not mean that we should not be concerned about them, or try to change them. They are hurtful and damaging, and must not be treated with reverence, as sacrosanct, not to be tampered with. With one blow all the age-old arguments that suggest that powerful and important people and structures reflect in some way the greatness and the glory of God are demolished. Analogies between God and the king, between God and ecclesiastical potentates, are laughable in their triviality, but serious in as far as they serve to inculcate passive obedience and resignation to lowly status, poverty and degradation on the part of many people. This spurious kind of theology excludes questioning and opposition as impious. Tawney seems himself to have imbibed something of the democratic theological world-view of the Puritans he studied so closely!

It is not that God has made human beings so puny and insignificant that their hierarchies and patterns of domination don't matter; God has in fact made human beings 'a little lower than the angels'. God has ascribed to human beings immense dignity and honour. Some element of celestial hierarchy seems to remain for Tawney, but human beings all together occupy a common position just below the angels. Human beings are equal because God ascribes equality of status and of worth to them, they have been *made* that way in creation. Equality is given. It is not a quality that many, or most, human beings have, like rationality or conscience. Nor is it a status that humans may achieve, or have achieved or deserved. Human beings are endowed with equal and infinite worth by God who made them. We *are* equal; equality is not something we have or possess or achieve, or will have. 'The essence of all morality', writes Tawney, 'is this: to believe that every human being is of infinite importance and therefore that no considerations of expediency can justify the oppression of one by another.' Once again he stresses: 'But to believe this it is necessary to believe in God.' And he continues:

> To estimate men simply by their place in a social order is to sanction the sacrifice of men to that order. It is only when we realise that each individual soul is related to a power above other men that we are able to regard each as an end in itself. In other words, the idea of 'humanity' stultifies itself. *The social order is judged and condemned by a power transcending it.*[12]

More than thirty years after the 1913 entries in the *Commonplace Book*, Tawney reiterates the theme, but now not so much as a direct implication of belief in the Christian God, as a central dimension of a Christian account of human nature: 'a strong sense of equality' is 'the necessary corollary to the Christian conception of man'.[13] This means that all human beings are of equal value, whatever their abilities and achievements or lack of them. The Christian understanding of human nature takes account of both the grandeur and the misery of which human beings are capable. It makes support of the class system 'an essay in blasphemy', and leads Christians to a distinctive view of society quite different from that taken by 'good pagans', unless the latter have been influenced, as many have been, by the Christian tradition. The 'necessary corollary' of a Christian account of human nature is 'a strong sense of equality', affirming that all people are of equal value. Class privileges and great inequalities of wealth, writes Tawney, are 'an odious outrage on the image of God'.[14]

Tawney also makes the remark that as in modern times people have ceased to believe in God, they have invented distinctions and inequalities among people. This is, on the face of it, a strange comment for an historian to make. We all know that every society of which we have records has had some structure of social stratification, and therefore of inequality. But Tawney is perhaps thinking of the tendency in the modern secular world, which commonly rejects the idea of a transcendent power, to absolutize differences of status, rank and power.

Rulers in pre-modern times often had confessors at their side to remind them of their mortality and of their accountability to a higher authority and a higher law than the will of the earthly sovereign. Religion provided, sometimes at least, some constraint on the impact of inequality and power. The savagery of the Holocaust and the Gulag were produced by secular ideologies which, whatever their formulae, were in practice profoundly inegalitarian and free from external moral constraint.

Tawney uses here and elsewhere a rather undifferentiated notion of the divine transcendence when he stresses, 'But to believe this it is necessary to believe in God'. It would fit almost any version of monotheism. This is perhaps a little strange in one who had imbibed from his guru, Charles Gore, a highly incarnational theology. Tawney draws hardly at all on the kind of narrative material about the egalitarianism of Jesus and the early Christian movement that we have discussed elsewhere, or understandings of the incarnation as God in Christ humbling himself to take on the human condition, to love and save humankind. Nor does he refer, as far as I am aware, to the Trinity as a model of loving community, as developed in recent theology by Jürgen Moltmann, Leonardo Boff and Miroslav Volf in particular.[15] These themes will be explored elsewhere. But meanwhile we should simply note the importance of Tawney's stress on the Christian grounding of the idea of equality.

Tawney on the nature of equality

The equality that Tawney advocates is called by Rae (rather awkwardly) 'person-regarding'.[16] It affirms the equal worth of persons in community – Tawney cannot conceive of an isolated individual; he is fundamentally convinced that people find fulfilment in fellowship. Equality for Tawney is necessary for right relationships between people, for the establishment and maintenance of community. People, for him, are people-in-relationship, in fellowship. His convictions about equality rest, according to Terrill, on three pillars: common humanity, the freedom for self-fulfilment, and the fact that everyone has a function, a role, a contribution in the community.[17] Each human being is entitled to respect. All human beings, by virtue of their common humanity have a right to provision for their needs, and society should seek to cultivate this common humanity by putting stress on institutions and procedures which 'meet our needs and are a source of common enlightenment and common enjoyment'.[18]

Equality does not mean a dreary sameness; uniformity of lifestyle or provision; it does not mean identity of treatment. Indeed, Tawney's vision of equality is one which encourages a lively flowering of individuality and freedom, and sees equality as the presupposition of this flowering. Differences of character, intelligence and need will be taken very seriously; such, for Tawney, is an implication of equality.

Equality, for Tawney, is the necessary condition for fellowship and true community. Inequality divides communities and creates all sorts of barriers of suspicion and rivalry. Extreme inequalities

[d]ivide what might have been a community into contending classes, of which one is engaged in a struggle to share in advantages which it does not yet enjoy and to limit the exercise of economic power, while the other is occupied in a nervous effort to defend its position against encroachments.[19]

Thus inequality is destructive of fraternity by breaking the ties of friendship and common purpose, and by setting groups and individuals in conflict and competition with one another. The inequality that Tawney targeted was specifically that produced by capitalism. His thought on equality was thoroughly contextual.

Equality of opportunity, the *carrière ouverte aux talents*, a meritocratic society, is not a sufficient way of establishing the kind of equality Tawney seeks. Historically, equality of opportunity has certainly played an important and positive role in breaking up structures of hereditary privilege. But now it does not in any substantial way alter the unequal structure of society, but simply makes the 'plums' and the 'glittering prizes' slightly more generally accessible. This greater accessibility to resources and position, however, is more apparent than real, for Tawney is perfectly sure that only in a more equal society in which equality of worth is generally recognized can some people's handicap at the starting-post or disastrous outcome at the finish be adequately provided for. True equality of opportunity may be an important component of the notion of equality, but it is by no means the whole story. The ideal of human equality must not be reduced to equality of opportunity. For the most part, equality of opportunity operates as a kind of lightning conductor which deflects a little of the damage done by social inequality, but does little more. It obscures some of the more glaring and obnoxious examples of the 'disease of inequality' at the expense of making the condition of the unsuccessful even worse. Tawney ridicules equality of opportunity as the 'Tadpole Philosophy':

> It is possible that intelligent tadpoles reconcile themselves to the inconveniences of their position, by reflecting that, though most of them will live and die as tadpoles and nothing more, the most fortunate of the species will one day shed their tails, distend their mouths and stomachs, hop nimbly onto dry land, and croak addresses to their former friends on the virtues by means of which tadpoles of character and capacity can rise to be frogs. This conception of society can be described, perhaps, as the Tadpole Philosophy, since the consolation it offers for social evils consists in the statement that exceptional individuals can succeed in evading them.[20]

Equality of opportunity in itself does not build the kind of caring relationships between people that Tawney seeks. While it provides self-fulfilment for a few, it has no fulfilment to offer to the majority. What is needed instead of, or in addition to, equality of opportunity are 'collective movements to narrow the space between valley and peak'.[21]

For Tawney, equality is not antithetical to liberty, but rather essential to the maintenance and diffusion of liberty. Frequently in the past, he believes, liberty has been regarded in too narrow a fashion. People have forgotten the social constraints and controls that ensure that one person's freedom is not used to harm others or to constrain their freedom. 'Freedom', he said in another of his aquatic metaphors, 'for the pike is death for the minnows'.[22] Liberty must be extended rather than being regarded as the possession of one class or group. Tawney had no time for an equality imposed in such a way as to diminish or destroy freedom; indeed that would not for him be equality at all. The liberty he speaks of is 'equality in action' – all are equally protected against the abuse of power, whether that power be political, social or economic. Liberty and equality complement one another and must be held in balance as the twin piers on which a better community may be reared.

If he says less about freedom than he does about equality it is because he sees it as less in need of defence than equality; and more, Tawney believes that the neglect of equality has encouraged a narrow and distorted understanding of freedom as well. Enlarging the freedom of the majority might be at the cost of restricting somewhat the freedom of the strong, particularly their freedom to do what they want at the expense of the weak. Freedom, he believed, involved equality of status, but it also required diversity of function and of contribution.

Both equality and freedom suggest that power should be widely dispersed. Power, more equally distributed, should be used for the common good rather than selfish purposes pursued at the expense of the neighbour. He develops this theme further in his *Commonplace Book*:

> A belief in equality means that because men are men they are bound to acknowledge that man has claims upon man, that nothing can justify my using power which chance gave me (the chance of a majority as well as of wealth or birth) to the full, that nothing can justify my using my neighbour as a tool, or treating him as something negligeable [*sic*] which may be swept aside to realise *my* ends, however noble these ends may be. It means that of all revolutionary schemes there is one awful criterion: 'It were better that a millstone were hung about your neck and that you were cast into the sea than that you should offend one of these little ones'; that I may not *force* any man to do right, because, even though he [be] rich and wicked, he is still a man; that I may not compel any man, however foolish, to think as the wise think, because truth has been hidden from the wise and revealed unto babes. It means that not wealth or power or numbers or learning is the standard by which conduct must be judged, but the conviction of the individual conscience; and that mercy, humility, peace, love shall judge cleverness and strength and numbers.[23]

Tawney was not a utopian who believed that the immediate realization of equality at any cost was either desirable or possible. His plea is that society should take equality as one of its major objectives and make determined moves towards greater equality even if absolute equality was out of the question. The present degree of social inequality he regarded as quite unacceptable, because it was socially divisive and individually dehumanizing as well as theologically offensive. Social goals are important as giving a sense of direction, even if they are never fully attained:

> What matters to the health of a society is the objective towards which its face is set, and to suggest that it is immaterial in which direction it moves, because whatever the direction, the goal must always elude it, is not scientific but irrational. It is like using the impossibility of absolute cleanliness as a pretext for rolling in a manure heap, or denying the importance of honesty because no one can be wholly honest.[24]

Out of the understanding of God comes a task which, according to Tawney, is to diminish inequality with all deliberate speed in order to permit human individuality, freedom and fellowship to flower. To this end he proposes what he calls a 'Strategy of Equality', to which I will turn shortly.

Tawney's influence

Tawney's thought, perhaps largely because of the compelling power of his passion for justice, had a deep and continuing impact on British public life. In his writings published in his lifetime he deployed few overtly Christian arguments, perhaps because he needed to communicate with an increasingly secular public. But his own Christian commitment was well known, and he played a major role in the development of the British churches' social thinking in the 1930s and 1940s. Those who probed below the surface of his writing in books such as *Equality* found a motivation and a set of values as well as distinctive arguments which were profoundly Christian. And on questions of equality, at least, 'he, being dead, still speaketh.'

An equal love

Søren Kierkegaard, that strange early-nineteenth-century Danish theological *savant* who has had a prodigious influence on modern

theology and is one of the founders of existentialism, developed a distinctive theology of equality, which continues to be significant.

His starting-point is the affirmation that love demands equality
between the lovers. If there exists a great difference of wealth or power
or social standing between the would-be lovers, it is hard for love not
to be distorted or eroded by the inequality. The rich and powerful
person finds it hard not to be patronizing to a poor and weak beloved;
the person of low status whose family is in the grip of poverty is
tempted to manipulate the situation to the benefit of the family, and in
the process make authentic, disinterested loving hard or impossible. In
Philosophical Fragments Kierkegaard develops this theme in relation to
the incarnation by producing a parable about a king who sought to love
a poor and humble maiden. The king, in all his power and splendour,
knows that 'love is exultant when it unites equals, but it is triumphant
when it makes that which was unequal equal in love'.[25] His courtiers
tell him he is about to confer a vast favour on the girl for which she
should be eternally grateful. The king, understandably, was deeply
disturbed by this. Is his love a condescension to which the proper
response is gratitude rather than reciprocating love? Would his beloved
be happy at his side? Would she ever be allowed to forget that he was
king and she owed everything to his patronage? Would she perhaps
be happier if he left her alone to marry a man who was in fact and in
reality equal to her? Would that not be the only way in which true love,
the love which demands equality, could flourish? And what, if coming
from backgrounds so different, the king and the humble maiden could
not understand one another?

Consider, Kierkegaard continues, the possibility that the king
should reveal himself in all his majesty to the maiden. Would not this
overwhelm her, and make love between them impossible? Or perhaps,
suggests Kierkegaard, the maiden can be raised up, taught to speak and
dress properly, and 'pass' in good society, like Eliza Doolittle in
Bernard Shaw's *Pygmalion*. But here again, the distance and the
inequality, the condescension, for whatever reason, of the king make
love impossible. The only way of enabling a loving union is for the king
to descend and identify with the maiden, and share her lot, her
suffering and her poverty. He must take the initiative and become equal
to her if they are to be able to love one another. The king must become
equal to the humblest. And this can be no play-acting, or deceit. It is

not enough to have a beggar's cloak which the wind sweeps aside to reveal the royal garments underneath; it must be the true condition of the king, alongside his beloved in all respects: 'For this is the unfathomable nature of love, that it desires equality with the beloved, not in jest merely, but in earnest and in truth.' [26]

Kierkegaard is, of course, speaking primarily of the incarnation, of God in Christ taking the form of a servant that God's love for all might be expressed. But he is also teaching more general lessons about love, morality and equality, lessons which he believes are of general truth and significance. The first lesson is this: God loves everyone equally, and thus establishes human equality, which we should recognize, affirm and express:

> Christianly, every man (the individual), absolutely every man, once again, absolutely every man is equally near to God. And how is he equally near? Loved by Him. So there is equality, infinite equality between man and man.[27]

This does not mean the erosion of *difference*. Far from it. Difference is necessary also for loving. For Kierkegaard difference and individuality are of the greatest importance and significance. Loving demands both equality and difference.

The command to love the neighbour

We are to see each other human being as our neighbour, as one God loves, and one we also ought to love. But these neighbours are also all different from one another. We must be able to see and understand and affirm both the neighbourly equality and the precious differences. Kierkegaard explains his point, characteristically with the use of a vivid image:

> Take many sheets of paper, write something different on each one; then no one will be like another. But then again take each single sheet; do not let yourself be confused by the diverse inscriptions, hold it up to the light, and you will see a common watermark on all of them. In the same way, the neighbour is the common watermark, but you see it only by means of eternity's light when it shines through the dissimilarity.[28]

In the neighbour's difference and equality you do not find one for whom you may have a 'passionate partiality'. But you are bidden to love the neighbour whom God has made equal to you. The barriers to love between people must be torn down if we are to obey the divine command. We are given the neighbour whom we are commanded to love. And we discern the neighbour, with the neighbour's needs, and quiddities and excellences only in the light of eternity.

Differences are important, and they are interesting. But for Kierkegaard, the differences are 'only a disguise'. The underlying reality is equality. The differences should 'hang loosely':

> When the difference hangs thus loosely, then that essential other is always glimpsed in every individual, that common to all, that eternal resemblance, the equality. In being king, beggar, scholar, rich, poor, man, woman and so on, we do not resemble one another, for just therein lie our differences; but in being a neighbour we all unconditionally resemble one another. The difference is the confusion of the temporal existence which marks every man differently, but the neighbour is the mark of the eternal – on every man.[29]

Kierkegaard is exploring with great subtlety the Bible's teaching on the neighbour. The root meaning of the word, 'neighbour' is, of course, some one who lives close by, and therefore in all likelihood is very similar to one, equal to one, from the same sort of background and culture and condition. The Bible then, through a series of steps, expands the meaning of the neighbour. The neighbour is the stranger, the different one, the person who is at the margins of the community, so that this neighbour may not live physically close by. In India, where commonly the former Untouchables are not allowed to live in the village, but live in their own settlement, the *cheri*, some distance off, the geographical separation is established as if to declare to the caste people in the village that the ex-Untouchables are *not* their neighbours. But the Bible is emphatic that they are indeed neighbours, that the ex-Untouchables are equal to the caste people in the main village, that there are reciprocal responsibilities between the caste people and the ex-Untouchables. The Bible steadily expands the notion of the neighbour. The alien, so often understood as threatening, so often the victim of pogroms or public hostility, is a neighbour with a neighbour's rights

and claims. And finally, the enemy is declared a neighbour, the neighbour we are commanded to love. All these are given to us as neighbours,
and we are commanded to love them! God has made us all equal in
neighbourly equality so that love and community may be possible. For
God loves us all equally. Kierkegaard makes the point with clarity:

> The neighbour is your equal. The neighbour is not your beloved for
> whom you have a passionate partiality, not your friend for whom
> you have a passionate partiality. Nor, if you are an educated man, is
> your neighbour the one who is educated, with whom you are equal
> in education – for with your neighbour you have human equality
> before God. Nor is the neighbour the one who is more distinguished
> than yourself, that is, he is not your neighbour just because he is
> more distinguished than yourself, for loving him because he is more
> distinguished can then easily become partiality, and insofar
> selfishness. Nor is your neighbour the one who is inferior to you,
> that is, insofar as he is humbler than yourself he is not your neigh-
> bour, for to love one because he is inferior can easily become the con-
> descension of partiality, and insofar selfishness. Loving your neigh-
> bour is a matter of equality…The neighbour is every man; for he is
> not your neighbour through the difference, or through the equality
> with you as in your difference from other men. He is your neighbour
> through equality with you before God, but every man uncondition-
> ally has this equality, and has it unconditionally.[30]

The strategy of equality

Both Tawney and Kierkegaard insist that equality is something to be
recognized and expressed in practice and in behaviour. Kierkegaard
emphasizes the command to love the neighbour; Tawney develops a
politically realistic 'strategy of equality' in some detail.

Tawney feels impelled to move from the realm of values and beliefs
to the political sphere, from ideals to implementation. He took very
seriously his own advice that 'to state principles without indicating
their relevance to specific situations is irresponsible'.[31] He was also
aware, as many of his later disciples were not, that any serious moves
towards equality would encounter determined resistance from vested

interests which, if they could not stop egalitarian measures, would attempt to subvert them. It becomes clear at this point that Tawney, unlike some of his more secular and idealistic disciples, has a large place for human sin in his understanding of human nature, politics and society. He believes that there is a deep-seated selfishness in human beings which resists any giving up of privileges and status, and is often entrenched in institutions.

Tawney also believed that capitalism was inherently inegalitarian, and that egalitarian policies should be recognized as subversive of capitalism. He believed in redistribution of economic and political resources and argued that the economy must be made more account-able to the public. The welfare state for him was an egalitarian institu-tion. And the educational system, particularly the private schools must be tackled as they were bastions of inequality: The private schools, in England quaintly called 'public schools', are

> at once an educational monstrosity and a grave national misfortune. It is educationally vicious, since to mix with companions from homes of different types is an important part of the education of the young. It is socially disastrous, for it does more than any other single cause, except capitalism itself, to perpetuate the division of the nation into classes of which one is almost unintelligible to the other.[32]

In the 1940s Tawney was calling on the churches to support 'measures designed to ensure that all children and young persons, from birth to eighteen, shall be assured, as far as social action can secure it, equal opportunities ... of making the best of the powers of body, mankind and character with which they have been endowed'.[33] Thus far, and in this way equality of opportunity remained on his agenda.

Tawney's strategy involved controlling the 'commanding heights' of the economy in the public interest, extending the system of social security and using it explicitly as a form of social engineering, reform-ing the educational system to ensure that it did not continue to per-petuate privilege and inequality, and ensuring through taxation that differences of wealth and income were progressively reduced.

But the strategy of equality was not to be carried through by state action alone. There was a place for voluntary organizations, for local government and for community groups. The individual citizen, too, was an important agent of the strategy; attitudes had to be reformed if an active citizenry were to share in carrying through the strategy of equality. On the one hand he eschewed the paternalism of the Webbs and many Fabians; on the other, he rejected a romantic view of the poor and needy. Like everyone else, they were sinners and could not be relied upon to be altruistic. Along with the state, many other institutions and people had to co-operate if the strategy of equality were to be successful.[34]

Tawney is quite clear that if we are commanded to love our neighbours equally and to recognize the equality that God has established, we should also seek to build social structures that express equality. On the other hand, some people suggest that Kierkegaard is concerned simply with a spiritual sphere and with interpersonal ethics. It is certainly true that Kierkegaard *is* deeply concerned for 'the individual' and for diversity; he consistently resists the absorption of the individual into the mass, or the erosion of difference into uniformity, or the premature attempt to realize the Reign of God. Accordingly he draws a sharp distinction between 'Christian' and 'worldly' equality. Most of the specific measures in Tawney's 'strategy of equality' he would, I think, label as concerned with 'worldly equality'. But it is not hard to see Kierkegaard's critique as offering a more profound challenge to existing structures of inequality than does Tawney:

> Worldly equality, even if it were possible, is not Christian equality. And to bring about a perfect worldly equality is an impossibility. The well-intentioned worldliness itself readily admits it; it rejoices when it succeeds in making temporal conditions more and more equal, but it recognises that its attempt is a pious wish, that it has set itself a tremendous task, that the chances of success are remote ... Christianity, on the contrary, by the help of the short cut of eternity, is immediately at the goal: it allows all the differences to continue, but it teaches the equality of eternity. It teaches everyone to *rise above* the earthly distinctions ... Christianity always allows the differences of the earthly life to persist, but this equality in rising above earthly differences is implicit in the commandment of love, in the loving one's neighbour.[35]

Certain ways of expressing equality in social structures would for Kierkegaard be ruled out on these grounds. Some things he says can be interpreted as suggesting that his teaching on the command to love one's neighbour cannot be transposed into social and political structures; the love command relates simply to the interpersonal and religious dimensions of life. Does Kierkegaard propose equality before God as a kind of solace for those who suffer from the inequalities of 'the world', and something which has no relevance to, or direct bearing on, social forms? If the equality of neighbour love cannot and must not be reduced to social and economic structures, is it not possible that it is inevitably corrosive of structures of inequality? Before God, Kierkegaard says, 'all these human differences are a joke, a nonsense, often leading to perdition'.[36] Some passages suggest that Kierkegaard believed that Christian equality was indeed radically subversive of worldly unequal social structures, precisely because God has a special concern for the weak and the poor and the forgotten:

Man is 'a social animal', and what he believes in is the power of association.

The human idea is therefore this: Let us all unite – if possible, all the kingdoms and countries of the earth, and this union in pyramid form, which evinces the ever higher and higher, supports at its peak an Over-king [*Over-Konge*]. He must be considered closest to God, so close indeed as to make God anxious and pay him attention.

In Christian terms the situation is just the reverse. Such an Over-king will stand furthest from God, just as the whole enterprise of the pyramid is something to which God is exceedingly opposed.

The despised, the cast-offs of the race, one poor single abandoned wretch, and outcast – that, in Christian terms, is what God chooses, what is closest to him.

He hates this business of the pyramid. For just as God is infinite love, and his paternal eye readily sees how cruel this human pyramid-idea can easily become towards the unfortunate, those in the human race who are set aside, etc. (therefore precisely those a God of love looks after), so is he too infinitely wise a majesty not to see that if this pyramid notion found the slightest acceptance, as though there were some truth, even the smallest crumb of truth, to the idea that, the higher the pyramid rises, that little closer one comes to God, then man would be unable to avoid thinking that one day, by raising the pyramid high enough, he will think himself capable of pushing God off the throne.

So God pushes the pyramid over and everything collapses – a generation later man begins again with this pyramid business.[37]

Kierkegaard launches a strenuous attack on what he calls 'equalization', or levelling, which is 'the false anticipation of the eternal life, which people have done away with as a "beyond" and now want to realize here *in abstracto*'.[38] The problem, as Kierkegaard sees it, is that politicians and economists have only too often shallow understandings of equality and how it might be expressed in social structures, but nevertheless tend to absolutize their programmes of reform. And Kierkegaard is right in this. Absolute equality is not achievable here and now, but if social reform is to be well-grounded and effective an eye must always be kept on the absolute and the coming Reign of God, lest politics become banal and dehumanizing. Hannay suggests that Kierkegaard is not advocating equality as only applicable in a religious sphere, or suggesting that the equality of which he speaks is without political implications. A politics of equality which does not consider the issue *sub specie aeternitatis* is radically flawed, and can be acutely harmful.

Kierkegaard's attack on 'equalizing' or 'levelling' is not a suggestion that the ethic of treating people as equal neighbours is incompatible with political and economic equalizing measures. But such measures may arise from envy and mean-spiritedness – the *ressentiment* which Nietzsche suggested was at the heart of Christian ethics – rather than being a loving response to God's command to love the neighbour as oneself. What he is acutely afraid of is the suggestion that political and economic equalizing measures may make in many people's eyes the actual concrete acts of neighbour love by individuals redundant, and that the implementation of the policies would be actually lacking in compassion while presented as unqualified manifestations of the Reign of God, of the absolute command to love the neighbour as oneself.

The levelling that Kierkegaard resists could be called, writes Hannay, 'a reduction of the individual to the ranks'.[39] The individual and the concrete act of recognition of the neighbour's equality must never be forgotten; but that is not the same as to suggest that measures of policy which implement a relative equality in an appropriate way are excluded by Kierkegaard. Levelling measures should be promoted, as long as steps are taken to ensure that differences are preserved, and there is not an over-investment of expectation that the outcome of policy will be the full realization of equality. Egalitarian policies must not become, says Kierkegaard, 'a false anticipation of the eternal life'.[40]

Kierkegaard roots human equality firmly in the divine command to love the neighbour as oneself, always inseparably linked to the command to love God. In the command to love the neighbour as oneself, God gives an infinite number of diverse neighbours and declares that they are equal to us, in all their difference. The command implies and declares the equality of the neighbours. The command calls for loving action on our part, based on the recognition that God has established the equality which is the condition for loving. But Kierkegaard's equivocation as to whether this God given equality should have a reflex in earthly structures and arrangements deserves further examination.

Let me return to the discussion in the Prologue of the problems of establishing a loving relationship between Munuswamy and myself. I feel guilt and confusion because I know that I am commanded to love Munuswamy, and I believe that God has, in all the important senses that matter, made us equal. And yet we cannot love one another. Why? The factors that keep us apart and frustrate our loving are largely structural factors to do with wealth, and social stratification, and culture – all obstacles that can be modified, and sometimes removed, by imaginative legislation and visionary leadership. But there are also limits to the adequate fulfilment of the love command simply in terms of individual action. There are loving things that I should do for Munuswamy and he for me which must be done in a general way, anonymously, judiciously rather than passionately. The boundary between love and justice is in practice often impossible to demarcate, and loving is often best expressed in the doing of justice. So Kierkegaard's cautions about hopes of establishing God's Reign of peace and love today, anticipating the final coming of God's Reign and assuming that all the responsibility lies in our hands, are well taken. Nor may we expect a nation to act always lovingly. But surely obedience to the love command involves more than individual activity and face-to-face relationships; its force should be felt in the temporal as well as the spiritual sphere. In additional to our individual frail attempts to love our neighbours, we need something like Tawney's strategy of equality if we are to be properly responsive to the divine command.

The preferential option for the poor

The liberation theology that has emerged out of Latin America seeks to do theology from the perspective of the poor. It uses rather sparingly terms like equality and inequality. It prefers to speak rather of poverty, oppression and exploitation, of poor people and the causes and possible remedies for their condition. It tries to avoid abstraction and idealism in order to concentrate on the human realities of a degrading and unchristian situation. It calls for what is called a 'preferential option for the poor', which is aimed at challenging and overcoming the structures of oppression and exploitation, the processes which condemn so many to squalor, illiteracy, poor health and early death. It is in fact a kind of *conversion* to the poor that is envisaged, or at least recognition that in the Christian view of things the poor on account of their serious disadvantage have a special claim to preferential treatment in order to redress their disadvantage and establish a greater degree of equality.[41]

The preferential option calls for believers and the church to stand with the poor and oppressed in their struggle for basic rights and a decent way of living. The structures of oppression are to be overthrown and replaced with a system which is more just and decent. They are not to be simply reversed, so that today's oppressed will be tomorrow's oppressors. The new system will be marked by a high degree of equality.

Latin American liberation theology emerged out of situations of extreme inequality, poverty and human degradation. Alongside great affluence and luxury for the few, huge numbers of human beings were condemned to struggle for existence in conditions of great squalor and hardship which eroded human dignity and were correctly assumed to be contrary to any civilized standards of decency, and to Christian morality. The poor were condemned to be treated as 'nonpersons', devoid of human dignity, the victims of what Gutiérrez calls, 'a "savage capitalism" that crushes the dignity of human beings under foot, turning them into the victims of a cruel and sacrilegious cult'.[42] It is this, the avoidable suffering and poverty of millions of people, which forces liberation theology to adopt a new agenda.

Gustavo Gutiérrez argued that Western theology responded primarily to the challenge posed by the unbeliever and by unbelief; it was concerned first of all with the religious sphere, with how to revitalize religion and faith so that it could effectively be commended to the sceptical and to unbelievers in a secular age in which for many faith of any sort has lost its plausibility. Bonhoeffer asked the question which has become central in the West: How are we to proclaim God in a world come of age? But the theological agenda may be very different elsewhere, where the challenges and opportunities presented by the context are quite different. Gutiérrez continues:

> In a continent like Latin America, however, the main challenge does not come from the nonbeliever but from the *nonhuman* – i.e. the human being who is not recognized as such by the prevailing social order. These are the poor and exploited people, the ones who are systematically and legally despoiled of their being human, those who scarcely know what a human being might be. These nonhumans do not call into question our religious world so much as they call into question our *economic, social, political and cultural world*. Their challenge impels us toward a revolutionary transformation of the very bases of what is now a dehumanizing society. The question, then, is no longer how we are to speak of God in a world come of age; it is rather how to proclaim him Father in a world that is not human and what the implications might be of telling nonhumans that they are children of God.[43]

For Gutiérrez and the other liberation theologians, the starting-point, the issue that gives contemporary theology its agenda is the existence of so many millions of poor people living in dehumanizing contexts of extreme deprivation. *This* is the situation that theology has to address. And the challenge is not primarily or mainly a call for more clarity of thought, or greater rigour of theological argumentation. It is rather that theology should serve the poor by enabling and encouraging acts of solidarity and by recalling the church to its calling to be the church of the poor. The Canadian theologian, Gregory Baum, makes the point incisively: 'When confronted by a conflict between rich and

poor (or powerful and powerless, or masters and slaves), then the
Gospel demands ... that [one] side with the oppressed'.[44] In the book
that was the initial manifesto of the Liberation theology movement,
Gutiérrez wrote:

> All the political theologies, the theologies of hope, of revolution and
> of liberation, are not worth one act of genuine solidarity with
> exploited social classes. They are not worth one act of faith, love and
> hope committed – in one way or another – in active participation to
> liberate man from everything that dehumanizes him and prevents
> him from living according to the will of the Father.[45]

The primary issue for theology is thus not an abstract concept, even
'poverty', 'inequality' or 'justice'. It is rather poor *people*, and the
question why they are poor, and what can be done about it. Liberation
theology is a practical theology in as far as it starts from the practices
which support an unacceptable situation of human degradation, and
seeks practical, loving and just responses to that situation, ways of
telling 'nonhumans' that they are children of God, and demonstrating
that reality to them.

But who are the poor? Clodovis Boff and Jorge Pixley suggest that
the poor exist in collectivities, that they are the 'losers' in social conflict,
and that they call for a new social order. The poor belong in a class or
classes – in Latin America the huge majority of the population; in
Europe and North America a minority, even if a large one, and therefore politically weak. Marxist analysis encouraged the liberation
theologians to emphasize the necessity of understanding the poor as
part of a class system of social stratification, which is itself inevitably
locked into class conflict. As the losers in this conflict, the poor 'have
been reduced to poverty (im-poverished) or held in poverty by a
system of domination'.[46] We should not, however, idealize the poor,
and we should see them as they really are. 'Are we really for the poor
and the oppressed,' asks José Míguez Bonino, 'if we fail to see them as
a class, as members of oppressed societies? If we fail to say *how* we are
"for them" in their concrete historical situation? Can we claim a solidarity which has nothing to say about the actual historical forms in
which their struggle to overcome oppression is carried forward?'[47] And
finally, in clearly Marxist terms, the poor are seen as 'indissolubly
wedded to the idea of revolution, in the real sense of a *basic* change in

the social system'. All over the world, Boff and Pixley write, 'the poor are rising up and organising themselves for their collective liberation'. They know that the new society of justice and equality can be built, for humankind has the resources, the know-how, and we hope the commitment.[48] These words, first published in 1987, ring rather hollow today. We are no longer so confident that a coming social transformation is just around the corner. But Boff and Pixley are theologians, not Marxists. They root their understanding of the preferential option for the poor in Christology and in Mariology. 'At root', they write, 'it is because Christians opt for Christ and for the Father of Jesus Christ that they opt for the poor.'[49] Opting for Jesus Christ means opting for the poor and opting for justice; it is a direct implication of faith in Jesus, and thus lies close to the heart of the Christian faith.[50] The Mary of the Magnificat is 'a model of a poor person identifying with the cause of the poor, a woman who was poor and believing'.[51]

Pope John XXIII at the Second Vatican Council called for the church to become the church of all, and in particular of the poor. The church which, according to *Lumen Gentium* (1964) is 'a kind of sacrament or sign of intimate union with God, and of the unity of all [hu]mankind',[52] should first endorse a preferential option for the poor as the way to unity and reconciliation. Indeed, Boff and Pixley affirm that 'through knowing the poor better, the Church knows its divine founder and Lord better'.[53] The church may be judged by the poor, but it is easier for the church to be a church *for* the poor than a church *of* the poor.

The Conferences of the Latin American Catholic Bishops at Medellín (1968) and then at Puebla (1979) strongly affirmed the preferential option for the poor, rooted in God's love which is both universal and preferential, as expressed particularly in the exodus and the incarnation. This option was both an expression of Christian faith and a foundation for a new kind of theology. As in the classic Anselmian understanding of theology as faith seeking understanding, so now liberation theology saw its role as interpreting and seeking to understand more deeply the linked commitment to Christ and to the poor, with the aim of purifying and strengthening faith and practice. The preferential option is, of course, far more than a commitment to charity or almsgiving. For the liberation theologians it involves a deep solidarity with the poor in their struggles for justice and equality.

Boff and Pixley agree that the option for the poor 'is one form – and today the decisive one – of Christian love'.[54] They affirm with the Vatican that God's love is universal as well as preferential; its universality demands that it be preferential and adapted to need.[55] But along with the other liberation theologians they are reluctant to regard the preferential option as essentially a charitable disposition towards the poor, and something that the church has consistently expressed down the centuries. The church, they believe, has often deserted the poor, or patronized them, or effectively denied them a place of honour in the church. The time has come, they believe to take conflicts of interest and class conflicts seriously. The church and Christians must work out where they stand: are they alongside the poor, in solidarity with them in their sufferings and in their struggle, or are they by default against the poor?

Archbishop Romero, in an address at Louvain, affirmed the preferential option for the poor in entirely non-Marxist terms, and argued that it was a way of avoiding 'false universalism' and expressing the universalism and equality of God's love:

> The world of the poor, with its very concrete social and poitical characteristics, teaches us where the world can incarnate itself in such a way that it will avoid the false universalism that inclines the church to associate itself with the powerful. The world of the poor teaches us what the nature of Christian love is, a love that certainly seeks peace but also unmasks false pacifism – the pacifism of resignation and inactivity. It is a love that should certainly be freely offered, but that seeks to be effective in history. The world of the poor teaches us that the sublimity of Christian love ought to be mediated through the overriding necessity of justice for the majority. It ought not to turn away from honourable conflict. The world of the poor teaches us that liberation will arrive only when the poor are not simply on the receiving end of handouts from governments or from the church, but when they themselves are the masters of, and protagonists in, their own struggle and liberation, thereby unmasking the roots of false paternalism, including ecclesiastical paternalism.[56]

The Vatican was quick to attempt to tone down and spiritualize the Latin American understanding of the preferential option for the poor. In an address to the cardinals in 1984, John Paul II traced the preferential option back to the Vatican II document, *Lumen Gentium*, which states that the church 'recognizes in the poor and the suffering the likeness of her poor and suffering Founder. She does all she can do to relieve their need and in them she strives to serve Christ.'[57] According to the *Instruction on Christian Freedom and Liberation* published in 1986, nothing new or different has occurred; the church has always cared for the poor:

> Those who are oppressed by poverty are the object of a love of preference on the part of the Church, which since her origin and in spite of failings of many of her members had not ceased to work for their relief, defence and liberation. She has done this through numberless works of charity which remain always and everywhere indispensable ... The Church shows her solidarity with those who do not count in society by which they are rejected spiritually and sometimes physically. She is particularly drawn with maternal affection toward those children who, through human wickedness, will never be brought forth from the womb to the light of day, as also for the elderly, lonely and abandoned... The special option for the poor, far from being a sin of particularism or sectarianism, manifests the universality of the Church's being and mission. The option excludes no one.[58]

The Vatican was deeply concerned because it believed that the liberation theologians accepted and endorsed uncritically a Marxist understanding of class struggle which saw the only way forward as direct action ultimately often involving violence on the part of the poor and their allies. The implications of such an understanding were felt to be alarming. The preferential option, the Vatican thought, had become a political alliance to struggle for the overthrow of the existing social and economic order. This, they suggested, was a radical politicization of the gospel, and rested on a misunderstanding of the nature of the church and its calling. The weakening of Marxist movements world-wide in the aftermath of the collapse of the old Soviet Union and its satellites, together with economic and political changes in many countries of Latin America have made expectations of radical social change as a consequence of class struggle less plausible today. But if the idea of the preferential option for the poor as meaning primarily identification with the poor in a class struggle to usher in a new order is no longer compelling, a more theologically rooted and sober account of the preferential option remains influential.

This asserts, on biblical and theological grounds, that our option for God in Christ is inseparable from an option for the poor and needy, and both rest upon God's prior choice of us and of the poor. In the incarnation we have a model of what the preferential option means, a model which can take a diversity of shapes in varying contexts. For some it involves a radical identification with the sufferings and the struggles of the poor. But even Gutiérrez does not insist that for everyone this is the necessary expression of the preferential option. For some who stay in their ordinary vocations, it means a thoroughgoing reordering of priorities and of lifestyle, to put commitment to Christ and to the poor in the controlling position.

The notion that God has a partiality for the poor has attracted much discussion. Does this mean that God does not love the rich? Is God's love universal, or is it selective? This is, of course, parallel to the discussion in social theory on whether partiality and justice are compatible with one another, and whether one can have equality along with special preferential treatment for some.[59] In an important article, Stephen J. Pope argues that the partiality of the preferential option for the poor is in fact 'morally justified and, indeed, required'.[60] It does not conflict with the universality of God's love or with the equality with which human beings are endowed because it responds to people and groups in relation to their diverse needs – as does the love of God. It is therefore not exclusive. And I would add that the discrimination and partiality involved is necessary for the establishment of a more equal situation. The preferential option for the poor is in significant part a form of positive action to redress inequalities.

Pope argues that the preferential option for the poor is not an arbitrary bias or a denial of the universality of God's love. At the intellectual level, it ensures that the experience of the poor and the powerless is taken into account. It encourages 'moral inclusiveness' by insisting on full participation of all in the life and decision-making of the community. And it promotes 'religious inclusiveness' by affirming both God's universal love and his preferential care.

Relative equality in Roman Catholic social teaching

Liberation theology presents itself as a 'theology from below' deeply rooted in the life and struggles of the ordinary poor people of Latin America. That, of course, is only part of the story. The leading liberation theologians were highly educated theologically, particularly at Louvain or in the circle around Karl Rahner in Germany. They were also committed to Marxist-style social analysis, and indeed the methodology of liberation theology demanded rigorous social analysis and theological reflection of a sort which could only be undertaken by people with a thorough academic training. This is not to deny that they attended to the poor, and sought to articulate their aspirations and the realities of their day to day existence. They saw themselves as 'organic intellectuals' (to use Gramsci's term) whose existential commitment to the poor and to the church of the poor was essential to the fulfilment of their task as theologians, the development of an *engagé* theology which was committed both to the poor and to the church. Although some of the theoretical tools and the academic articulation came directly from the academy, much of the content and thrust of liberation theology in fact came from below, and was rooted in and related directly to specific contexts of oppression, suffering and pain.

The official teaching of the Roman Catholic Church is often seen and experienced as theology from above, handed down by the Pope, not always after consultation with the bishops as other guardians of the heritage of faith. Consultations of experts and others doubtless takes place, but the Pope is at liberty to reject the advice given him in these consultation exercises, as he did in the case of the encyclical *Humanae Vitae* (1968). The teaching office tends increasingly to be concentrated in Rome, and particularly in the person of the Pope, whose formal pronouncements on matters of faith and morals had been declared by the First Vatican Council to be infallible. The teaching of this magisterium tended until quite recently to be presented as universal truths, valid always and everywhere, and in the case of moral and social teaching, founded on the principles of natural law which were accessible to all rational beings. In many instances, such teaching related quite closely to the circumstances of the day, but rarely recognized its own contextuality and time boundedness.

Official Roman Catholic social teaching since *Rerum Novarum*

(1891) tended to tread a middle way between socialism and market capitalism, which were both rejected, for rather different reasons. The alternative advocated seemed at times compatible with the corporative state, or even with Fascism. Every individual and group should know its proper place in a rigidly stratified society which in many ways reflected the hierarchical structuring of the church. There was, of course, a considerable stress on charity and on the duties of the wealthy to assist the less fortunate. The social and economic structures were generally regarded as given, although the excesses of the market were to be curbed, and the interests of the workers were to be protected. Modern Catholic social teaching at the start was part of a sustained protest against modernity, and especially the effects of urbanization and industrialization. The implied goal was to restore something like the social order of medieval European Christendom. And the method of the early social encyclicals was scholastic natural law teaching of apparently timeless social truths which were believed to be applicable everywhere and always.

The change came with the remarkable pontificate of John XXIII. John in his encyclical, *Pacem in Terris* (1963) and then in various contributions to the deliberations of the Second Vatican Council, attempted to 'discern the signs of the times' in the light of the gospel, rather than continuing natural law reasoning. John saw God at work in some of the great developments of the day, and attempted to attend to 'what the Spirit was saying to the churches'. From then on, social encyclicals and social teaching more generally tended on the one hand to be structured around biblical rather than natural law themes, and on the other hand to analyse with some considerable care and insight the dangers and opportunities involved in the circumstances of the day.

One consequence of this change of style and theological approach was that the older stress on hierarchy and social gradations was virtually replaced with a new emphasis on the need for what Drew Christiansen in an important article calls 'relative equality'.[61] Christiansen argues that around 'a norm of solidaristic equality' the various norms of economic justice clustered and justified themselves as necessary for the achievement of the human solidarity which had been introduced into Catholic social teaching by Vatican II and Paul VI, and then firmly emphasized by John Paul II.[62] Relative equality requires regular redistribution of wealth to lessen the economic disparities between classes, groups and nations. John XXIII, for all his antipathy to communism, insisted on redistributionary moves towards greater equality, and understood the common good in clearly egalitarian terms. Christiansen argues that Catholic social teaching under John XXIII adopted what he calls 'a strong sort of egalitarianism' which sees an equal allocation of resources as a norm, and advocates 'redistribution of wealth from rich to poor towards a mean.' It is *relative* equality because it sets limits to acceptable inequality rather than advocating an absolute equality. This is presented as for the sake of community; great disparities of wealth and other resources are seen as corrosive of fellowship. What is needed are socioeconomic structures which enable and encourage the development of community through more just sharing of material and other resources. A main, but not the only, agent of redistribution must be government. Catholic social teaching accordingly endorses the mixed economy and a measure of government regulation of the economy.

The reading of the signs of the times since Vatican II had suggested, according to Christiansen, that earlier social teaching had had little impact on the injustice and social corrosiveness of radical inequality. A turn to a more radical stance is now appropriate and necessary. John XXIII, Paul VI and Vatican II saw inequality as socially divisive and 'inconsistent with common humanity'.[63] It should be unacceptable to Christians, and governments are urged to take firm steps towards 'relative equality'.

Recent social encyclicals of Pope John Paul II have moved in a more conservative direction, and there has been markedly less stress on 'relative equality', and on the role of the state in moving towards equality. The change of mood has, however, been gradual, and it would be an exaggeration to say that Rome has turned its back on equality. What is depressing is that with Rome – as indeed with other Christian churches – there is such an obvious gap between the equality that is commended to society and the way the church itself operates.

I have in this chapter discussed a diverse group of modern theologies in the hope that they may suggest a helpful account of the Christian shape and grounding of human equality. The theologies I have examined have been very different, but they have concurred in affirming that there are Christian roots and a Christian shape for human equality which they believe can make a constructive contribution to the resolution of some contemporary dilemmas, and introduce a different voice to modern secular debate. Equality is a central value in this tradition of discourse and of action. A family-like community which is bound together by neighbour-love demands equality. Love and justice belong inseparably together.

Equality is not merely an application of Christian truth, or an afterthought. Its roots go right to the very heart of Christian belief and practice. It is anchored in the love-command and in the ideas of community for which believers strive and which are to be given at the end. It is not, of course, a narrowly religious concept, but has always been understood as something which must find expression in the life of the world. And in life 'between the times', it seeks embodiment and expression in human behaviour, in the life of the church, and in society, as we shall see in the next three chapters.

Part Three:
Fruits of Equality:
Practices and Policies

Introduction

What Should We Do Now?

Lenin's question cannot be dodged in a book such as this. But while I attempt to address this question in relation to personal and family lifestyle, the structure and the calling of the church, and egalitarian public policies, broader issues inevitably arise. This Part is not simply a postscript to the main body of the book. For in discussing how a belief in equality may work out in practice, may be embodied, I am not simply concerned with applying an already established theory of value and suggesting how it might be applied; rather, in the discussion of practice issues of the meaning and justification of equality continue to arise, and may gain substance and clarity. Alasdair MacIntyre is surely right to suggest that:

> In moral enquiry we are always concerned with the question: what *type* of enacted narrative would be the embodiment, in the actions and transactions of actual social life, of this particular theory? For until we have answered this question about a moral theory we do not know what the theory in fact amounts to; we do not as yet understand it adequately.[1]

And a similar point was made by R. H. Tawney, when he suggested that stating principles without their application is irresponsible and unintelligible.[2] Accordingly in this Part I am concerned with some of the ways in which, in today's world, equality might be expressed or implemented, with 'enacted narratives', which embody, or might embody, equality in 'actual social life'. How can convictions about the equal worth of human beings, especially such as those whose ground and shape we have explored, be expressed or implemented?

I am not attempting, even if it were within my competence, to present a comprehensive blueprint for an egalitarian society. Rather, I am offering some suggestions and examples of possible ways forward, some of them small steps, others huge leaps; some of them tentative possibilities for experiments in equality, others major steps for society. In the process of this exploration, I expect to say something about the fruits of equality, and to point to areas and experiments that suggest that equality works, and that it has shown itself to be a good thing.

For Christians, this Part may be understood as being about faith becoming active in love, and about the social establishment of the conditions for loving. But it is equally important for others, who are convinced on different grounds of the importance and goodness of equality. For our value commitments need to find expression. And people are rightly suspicious of theories and values which do not seem to have a bearing on life, and do not seek embodiment in practices and policies in which they may be expressed and tested.

Our practices reveal the kind of people we are – our characters and our values. People are usually sceptical of those who proclaim their commitment to high-sounding values and theories but do not allow these to shape or constrain their behaviour in any significant way. There is something dishonest in expecting institutions to follow standards more stringent than those we apply to ourselves. It is a good principle to practice what you preach, even if in a sinful world there is almost always a gap between aspiration and action – the gap that, when frankly acknowledged, can be healed by forgiveness and grace. Legalistic and imposed egalitarianism can do much damage; far better is what one might call the egalitarianism of grace.

The practices, structures and priorities of the church can and should display loving and gracious egalitarianism as well as nurturing a passion for justice. The church as a sign and foretaste of God's Reign should demonstrate in the way its own life is arranged that it takes seriously the values of God's Reign and shows that equality is the ground of fellowship and love. And in the church, as much as in the family and private life, a blatant gap between what is proclaimed and taught and what is done, is often an occasion of scandal. I will explore at least some aspects of the church as an exemplary and anticipatory egalitarian community, that is called to witness to equality in the way it structures its life and deploys its resources as well as in the message it proclaims and the tradition of which it is the steward.

Social policies and social practices display the kind of society we are and how far we are shaped by the values we affirm. 'A decent concern for the poor is the true test of civilization', proclaimed Dr Johnson. And he was right. For a society which humiliates and degrades rather than honouring a category of its citizens is not expressing equality. The stated values of a society should penetrate and shape policies and practices. There is, of course, a threshold between principles and values, on the one hand, and policies on the other. Some people argue that theologians and others who are not expert in the policy formulation and implementation process should not cross this threshold, for the laying down of values and general principles represents the limit of their competence. While I recognize some validity to this boundary, it seems to me that in a democracy one cannot leave the whole business of policy to the experts and the politicians. An active citizenry has a responsibility to interest itself even in technical matters and the constraints of the so-called 'real world'. The experts and the politicians are responsible to the public, and an active citizenry cannot accept exclusion from technical and detailed discussion of policy issues. In this book I do no more than consider some policy areas that have a particularly clear significance for issues of equality and human worth. As in the rest of this Part, I do no more than offer pointers to possible ways forward towards a more equal society.

People concerned for equality are often uncertain what to do, how to express and embody their convictions. Behind this uncertainty there is often a residue of fear. We are afraid that change may destroy our security and that of our families, that moving towards equality may make us significantly less well off, that we may find equality involves a more radical sharing than we may find acceptable. But, as we have seen, poor people also are frightened, frightened of present realities and afraid that the future will be no better than the present, and perhaps worse. Poor people are afraid of poverty and inequality, afraid of what it means for them and their families, angry or confused at finding themselves in a 'poverty trap' from which they cannot escape.

The realities of inequality should disturb us. And then they may make us variously angry, frightened or threatened. For it is our interests and possessions and position that are involved. Because of this it is in this area particularly difficult to bring every thought and prejudice and attitude into captivity to Christ, and overcome 'every proud

obstacle raised up against knowledge of God'.[3] But this is precisely
what Christians are called to do. And only so may they make a distinctive contribution.

6

An Egalitarian Lifestyle

From scholars and clergymen on my mother's side I inherited a belief that, in the very radical sense of the gospels, all men were equals as children of God, and should be met and treated by us as our masters.

Dag Hammerskjöld[1]

We cannot regard men as brothers unless in some sense we share their lives.

R. H. Tawney

The claim of the neighbour

When in this book we have been discussing Munuswamy and the inequalities which impede a proper relationship between him and me, the primary question has always been, 'What can, what ought, I as an individual to do?' But then we have several times noted that there are limits to what such a personal response may achieve. Even the best and most carefully considered, and generous of personal responses needs at least to be supplemented by policy initiatives and communal action. We should not exaggerate what the individual is capable of achieving.

But personal responses to real human situations are nevertheless important. That is something that perhaps needs to be emphasized. If we are to respond to people as people we need to be willing to put our own lives and interests on the line. If we are people of faith, we know that faith must become active in love, and that turning away from need when we are capable of helping is a denial of our faith. And we are taught (as Kierkegaard insistently reminded us) that loving demands equality. If we simply believe, on whatever grounds, that equality is a good thing, this goodness should be shown in the way we conduct our lives as well as in the way we believe society should be organized.

We ought, then, first of all to be willing to show in action that we take seriously what we believe and teach about the worth of human beings, about breaking down barriers, about overcoming divisions of status, about sharing resources in order to express neighbour love here and now. We all, of course, have difficulty in co-ordinating our lifestyle and our belief. In a broken, sinful world it is almost impossible not to be to some extent a hypocrite. Paul points to the central paradox of Christian morality:

> I can will what is right, but I cannot do it. For I do not do the good I want, but the evil I do not want is what I do … For I delight in the law of God in my inmost self, but I see in my members another law at war with the law of my mind, making me captive to the law of sin that dwells in my members. Wretched man that I am! Who will rescue me from this body of death? Thanks be to God through Jesus Christ our Lord![2]

But this is no excuse for not trying to live in accordance with the command to love the neighbour. It suggests that we should expect failures, but this should not drive us to despair. For God in Christ can forgive us, and rescue us 'from this body of death', and enable us to live as forgiven disciples, and to try again.

The command to love the neighbour comes to each of us as a challenge and a summons to action. The command is addressed to us in concrete situations, and calls for a personal response. I have suggested again and again in this book that a purely personal, direct and individual response is not enough, for the problem that keeps Munuswamy and me apart is to a significant extent a structural one. We have also to examine ways in which statutory, communal, economic and political responses are required if relationships are to be healed and human beings are to flourish together in community. But personal attitudes and individual behaviour are still important. One could, for example, imagine a situation in which the welfare system and the public policies were enlightened and generous, but in which the individual citizens and those who applied the policies were often callous and uncaring. That would be a society in which although the social structures were in principle just, needy and vulnerable individuals and families were humiliated and their worth denied in practice on a daily basis. So we have to be concerned that people in their practices should recognize others as equals. And we should be concerned also about the ways of

nurture, education and formation in the family and elsewhere that produce such people, and confirm that egalitarian behaviour is good.

The issue of the egalitarian lifestyle for disciples is explored in the
New Testament particularly vividly in two stories, the parable of the
Good Samaritan,[3] and the story of the Rich Young Ruler.[4]

The familiar parable of the Good Samaritan starts with a lawyer, a
professional in such matters, who wants to test Jesus, to catch him out.
He asks what he must do to inherit eternal life. Jesus lobs the question
back to him: 'What does the law say?' he asks. The lawyer replies,
correctly of course, by stating the twofold command to love God and
the neighbour. 'That's right – go and do it', says Jesus.[5]

The lawyer is the religious expert; he knows already, of course, what
the law says. He might have left the discussion at that, but he wants 'to
justify himself', he wants to win an argument, perhaps expose Jesus as
in some way unorthodox, or ignorant, even as a charlatan. 'Who is my
neighbour?' he asks. This question betrays a fundamentally mistaken
or confused attitude to others, and to God as well, on the part of the
lawyer. If he does not know who his neighbour is, he cannot love him.
The lawyer doesn't ask who God is. Presumably he thinks he knows
that well enough. But it is impossible for one who does not know and
love the neighbour to love God. The lawyer's efforts to 'justify himself'
are really incompatible with love to God or to neighbour. He is trying
to justify himself rather than taking the claims on him of God and
neighbour with ultimate seriousness.

As Jesus tells the story, one might expect the lawyer to be guided by
the parable to see in the Jew lying wounded by the roadside an opportunity given to him, the Jewish lawyer, in his strength to do good to
his weak and needy neighbour. But instead, Jesus' story invites the
lawyer to see himself as lying by the roadside, vulnerable and without
resource, the recipient of compassion from the alien, the stranger, 'who
makes no claim at all, but is simply helpful'. Only so could the lawyer
have been set free from self-righteousness, set free to accept God's
compassion. And in recognizing his own need for a neighbour he would
have been enabled in his turn to love God and the neighbour. The
lawyer was called by the parable to break through the primordial
barrier between Jew and Gentile, to establish an equal relationship, to
be modest enough to accept his need of the Samaritan, to enable neighbour love.

Like all of us, the lawyer enjoyed talking about what is right and good, but did not obey. Just as much as the priest and the Levite, he knew the law. But, like them, he was unwilling to break through the barriers in order to obey the command. The lawyer seemed reluctant to put his life on the line, to take seriously in his lifestyle and behaviour what he believed and taught, what he knew to be true. He had asked an 'academic' question, hoping to score an academic point. Instead he received an existential challenge to a fundamental change of lifestyle and of practice. In him, as in the priest and the Levite who passed by on the other side, and in us, there was a deep-seated resistance to doing anything risky. We feel, correctly or incorrectly, that the situations we face are more complex and ambiguous than that presented by the wounded Jew the Samaritan found by the side of the Jericho road. That means that our reasoning, unlike the lawyer's, should start from the question, What should we *do* here and now?

This is the first thing to be said: those who believe that they ought to love the neighbour, whether they recognize this as a command of God or not, should do something to put their lives on the line, express their convictions in action and in the way they lead their lives, putting their money where their mouth is, for example.

The second story is of a rich ruler who came to Jesus asking with urgency how he could inherit eternal life. Like the lawyer, he knows the commandments, and says he has kept them from his youth. The discussion is already more grounded in reality than the first lawyer's attempt to trip Jesus up. On hearing the ruler's reply, we read in Mark, that Jesus loved him. But Jesus' verbal and loving response is still demanding:

> There is still one thing lacking. Sell all that you own and distribute the money to the poor, and you will have treasure in heaven; then come, follow me.[6]

The daunting command to give up all, to redistribute one's wealth, and then to follow Jesus is too hard for the ruler – and for most of us. The text does not suggest that this command of Jesus is for everyone; it is addressed to a particular person in a specific situation. Yet the specific commands of Jesus that come to us are always demanding and concrete, and they often relate to issues like money and status. We must not underestimate the strength of the ties that hold us in unjust structures.

Discipleship is difficult; and so we compromise. But the call is there as a stark reminder of the cost of discipleship.

Renunciation of status

This is, in Theissen's recent book, along with neighbour love one of 'the two basic values of the primitive Christian ethic'.[7] An impressive example of principled renunciation of status today is Bob Holman. Bob was Professor of Social Policy in the University of Bath, secure in a tenured academic post. I first came across him many years ago when I read a book on poverty which struck me as particularly sensitive and full of insights and relevant challenges. When I came to the last chapter I discovered, not altogether to my surprise, that he felt people should be honest about where they are coming from. He was a Christian, and he briefly outlined how he felt his faith illumined issues of poverty in a challenging way.[8] Shortly after that he resigned and became a community worker, first in a housing estate in Bath, and then in Easterhouse, an area of multiple deprivation in Glasgow, employed by a local community action group and living in the area. He is quite explicit about the roots of his egalitarian lifestyle:

> The impact of Jesus Christ stemmed not just from his teachings and his miracles. It also came from the kind of life he lived. His attitudes, his practices, his behaviour, were entirely in accord with the values he proclaimed. He told his disciples to be like servants – and he washed their feet. He gave the commandment to love – and he embraced the leper, the prostitute, the outcast. He told the wealthy not to put their trust in money – and he lived modestly and refused to accumulate possessions ... There was a loving consistency about Jesus ... The New Testament likewise expects his followers to show behaviour which is in line with Christian codes of conduct.[9]

Renunciation of status and identification was for Holman a way of taking sides, a form of what R. H. Tawney called 'an intellectual conversion'. By breaking through barriers not only did he find new insights, but he was able to give voice to people who had been deprived of a voice, or whose voice was never listened to.

Bob Holman is a disturbing figure, challenging our own individual compromises, and demonstrating that the problems of our society are not 'out there', among the poor and weak, so that we, the strong, powerful and prosperous, can solve them, but they are afflictions of the society as a whole, processes in which we are implicated. Holman calls for consistency between belief and behaviour, even while recognizing that '[p]robably everyone is a hypocrite to some degree'. But he both affirms and demonstrates that '[I]ndividuals can live in ways which uphold the principle of equality and, in so doing, persuade others to do the same.'[10]

Holman has recognized that social barriers are also barriers to communication, and that much academic discourse is not only often unnecessarily abstract and obscure, but also often actually and quite unnecessarily humiliates. His renunciation of status has enabled in a small area at least the breaking down of some serious barriers to communication so that ordinary people are enabled to speak without fear of coercion or ridicule, and academics and clergy are enabled to attend to people in such a way as to appreciate the human meaning of social problems. 'Only a society which can imagine the plight of its weakest members and legislates for their inclusion into society rather than their virtual exclusion from it can call itself a just or equal society', writes Margaret Drabble.[11]

Holman presents a disturbing challenge. 'Any religion, any set of beliefs, any political creed,' he says, 'has to be judged according to the way adherents put principles into practice. Both Christianity and socialism hold as central the reduction of poverty and inequality and their members should be expected to live in ways which further these ends.'[12] If lifestyle is not taken seriously, we are constantly open to charges of hypocrisy. How can a political movement or a church 'be serious about challenging poverty and inequality when leading members enjoy lives of luxury?' While there may not be one pattern of egalitarian lifestyle valid for everyone, luxurious lifestyles reinforce social ills and legitimate greed, as well as creating distance from people with low incomes or who live in deprived areas:

> By mixing largely with the privileged they become immune to the fact that children die young, that families are split asunder, that lives are warped by poverty and inequality. They lose the sense of anger that should insist on radical action.[13]

Holman's challenging voice is one that must be attended to. His may not be everyone's calling, but all Christians and people of good will should seek to express in their lifestyle their deepest convictions and values.

Sharing and solidarity[14]

The example of personal lifestyle may be the surest way in which any-one and everyone may proclaim their commitment to the values of God's Reign. Excesses of wealth and poverty result in different forms of exclusion from the community, and a lifestyle which recognizes this and which respects the value of community will be a lifestyle of sharing and moderation.

There is nothing wrong with money in itself. But it is hard for a rich man to enter God's Reign, basically because of the temptation to use money in selfish ways. We must not disregard ourselves and those for whom we have special responsibilities, but judge what is appropriate for ourselves by first appreciating the needs of our neighbours.

Moderation should not itself be conspicuous; how the individual pursues it will vary in emphasis. Some will focus on personal sharing and serious giving, which is a form of voluntary redistribution. Others will express their commitment to sharing by striving to live as respon-sibly as possible towards the environment, consuming the minimum of non-renewable resources. All should be guided to live hospitably, and in harmony with their surroundings.

Moderation in personal lifestyle means, in terms of the fine slogan, 'living simply that others may simply live'. It should be a way of recog-nizing that the hungry, the poor and the powerless are our neighbours and equals, and that our patterns of consumption affect them. In addition to generous and unpretentious giving, this involves a call for simple moderation, for a life with as little waste or conspicuous con-sumption as possible. This has, of course, implications for family life. Is the allocation of resources within the household openly discussed and agreed? If both partners work, how is the unpaid domestic work allocated? What value is put by the earners on the unpaid work per-formed by others, and is the unpaid work shared? And questions need to be asked about regular income: Am I on the fiddle in any way? Am I being entirely honest about my tax liability? Do I grudge contributing through taxation to the welfare of others? Do I respond in my pattern of giving to the injustices and the inequalities of the world?

Life is to be celebrated. The search for a moderate lifestyle should not make us gloomy. Sharing is for the sake of conviviality. We should seek ways of making our lives celebrations of our relationships with neighbours near and far.

Political action

Democracies, for their proper functioning, require an active citizenry. If citizens are passive, uninterested in what goes on in the public sphere, and willing to leave matters between elections simply to the discretion of the government – this is a recipe for the collapse of true democracy. Citizens should hold government accountable. It is responsible to them, and in a democracy the government is responsible to the citizens for its actions. During the Scottish Reformation, John Knox, in addressing 'the dear commonalty of Scotland' made precisely this point, which lies at the root of modern democracy:

> And if ye think that ye are innocent because ye are not the chief authors of such iniquity, ye are utterly deceived. For God doth not only punish the chief offenders, but with them doth He damn the consenters to iniquity; and all are judged to consent that knowing impiety committed give no testimony that the same displeaseth them. To speak this matter more plain, as your princes and rulers are criminal with your bishops of all idolatry committed, and of all the innocent blood that is shed for the testimony of Christ's truth, and that because they maintain them in their tyranny, so are you (I mean so many of you as give no plain confession to the contrary) criminal and guilty with your princes and rulers of the same crimes, because ye assist and maintain your princes in their blind rage and give no testimony that their tyranny displeaseth you.[15]

It is not inappropriate to see in such an affirmation of the collective responsibility of the whole community roots of modern democratic politics, and a remarkably early call for an active citizenry.

An active citizenry in a modern democracy should not simply pursue individual and group interests. There is a widespread assumption that citizens do just this, that whatever they say in opinion polls about willingness to pay extra taxes for an improved health service, or for world development, or for better schools, in the privacy of the polling booth people vote selfishly, and follow what they believe to be their own short-term interests. There is indeed plenty of empirical evidence that this is how most people actually behave most of the time. But if this assumption is accepted, and by acceptance becomes respectable, the consequences for the polity and for democracy are devastating. Democracy becomes the tyranny of the majority; the interests of minorities are sidelined, except when they are able to hold a balance in the legislature. And in societies like most western democracies where the poor are not only a minority of the population, but politically passive, and unlikely to vote, the interests of the poor can easily be neglected while the more powerful and vocal groups have their interests attended to. This is, in Alasdair MacIntyre's telling phrase, politics as 'civil war carried on by other means'. The aim of such a war is total victory, and the spoils belong to the victors.

A democracy needs an active citizenry that is willing to put the common good before sectional and individual interests, and sometimes make sacrifices for the benefit of others, and for a greater good. Usually this is only possible when many people are gripped by a vision, and feel a sense of solidarity, shared destiny and mutual accountability. But it also depends on visionary leadership, for political leaders who have convictions which they can share and a vision, a dream, of the future of the society that is infectious, like Martin Luther King's, or Desmond Tutu's.

Symbolic action

Symbolic action can be remarkably significant in the public forum. Personal, generous, perhaps sacrificial, sometimes risky actions may actually affect the way things go, even if at the time they often seem impotent gestures. I am speaking here both of protests and of action to advocate a particular policy. Formal protests against apartheid in South Africa were backed up by boycotts – in sport, in academic life, in the purchasing of South African goods. It would be naïve to suggest that these things were able to exert significant political or economic pressure on the apartheid regime (although successful pressure for disinvestment did have considerable impact on the South African economy), but they did have a powerful effect in two ways: first, in sending out a message of solidarity to black South Africans and those who were struggling for justice inside South Africa, backed up with token little sacrifices in abstaining from South African goods; and, secondly, in sending, particularly through the sporting boycott, a message which was heard because it hurt white South Africa, that apartheid was not acceptable to the rest of the world.

One of the most interesting past examples of symbolic action on a political and economic issue which was spearheaded by evangelical Christians, mobilized large sections of the British churches, and was often couched in explicitly Christian language was the nineteenth century campaign against the slave trade. Like the later campaign against apartheid, this involved a boycott of slave-produced sugar, a massive programme of education about the human reality of the slave trade and of plantation slavery, and direct, insistent pressure on government and on legislature.

And in more recent days, in the Jubilee 2000 campaign we have seen an extremely well-orchestrated peaceful campaign which has certainly had impact on governments and to some extent at least on the international economic agencies such as the World Bank and the International Monetary Fund. Symbolic acts, indicating that people are willing to make at least token personal sacrifices, play an important role in various ways. They demonstrate to politicians that considerable numbers of people care passionately about others who are suffering. They give people an opportunity to 'go public' about what is important to them. They educate people about the realities of the situation. Particularly if the action elicits any kind of positive response, there is a reduction in the sense of impotence that is so destructive of healthy democracy. And they engender at least the beginnings of an egalitarian sense of solidarity, of belonging together and being accountable to one another between people who are otherwise divided by an ugly ditch of inequality.

Nurturing equality

Most people imbibe their fundamental values and attitudes in the family first of all. And they do this not so much through words as through example, through the way the family operates, and the way they themselves are dealt with. In a good family the worth of each child is affirmed and celebrated. Differences of physical or emotional ability are recognized and affirmed, but not as matters that translate into higher regard for the achievers than for those who for good reason cannot be so successful. The way a family responds to serious learning or physical difficulties in a child, for instance, is crucial. In an egalitarian family children learn to respect one another, and to 'honour their father and mother'. Children are expected to contribute to the life of the family in appropriate ways. The parents and adults in the family circle take them seriously, listen to them, explain things to them. My mother, looking after four of her grandchildren while their parents were away for a break, had to deal with a case of bad behaviour. 'What do mummy and daddy do when you behave like that?' she asked the eldest. 'Oh, mummy and daddy just say, "Wah, wah, wah, wah: DO YOU UNDERSTAND?"' And the children all agreed. Their parents always tried to explain why behaviour was unacceptable. Their rulings were not arbitrary, or simply an expression of anger or impatience. They made sense, they fitted into a structure of meaning.

Both in storytelling and in the life of the family, models of virtue, and of vice, are offered to the child. Today much of this process takes place through TV – that's why soaps are so important – and computer games. Serious questions of course arise about the kind of models that are offered in and through the media. But that is another fascinating and complex story, which should, I think cause much concern because so many of the hero figures are aggressive and selfish, and few have a moral passion involving self-sacrifice or a commitment to the needs of others. And the peer group is, of course, of immense importance in determining values and behaviour, and in selecting role models.

This is how we receive our basic value orientation. We have, of course, a choice particularly in the teenage years whether to accept or reject what we have received. But early impressions run deep, and tend to last, for good or ill. And the most powerful of these are commonly things that are done, rather than things that are said, in the family. For instance, children notice if the family gives a proportion of resources to church or charity, and if they are expected to think about giving away a proportion of their own pocket money, and of anything they earn. They notice if the family cares about others as well as its own members. Indeed, children will often at the time resent it if mum gives a lot of her time to a neighbour whose own child is seriously ill – they need to have the situation explained to them. And when it is, it makes a little dent in their selfishness, often for years.

I myself was profoundly influenced by the experience when I was a little boy of having an exiled German Jewish family living with us for some months in 1939 and 1940. I remember at the time resenting them, and the energy my parents gave to making them feel secure and cared for. I had a sense that my home was no longer my home. I remember vividly, too, hearing from them something of the horrors of Nazism. And I remember with gratitude the extraordinary generosity with which, as soon as they arrived in the United States, and before they had employment, they cabled my parents offering to look after all five of us children in the USA for the duration of the war. Family experiences like that are formative. For they eat away at some of the selfishness that is in us all, and they suggest that the egalitarian family must be open and hospitable to the needs of others.

Formal education matters too, of course. R. H. Tawney was, I think, right to argue that the segregated British educational system was one of the great bastions of inequality that implanted in British society the assumption that inequality is a natural and good thing. Segregated education, Tawney argued, is divisive and destroys the kind of egalitarian fellowship which is necessary in a decent society in which citizens are not humiliated. Segregated education, whether the segregation be in terms of wealth, or class or religion or whatever, not only increasingly reinforces inequality and confirms social divisions, but it encourages dangerous misunderstandings of the other groups which are educated separately. I know this from my own experience. Up to the age of 13 I was educated in private schools in my home town. I still remember the assumption which was rife among the pupils of these schools that the other children in the town who went to what we call in Scotland, correctly, the public schools, were different, strange, rather threatening, and liable to be violent. We called them the 'keelies'; and 'keelie' was a term of abuse for any of our number who departed from group norms. Then at 13 I went to the local high school, and discovered, rather to my surprise, that the keelies were just like me, and good friends to boot.

If equality is to be nurtured, we need to have a radical change in the educational system. Tawney was, I think, right in suggesting that 'The English educational system will never be one worthy of a civilised society until the children of all classes in the nation attend the same schools.' A separate school system effectively reserved to the children of the wealthy exists to the same scale in no other country other than Britain. It is, Tawney argues,

> at once an educational monstrosity and a grave national misfortune. It is educationally vicious, since to mix with companions from homes of different types is an important part of the education of the young. It is socially disastrous, for it does more than any other cause, except capitalism itself, to perpetuate the division of the nation into classes of which one is almost unintelligible to the other.[16]

Egalitarians should wish for a system of schooling which ensures that the kind of opportunities which any good parents wish for their own children should be available for all. According to David Donnison, who was for a time chairman of the Public Schools' Commission, parents often have to choose between being good parents and being good citizens. He remembers hearing evidence from a group of parents in Edinburgh, which had, and has, one of the most stratified school systems in Britain:

> Their message was simple: 'For the sake of our children', these mainly middle class people said, 'we are compelled to compete to get them into the best schools available, knowing that those at the bottom of the pecking order have had so many of the talented pupils and teachers creamed out of them. We hope your recommendations will help to create a comprehensive system in which every school will give its pupils the opportunities we want for our own children. Then we shall no longer have to choose between being good citizens and good parents.'[17]

Parents who believe in equality have to take sometimes difficult and costly decisions about the education of their children. For they know that these decisions can cumulatively affect the prospects of children who suffer serious disadvantage, whose equal worth they wish to affirm.

Humility and self-respect

An egalitarian lifestyle means for many a conscious renunciation of status and privilege, but for others it demands an affirmation of self-respect. We have been reminded by feminist thinkers in particular that an enforced humility or social pressure on women to confine themselves to caring, largely in the domestic sphere, can be destructive of self-respect, of a proper sense of worth. The feminists are speaking of a subtle, socially-constructed process that I do not have the space to explore in any detail here. But it has to be mentioned, for religious or Christian pressures for humility can be for some people profoundly destructive, and do not in fact establish an equality of respect for others and respect for oneself. It is worth remembering that the command that we found to be so pivotal in the theological argument for equality was to love the neighbour *as oneself*, the implication being that one cannot truly love the neighbour unless one loves oneself, and therefore affirms one's own equal worth. As Iris Young puts it:

> People have or lack self-respect because of how they define themselves and how others regard them, because of how they spend their time, because of the amount of autonomy and decision-making power they have in their activities and so on ... Self-respect is at least as much a function of culture as it is of goods, for example ... None of the forms and not all of the conditions of self-respect can meaningfully be conceived as goods that individuals possess; they are rather relations and processes in which the actions of individuals are embedded.[18]

These relations and processes are perhaps another way of speaking about an egalitarian lifestyle, in which self-respect and a sense of worth are systematically promoted in the way relations are structured.

Exemplars of equality

Richard Tawney was born to the purple. Born in India, where his father was a servant of the Raj, Tawney was educated at Rugby and Balliol College, Oxford. In terms of contacts and friendships, he was clearly set to be a member of the 'establishment'. Then, at Oxford, his conscience was jolted. He discovered the reality of poverty and inequality in the East End of London. His life was changed. He went through a kind of conversion.

Tawney enlisted as a private in the First World War, and fought in the trenches. He was moved by the friendships he developed with working-class soldiers. He came to admire their generosity, their cheerfulness, their willingness to share, their modesty – in many ways so different from many of the officers who had been educated beside him in places like Rugby and Oxford. He concluded that 'an army does not live by munitions alone, but also by fellowship in a moral idea or purpose'.[19]

This sense of the value of egalitarian fellowship around a shared goal stayed with him for the rest of his life. Throughout the 1920s and 1930s he denounced the mammon-worship which condemned multitudes to poverty and degradation and despair. He called for a fraternal society, a community of friends, in which the equal worth of Dives and Lazarus, of every human being before God is fully recognized. And he himself, even when he was one of the most politically influential intellectuals in Britain, lived a life of great simplicity, practising what he preached. When he was presented for an honorary degree at Oxford he was compared to Diogenes, the Greek philosopher who lived in a barrel because Tawney and his wife had spent much of the Second world War living in a hen-house in great simplicity. In some ways it is tempting to call him a kind of saint, although the 'saintly idiom' of politics is hardly current in the West today.

One could go on, listing women and men who have lived out an egalitarian lifestyle, rather like the catalogue of the heroes of faith of the Old Testament in the eleventh chapter of the Letter to the Hebrews! But one last figure must be mentioned. Let David Donnison, the doyen of British social policy, speak in his own words:

Egalitarians are often accused of indulging in 'the politics of envy', and this tempts them to reply that they, too, deplore an envious world, and – unlike their critics – they are prepared to remove the massive and indefensible inequalities which are the cause of that envy: a justifiable debater's riposte, but too superficial to start anyone thinking afresh.

Seeking to create a more equal world does not *feel* like envy. It does not even feel as if money and material wealth were the central issues. So what is it about? It is about creating a world in which people find it easier to see and hear each other, not treating each other as objects; a world in which it is easier to treat people with respect and kindness, even when we disagree profoundly with them; a world, if you like, in which it is easier to be good and harder to be bad. But where does equality come in?

The world we actually live in so often seems almost to compel us to treat other people in, at best, a guarded fashion, and at worst with suspicion or outright hostility. Our critics regard these as permanent features of a race filled with original sin, living under governments powerless to make any significant impact on society. The wise man accepts that this is the world he must live in and, imbibing its poisons, acquires what immunity he can.

> The thoughts of others
> Were light and fleeting,
> Of lovers' meeting
> Or luck or fame.
> Mine were of trouble,
> And mine were steady,
> So I was ready
> When trouble came.

– as A. E. Housman said. Yet all are not compelled to swallow the poison or dish it out. We are all lucky enough to know people who seem to surmount these sad and crippling pressures. By luck, love or hard labour, people do change the worlds they live in, both for the better and the worse.

When I first joined the navy I spent time in barracks and transit camps where men flowed through, coming off ships for a few days or weeks before being drafted out to sea again. And it was an awful world. No one gave anyone anything: not even information. I lost right away the nice hair brush my mother had given me, and quickly learnt that we could not turn our backs upon our few possessions for one moment without losing them. Later I served in a destroyer, a minesweeper and other ships, and was moved by the kindness and comradeship of their crews. Your possessions were safe. People took care of each other. A man who came aboard drunk when the ship was in port would be told to turn in, and the fellow he was about to relieve would stand his watch for him – thereby working for twelve or sixteen hours at a stretch – rather than expose the ship to danger or his drunken comrade to punishment. And whether he liked the man or not played no part whatever in that comradely act. Then I went back to a transit camp on my way to another posting, and it was as awful as before. Yet, in a ship or a barracks, these were the same men....

We have all had similar experiences. Richard Titmuss's book, *The Gift Relationship*, gives a particularly telling example, describing the way in which blood donors have created a nationwide service, providing blood for unknown fellow citizens without asking for payment – whereas in other countries, where the health services work on more mercenary principles, blood donors too demand payment, and the risks of lethal infection from people who have nothing left to sell but their blood are much greater. The whole society is thereby morally impoverished

Every act – and certainly every act of governments – makes it a little easier or a little harder for all of us to treat each other as comrades: not as objects, but as people whom we really see and hear; people we respond to with respect, trust and kindness, whether we like them or not. Amongst comrades, differences in power, status and wealth – modest differences – can be cheerfully accepted without envy, if they are earned in some way by talent and hard work, by the happiness their possessors give the rest of us, or the responsibilities they bear on our behalf. Gross or inexplicable differences in power, status and wealth are not accepted – even for themselves – by people who value comradeship. They would destroy something that is more important.[20]

Donnison's experiences as a bicycling egalitarian Chairman of a major government organization, the Supplementary Benefits Commission, are recounted, sometimes hilariously, in his book, *The Politics of Poverty*.[21]

Donnison and others remind us that lifestyle matters, the way we relate to Munuswamy is important. In this chapter I have not attempted to outline and commend a particular egalitarian lifestyle, suitable for everyone. That would be arrogant and unconvincing. Rather, I have attempted to suggest a number of areas which people who believe in equality might consider when they are framing their consciences and considering what they are called to do and be.

Some of the areas we should consider involve money – payment of taxes, generous charitable giving, proper stewardship of material resources, acknowledging that we are not the unqualified owners of what we earn or inherit. The Iona Community has had from its early days an 'Economic Discipline', in which members accept accountability to the Community for their stewardship of their financial resources. Other areas involve political action, symbolic or otherwise: the kind of social policies we support, the taxation and benefits policies we advocate, and so forth. Others again concern education and the nurture of the next generation. Here the central issue is how to be as concerned for the education of our neighbours' children as for our own, and how to encourage an educational system, and forms of family life, which enable children to recognize the equal worth of others. Then there is the possibility of sitting light to status and in all one's 'walk' showing that one really believes in equality.

The Society of Friends, or Quakers, have throughout their history had a strong egalitarian commitment, expressed in simplicity of lifestyle, generosity in giving, and a recognition of the need for public witness to what they believe. A typical example of the Friends' way is the recent launch in Scotland of a 'Quaker Tax Witness Fund'. Their publicity starts by pointing out four key facts on poverty in Britain:

- Between 1979 and 1993 the number of children living in poverty increased from 1.4 million to 4.3 million.

- In the same period average household incomes rose by 40% above the rate of inflation, but for the lowest tenth of households income fell by 12.5% in real terms.

- At least 25% of children in Scotland live in households dependent on income support.

- 33% of pensioners live in poverty.

Quakers regard paying tax as a religious duty, and they have consistently urged that the tax system should be used to promote a more equal society, and they have opposed cuts in income tax. The Tax Witness Fund has now been set up 'as a corporate witness to this view'. The Fund has four objectives:

- To demonstrate the principle that progressive personal taxation is a key element in securing a society in which all citizens have access to good standards of health care, housing and education.

- To show through practical action that there is willingness to pay more income tax to achieve a fairer society.

- To give individuals a channel for their sense of injustice at tax reductions which favour the relatively prosperous at the expense of the poorest and weakest.

- To support local action which counters the effects of poverty and low income.

The funds collected will go to initiatives and projects which empower poor people and are effective in relieving poverty and disadvantage. Donors are left to decide the level of giving that is appropriate for them, but people are reminded that the standard rate of income tax has been reduced by one penny in the pound in each of the past two years.[22]

This project could well be a model for the kind of lifestyle initiatives which are appropriate for Christians who believe in equality.

But changes in individual lifestyle are not in themselves enough. The proper fulfilment of the command to love the neighbour must also be embodied in the life of the church, and expressed in policy initiatives.

7

An Inclusive Church

As in the Holy Trinity, so in this Parish:
None is before or after another,
None is greater or less than another.[1]

[From an Anglo-Catholic parish notice-board in London]

Egalitarian community

In the previous chapter I was discussing ways in which people who believe in human equality, who are convinced that all human beings are of infinite worth and entitled to respect, might behave. From the Prologue, where we wrestled with the problem of how to establish an equal and caring relationship with Munuswamy, and repeatedly since then, we have seen how difficult it is for individuals to break free from structures of inequality and establish equal relationships. The obstacles in the ways of individuals making an impact, swimming effectively against the stream of inequality, are huge, and sometimes lead people to despair. People of egalitarian principles need encouragement both from the support of others and from demonstrations that equality can work. We need a variety of egalitarian communities, experiments in equality, working models that show that equality is viable, that it works, that it can produce good fruits. And such communities will also, in all probability show up some of the problems and difficulties that must be faced if we are to live together as equals.

Perhaps, in speaking in this way, I am suggesting the need for, and the importance of, utopian communities. And, in a way, I am. But before going further down this road we need to take seriously the criticisms of utopian socialist communities that were made by Engels[2] and by Marx, and the experience in more recent times of communities and fellowships committed to equality and spirituality and a new way of living together which have either after a time broken up with some acrimony, or have become asylums or refuges from the inequalities and materialism of the broader society rather than agencies of transformation. Engels saw utopian socialist communities as failing to take seriously the entrenched power structures of the broader society, or the historical process. The utopian socialists felt they could win over the minds and hearts of the powerful to a voluntary renunciation of their power and wealth by showing a new and better way. The utopian communities were small-scale and largely bourgeois fellowships that tended to be rather self-indulgent, with little direct contact with the places and the people that were hurting most. In theological language that Engels would not, of course, have used, they failed to take structural sin in the society with adequate seriousness, and they were not conscious that sin infected their own membership and their own operations subtly and pervasively. Then, as now, utopian communities tended to lack staying power and were commonly rather short-lived. But let there be no doubt about this: the long-term influence of some utopian experiments like those of Robert Owen at New Lanark and elsewhere was considerable. They demonstrated that a humane mode of industrial production that built a caring community around the factory could indeed be profitable and competitive. And that lesson is still to be fully assimilated.

It would be wise also to learn from the successes and failures of egalitarian movements in Christianity and beyond. Counter-cultural movements can have an important role, even if they are short-lived, and protest movements can affect very deeply the way things go in the world. This is particularly true at times of crisis, when people are questioning the ability of the existing order of things to provide an opportunity for people to live a decent life in community. One might mention at this point Alasdair MacIntyre's now famous declaration at the end of *After Virtue* that we have entered a new Dark Ages in which, as in the first Dark Ages, community and moral integrity are disintegrating. The time has come, he insists, to stop trying to shore up the existing pattern of things, for the Barbarians have taken over and decency, and just, decent and loving community life have become impossible in the broader society. Accordingly, MacIntyre continues, 'What matters at this stage is the construction of local forms of community within which civility and the intellectual and moral life can be

sustained through the new dark ages that are already upon us.'³
Interestingly, MacIntyre points back to the monastic communities
that, he argues, sustained civility, morality and a sense of egalitarian
community through a very difficult period of cultural and political
breakdown. That is why he suggests that we need 'another – doubtless
very different – St Benedict'.

Others have seen the congregation rather than the monastery as the
major sustainer and generator in times of decadence and disintegration
of ideas of community with an egalitarian dimension. The congregation which is socially diverse and cannot detach itself from 'the world'
can yet produce and demonstrate notions of fellowship at times when
community seems in danger of being totally eroded. Sheldon Wolin,
for instance, argues that at the time of the disintegration of the Roman
Empire, it was the churches as communities of love which withdrew
from politics in order not to have to make compromises with power,
that revitalized Western political thought. These congregations were in
a real sense counter-cultural, and understanding themselves as the soul
giving life to the body they presented an implied challenge to the disintegrating political order. They offered an alternative, and 'a new and
sorely needed source of ideas for western political thought'⁴ by living
out 'a new and powerful ideal of community which recalled men [*sic*] to
a life of meaningful participation'. This kind of community contrasted
sharply with late classical and Hellenistic ideas on how human beings
ought to relate to one another. Michael Mann, in the first volume of his
ambitious *The Sources of Social Power* (1986), suggests that the congregations of the early church were unintentionally subversive because
'they were a rival social organisation to the empire', offering a better
sense of meaning and belonging, and better care and discipline, than
did the political and social institutions of the empire with which the
church was in unavoidable tension.⁵ In the church, women and men,
and people from excluded communities – children, soldiers, notorious
sinners, foreigners, and the ritually impure – were 'made at home in the
universe', as members of an egalitarian fellowship.⁶ 'The "home"',
writes Mann, 'was a social home, a community, but one that had universal significance in relation to ultimate meaning and morality. It
fused the sacred and the secular, the spiritual and the material to produce a transcendent *society*.'⁷ The church offered a resolution of the
profound crisis of social identity by manifesting an *oikumene* which was

equally open to all and transcended lesser loyalties. The church was a place where in principle everyone was at home, everyone was equal.

The church in the early centuries thus did not entirely abandon the sense of being an egalitarian community gathered around Jesus. It did not give up its engagement with the power structures of the broader society; nor did it accommodate itself to a ghetto existence, condemning itself to irrelevance, in separation from the temporal city. It remained in significant ways an egalitarian movement, striving to affirm in practice the infinite worth of the neighbour, and an inclusive community that recognized the equality before God of all who bore God's image.

The church as sacrament, sign and instrument of equality

The Second Vatican Council rather daringly declared:

> By her relationship with Christ, the Church is a kind of sacrament or sign of intimate union with God, and of the unity of all mankind. She is also an instrument for the achievement of such union and unity.[8]

The wording is quite cautious, but it is unambiguous in suggesting that the church is, or is called to be, an exemplification of a kind of egalitarian community which is intended to encompass all humankind, and of which the church is also to be an instrument, helping to bring such inclusive community into existence as well as providing a preliminary manifestation of it. The term 'instrument' suggests that the church has a servant role, helping with the overcoming of ancient hostilities and the establishment of the kind of reconciled community in which human beings may flourish together in love and justice.

The Uppsala Assembly of the World Council of Churches in 1968 adopted similar language, declaring that 'The Church is bold in speaking of itself as the sign of the coming unity of mankind.'[9] These declarations were followed by years of careful study and clarification in the ecumenical movement. In particular it was increasingly emphasized that the 'sign' was 'a calling and a task', not something that was already complete and perfect, fully expressed in the visible church.

The church could only become an instrument for the healing of the nations 'as a community which is itself being healed'. Despite its divisions, which so often in fact reflect and exacerbate the divisions of the world, the church may be 'the foretaste of a redeemed creation, a sign of the coming unity of mankind, a pointer to the time when God shall be all in all.'[10]

These are vast and daunting claims made for the church. It is to be an anticipation of God's Reign, an earnest or down-payment, enabling people to glimpse and experience the authentic flavour of God's Reign. It is called to be an exemplary community, existing for the sake of the world. And more, it is to be an instrument, not so much for bringing or building God's Reign as for spreading throughout human society the values, social structures and attitudes which are characteristic of the Reign of God, which is still to come as gift and as grace in its fullness. But the church, in using such language, is committing itself to being a community which seeks to follow and exemplify the kind of egalitarian, inclusive fellowship which was characteristic of the disciples and others who gathered around Jesus. Only thus may it be a sacrament, sign and instrument of the equality and unity of all humankind.

Some recent theologians have developed the insight in the epigram at the head of this chapter – that the fellowship of the church, which is a foretaste of what is in store for all humankind, is modelled on, and rooted in, the loving fellowship of the Holy Trinity.[11] Recent theologians writing on the Trinity have tended to emphasize the equality of intratrinitarian relationships. In the trinitarian dance of love (or *perichoresis*) the constant self-emptying to give to the other makes it nonsense to speak of the 'greater' or the 'lesser'.[12] An implication of such an approach for an Orthodox theologian such as John Zizioulas is the call for a church that is characterized by 'non-pyramidal' structures of authority, so that the church provides a context of equality among believers in which disinterested love or *agape* may flourish. Authority and hierarchy within the church are 'born out of relationship and not of power'; they exist in this way for the expression of loving fellowship.[13] A similar point is made by Miroslav Volf when he speaks of 'symmetrical relations within the Trinity'. He continues:

> This yields the ecclesial principle that the more a church is characterized by symmetrical and decentralized distribution of power and

freely affirmed interaction, the more it will correspond to the trinitarian communion. Relations between charismata, modelled after the Trinity, are reciprocal and symmetrical; all members of the church have charismata, and all are to engage their charismata for the good of all others.[14]

Churches are already in communion with the triune God, and reflect a little of the loving equality which is characteristic of the Trinity. But Volf suggests further that 'ecclesial correspondence to the Trinity' become both a matter of hope, that it may be more fully realized now, and fully at the end, and also a task laid upon believers, to realize with ever greater fullness the quality of fellowship which participates in the love which binds the Trinity together.

The liberation theologian, Leonardo Boff, sums up the social implications of the mystery of the holy Trinity as follows:

> From the perichoresis-communion of the three divine persons derive impulses to liberation: of each and very human person; of society, of the church and of the poor, in the double – critical and constructive – sense. *Human beings* are called to rise above all mechanisms of egoism and live their vocation of communion. *Society* offends the Trinity by organising itself on a basis of inequality and honours it the more it favors sharing and communion for all, bringing about justice and equality for all. The *church* is more the sacrament of trinitarian communion the more it reduces inequalities between Christians and between the various ministries in it, and the more it understands and practises unity as co-existence in diversity. The *poor* reject their impoverishment as sin against trinitarian communion, see the inter-relatedness of the divine 'Differents' as the model for a human society based on mutual collaboration –all on an equal footing – and based on individual differences; that society's structures would be humane, open, just and egalitarian.[15]

The hope and task of being the church

On the face of it, the theological claims for the church that I have been discussing in the previous section seem to the commonsensical mind at least grossly inflated, and seriously lacking in plausibility when we measure them against the actual examples of what it is to be church with which we are familiar. The few old ladies gathering Sunday by Sunday in St Mungo's Outside the Gates, or the 'happy clappy' youngsters almost obsessed with their own feelings in a charismatic house church may seem to have little to do with the picture that we have painted. Many people turn to the church seeking authoritative pronouncements to set their minds at rest, and look to powerful figures working within an ancient and clearly stratified hierarchical structure to give them security. It would not perhaps occur to many people that they might turn to the church to find love and equality. The glaring divisions and the petty squabbles of the church are a public scandal, which does not go unnoticed.

Honesty makes us acknowledge that the church has been deeply penetrated and corrupted by the inequalities and divisions of the world. It has absorbed much of this into its own structures and ways of working. It reflects and reinforces divisions and inequalities in many situations around the world, today as much, if not more, than in the past. It is commonly reluctant to put its own house in order. In situations as diverse and as complex as South Africa, Rwanda and Northern Ireland the churches have done at least as much to exacerbate things as to proclaim and demonstrate reconciliation and love. There is a great gulf between the church as she ought to be and the churches as they are. Even among themselves, they are slow to seek true reconciliation, and are often suspicious and hostile towards one another. And churches develop their own institutional interests and wealth, of which they are often very possessive. The empirical, visible church is always in need of repentance and radical reformation.

All that, and more, is true and must be acknowledged, and grappled with, because it is, in the precise sense of the term, a scandal which in fact obscures rather than demonstrating the truth of the gospel. But it is also true that the church, in all its brokenness, lack of faith, and corruption is still a highly unusual sort of egalitarian fellowship, striving to be faithful to its calling. At its best, it is a repentant community trying to put its trust in God's grace rather than its own institutional power or wealth, or place in the broader community. Almost despite itself, it operates as a paradigmatic community. And it does this at the three levels at which the church operates – the local congregation or parish, the national church or denomination, and the ecumenical church that is emerging so clearly.

If the church is to be in any real sense an exemplary community, a community which demonstrates the possibilities and the blessings of loving fellowship, it must take very seriously in its own life the message and the principles it offers to the world. The church exists in a multitude of different forms and structures, but almost all of them are reluctant in various ways to allow the gospel to shape how they deploy power and wealth in their own structures, and this limits their ability to be exemplary communities. Often enough they are dismissed as hypocrites by people who observe the contrast between what they commend and how they themselves behave. Many churches faced precisely this issue in relation to investment of church funds in South Africa in the days of apartheid. Church financial managers argued that they had a simple task – to realize as much income as was prudently possible from the church's investments, so that stipends could be paid, buildings maintained, and the whole life of the church sustained; the effectiveness of their service of the church would be destroyed if all their decisions were to be circumscribed by ethical and theological cautions and prohibitions. Only gradually did some of them come to see that ethical investment could be prudent, and yield a respectable return, as well as sending out important signals which were closely related to the message that the church was proclaiming. Churches of all denominations today struggle, with variable success, to reduce large inequalities in stipends, and to grapple, as did Paul – with the problem that some congregations are rich while others are desperately poor in material and human resources, and that these differences usually mirror differences in the social composition of the parish area. Similar issues arise in relation to global inequality and development issues. Here two things can be said with some confidence. The first is that Christian development agencies have been pioneers not only in relief and aid, but in ways to encourage full participation in decision-making and allocations on the part of the receiving communities – ways, that is, of encouraging a sense of community between the wealthy and the poor; striving in moving towards a more equal sharing of resources to do justice, challenge the structures of oppression, and build community rather than give voluntary charity. The second thing to be said is this: there is much empirical evidence to suggest that Christians are

more generous in giving than the population in general, perhaps
because exposure to the gospel has given them a bad conscience about
the gross inequalities that disfigure the world today.

In relation to power, the situation is no less complex. Historically
churches have tended to mirror the power structures they find around
them; and since church power structures tend to change very slowly
indeed, we find still significant remnants of feudal or medieval structures of power in some churches, and many have in modern times
developed powerful bureaucratic structures which operate very similarly to bureaucracies elsewhere. It is sad, for instance, that while the
Roman Catholic Church proclaims the virtues of subsidiarity, that
is, that in a healthy community decisions should be taken at as low a
level as possible and as many people as possible should participate in
decision-making, its own structure has in recent decades become
increasingly authoritarian and centralized. But all traditions face similar problems of failure to implement in their own structures and ways
of working the principles they offer to the broader community for its
guidance. We should not, perhaps, be totally surprised at this. For
churches and church leaders are also infected by sin, and it is no more
easy for modern disciples than it was for the original disciples to accept
Jesus' call for a renunciation of status, and for all power to be for the
service of God and human flourishing.

Yet for all its failings and hypocrisy, the church of Jesus Christ in all
its various forms is still an extraordinary community which often witnesses to equality in powerful and unusual ways. At the local level in
any Western country, the church is virtually the only organization to
include in it membership some of the poorest, weakest and most
marginalized, and some of the wealthiest and most powerful. Often, of
course, they are kept apart, even by the way the church organizes itself.
But when they attend to one another a highly unusual kind of communication takes place which can have significant consequences. Let
me give two examples from my own experience.

After the publication of *Just Sharing*, the report of a working group
on the distribution of wealth, income and benefits sponsored by the
Church of Scotland Church and Nation Committee we had discussions
with a wide variety of church groups, with politicians and with business
people. In each case the constituency was different, and the discussion,
although always vigorous, followed different lines. Then came an

invitation from local community and political groups and the local churches in an Edinburgh area of deprivation to come as their guests, and hear about their lives and their reactions to our work. At this stage we were approached by a group of Christian business people who were concerned for the future of Edinburgh: 'Could they come to the conference?' After consultations, we replied, 'Yes, you are welcome, on two conditions: first, that there are not too many of you; and, secondly, that you spend most of the time listening rather than talking.' A small group of wealthy and influential business people came, more or less in mufti. They had the grace to listen quietly and attentively while often angry local people spoke of housing conditions, transport, education, medical care in their community. For some of the business people this was their first exposure to the human realities; for all of them it was the first time they had sat at the feet of poor and disadvantaged people, and simply listened. For one or two this was perhaps the kind of experience that R. H. Tawney called an 'intellectual conversion'.

A few years later, that largely middle class and rather mundane council, the Presbytery of Edinburgh invited a group of people from congregations in the peripheral housing schemes to speak to Presbytery. They talked about housing, education, transport, health care as well as the problems of maintaining the church building and how to witness to Jesus Christ in conditions of extreme inequality. And as they talked, one could feel the respectable middle class members of Presbytery becoming palpably angry, not simply that fellow Christians but that women and men and children in their city should have to cope with such an interlocking and humiliating network of disadvantage. Communication of this sort, and at this depth, is not common anywhere, but it can happen in the church, and when it does, people can be changed and a new kind of engagement with issues of inequality may result.

The same is true at the national level. The church numbers among its members some of the many who are denied a voice in our society, and itself still has a not inconsiderable voice in public affairs. It can, and sometimes does, speak for the voiceless. The notable Anglican report, *Faith in the City* (1985), arose directly out of people from parishes in areas of deprivation telling their stories, and bishops and clergy feeling that something must be done to remedy flagrant and divisive injustice and inequality. That report had a vast impact, aroused a major national discussion, and made sure that urban problems would be high on the national agenda for many years. Similarly during the miners' strike of 1984, David Jenkins, at that time Bishop of Durham, one of the largest coal mining districts in the country, heard from mining parishes, and experienced for himself, what the policy of pit closures was doing to people and to communities. It was on this basis that he became such an outspoken critic of the Thatcher government, seeing it as his duty to speak for the voiceless, and calling on people to face up to 'what is going on, what is wrong in it, and what might be brought out of it'.

At the global level we have not only the central structures of the Roman Catholic Church and of what are called 'the world confessional families', but an embryonic but nevertheless real 'ecumenical church'. This is expressed not simply or mainly in the activities and structures of the World Council of Churches, but in a new and pervasive sense that Christians and churches around the globe are accountable to one another and responsible for one another. Just as Paul's collection for the poor Jerusalem church was intended to express *koinonia* and establish equality between the churches and thus display the kind of mutual care and solidarity which should characterize human community as such, so today churches around the world are beginning to address together the issues of global inequalities, and struggling to overcome their own divisions and suspicions, to ensure that they are not locked into one class, nation or culture, caught up into some form of modern tribalism. The famous Barmen Theological Declaration of 1934, produced as a direct challenge to Nazism and its largely successful subversion of the German church, put this point with great clarity:

All the churches of Jesus Christ, scattered in diverse cultures, have been redeemed for God by the blood of the Lamb to form one multicultural community of faith. The 'blood' that binds them as brothers and sisters is more precious than the 'blood', the language, the customs, political allegiances, or economic interests that may separate them.

We reject the false doctrine, as though a church should place allegiance to the culture it inhabits and the nation to which it belongs above the commitment to brothers and sisters from other cultures and nations, servants of the one Jesus Christ, their common Lord, and members of God's new community.[16]

This 'commitment to brothers and sisters from other cultures and nations' has found more concrete expression in the decades since the Barmen Declaration. There is still a long way to go, but under the influence of the ecumenical movement and with the assistance of modern communications, churches around the world are increasingly aware that the positions they take up and the public statements they make are noted and assessed by other churches around the world, to whom they are gradually feeling increasingly accountable.

A case in point in Britain was the Falklands War of 1982, and in particular the Service in St Paul's Cathedral to mark the end of that war. The government was well known to wish for a service of thanksgiving for victory. What in fact took place was a service which included a strong note of penitence, avoided any kind of triumphalism, and offered prayers for the people of Argentina who had lost relatives, and for all who suffered as a result of the war. All those who took part in the designing of the service were well aware that what was said and done would be noted by churches around the world, including those in Argentina. Mrs Thatcher and some other government leaders were furious that the service did not have a dominant and clear note of celebration of victory. My wife and I were on holiday in France at the time, and we found that French Christians were surprised and delighted that the British churches could, at least on this occasion, rise above nationalism and show themselves to be part of the *oikumene*.

Table fellowship

The eucharist is both the place where the church is most visibly the church, and also the focus down the years of constant disputes, which at their heart are differences about what it is to be the church of Jesus Christ. Increasingly there is among Christians a feeling that Jesus' table fellowship should be normative for today's eucharistic practice. Jesus' practice was a constant breaking down of barriers, establishing equality at the table. It was not a peripheral matter in the ministry and mission of Jesus, but close to the heart of what was going on. It is amazing the amount of space that is given in the Gospels to accounts of Jesus' practice of eating and drinking with all sorts of people, to the miracles of feeding, to the Last Supper and the resurrection meals; and in addition,

Jesus' stories are often about banquets, and the invitation to the table
extended to people from the highways and byways.

Jesus' table fellowship caused profound offence. The Pharisees and
the scribes complained, and said, 'This fellow welcomes sinners and
eats with them'.[17] At the table Jesus broke through traditional barriers
between the pure and the impure, the sacred and the profane, the dis-
reputable and the honoured, women and men. He challenged hierarchy
by welcoming all, and especially the marginalized, the despised and the
neglected, to eat and drink with him at his table. There was a special
invitation to the poor and the weak.

The table fellowship of Jesus was from the beginning seen as a
prefiguring of the heavenly banquet that would be spread in the
messianic age, and to which many from north and south, from east and
west would be bidden. Whereas in virtually every culture of which we
know, the rules as to what one may eat, and with whom are ways of
preserving boundaries and affirming status, Jesus' table fellowship was
calculated to have the opposite effect: he welcomed all at his table into
an egalitarian fellowship of love.

In Israel as depicted in the Hebrew Scriptures, and in observant
Jewish communities today, eating and drinking also play a central role.
The complex listings of pure and impure foods and the regulations
about the slaughter of animals and the proper ways of cooking contained in books such as Leviticus define in meticulous detail the boundary between the pure and the impure. But eating performs a positive
role as well. The Friday evening meal in the typical Jewish family is a
ritualized celebration to welcome the Sabbath, but it also functions as a
great focus and strengthening of family solidarity. Central among
Jewish meals, the Passover defines and reaffirms the identity of the
people through the ritual recapitulation around the table of the story of
the exodus. This history, repeatedly repossessed and enacted anew, not
only defines the people in terms of their story, but proclaims their
destiny and draws a boundary between the people of this story, and
people who have other stories or, worst of all, who have no story at
all.

The boundaries between Jew and Gentile were expressed very
centrally in food rules which made solidarity and easy social inter-
course between Jew and Gentile difficult, and suggested to many,
rightly or wrongly, that Jews regarded Gentiles as inherently impure,

and inferior in the divine ordering of things.[18] The overcoming in the practice of Jesus and the early church of the division between Jew and Gentile was seen as indicative of the establishment of a new form of loving, equal community.

It has been strongly argued by numerous New Testament scholars, most forcefully perhaps by F. Belo,[19] that Jesus directly confronted and broke through the structures of purity and pollution which were deeply entrenched in the Israel of his day, particularly in relation to eating and drinking. Indeed, the amount of attention given to Jesus' eating and drinking in the Gospels is quite extraordinary. The point was not simply that Jesus was a lover of food and drink – although he was accused of being a glutton and a wine-bibber – not at all the received pattern of the holy man! He seemed to worry little about the traditional purity rules in relation to eating.

But what was even more disturbing to traditionalists was that he ate with all sorts of people. He ate with Zacchaeus, and with Levi; he ate with Pharisees and he ate with quislings. The religious folk of the time were profoundly shocked that this Jesus was happy to share his table-fellowship with prostitutes and traitors and other notorious sinners, with people every respectable person of status despised and feared: 'Look at him, a glutton and a drunkard, a friend of tax-collectors and sinners!' they said.[20] And Jesus told stories about meals, which were just as shocking to those who took the traditional rules of purity and pollution seriously – stories of people invited to a banquet who invented excuses not to come, and whose places were taken by other people off the streets; stories of the great feast to welcome back the prodigal son, to the fury of his respectable elder brother; stories of the coming feast in the Kingdom to which multitudes from North and South and East and West would be welcomed without qualifying by belonging to a particular religious community.

When Jesus found himself in the country, far from any village and surrounded by multitudes of hungry and confused people who had been taught that they didn't matter and weren't worth much – the 'sheep without a shepherd' he called them – he fed them and he taught them because he was moved with compassion for them. Then, at Passover time in Jerusalem, facing the imminence of betrayal, suffering and death, Jesus gathered his disciples to eat a meal together in the upper room. One from this company around the table betrayed him.

Another denied him. And the rest made themselves scarce when the crisis came. This was the meal he linked for ever to his death and resurrection, the death of the true Passover lamb prefigured in the meal, and celebrated in *anamnesis* (memory) of that death and resurrection ever since. There are also the narratives of meals after the Resurrection: the risen Lord meeting with disciples on the Emmaus road and being made known to them in the breaking of the bread; or the breakfast by the lakeside. Eating and drinking were central aspects of Jesus' life and work, enactments of his message, the establishment of equal fellowship.

The significance of Jesus' table fellowship which broke through the barriers of purity and pollution, and all obstacles to the expression of inclusive fellowship, can hardly be exaggerated. Norman Perrin has argued for a direct connection between Jesus' pattern of eating and drinking and the calls for his death.[21] His table fellowship has been aptly called 'salvation by association'.[22] And it also involved a head-on confrontation with the accepted distinction between the holy and the profane, the pure and the polluted. The strange and complex relation between the meals and the death of Jesus suggests that it is not at all fanciful to see Jesus' meals as a significant part of the work of reconciliation, the breaking down of the dividing wall of hostility, the bringing near of those who were far off, the welcoming of strangers into the commonwealth of Israel, for 'He has abolished the law with its commandments and ordinances, so that he might create in himself one new humanity in place of the two, thus making peace, and might reconcile both groups to God in one body through the cross, thus putting to death that hostility through it'.[23]

If salvation was reflected and expressed in the table fellowship of Jesus in which ancient enmities and fears were overcome, the same should be true of the prolongation of that table fellowship in the life of the church. But from very early times there was vigorous dispute about whether the table fellowship of Christians need be as inclusive as that of their Lord. The apostle Peter himself clearly had persistent inhibitions about cutting free from the traditional regulations about eating and social relations with Gentiles. Peter had a vision on the housetop in Joppa in which he resisted the voice calling on him to eat: 'No, Lord; for I have never eaten anything that is common or unclean', and he is then told, 'What God has cleansed, you must not call common'. This is presented as the opening of the way to the incorporation of the Gentiles into the church and the inauguration of the Gentile mission.[24]

All the evidence suggests, however, that this was not the end of disagreement; the controversy waxed furious and long, and included a direct confrontation between Peter and Paul in Antioch, and a decree of an apostolic council in Jerusalem, to which the matter had been referred.[25] The principle that Gentiles on conversion need not take on the Jewish rules of purity which powerfully inhibited eating and drinking together, was only established gradually and with great difficulty. But the importance of the issue was vast. Max Weber wrote of the 'shattering of the ritual barriers against commensalism' as something that meant 'a destruction of the voluntary ghetto' and 'the origin of Christian "freedom", which Paul celebrated triumphantly again and again; for this freedom meant the universalism of Paul's mission, which cut across nations and status groups'. It also, he wrote, decisively influenced the shaping of Christian societies, making them in crucial ways egalitarian communities.[26]

For Paul, however, the importance of the principle had little to do with the shaping of societies and cultures. It was rather a necessary expression of the heart of the gospel and essential for the integrity of the church. To say that Paul won this controversy, that his victory enabled the incorporation of Gentiles into the church, and that eucharistic commensalism definitively shaped not only the church but also societies in which Christianity was a dominant influence is the beginning, not the end, of a complex, still ongoing, controversy in the Christian church.

Paul could be as savage about other divisions at the Lord's Table, particularly between rich and poor, as about the paradigmatic separation between Jews and Gentiles. In 1 Corinthians 11, Paul denounces the rich Christians for guzzling at the eucharistic meal while their poor brothers and sisters had nothing to eat. This behaviour divided the community and introduced an inequality which was subversive of *koinonia*. It involved contempt for the church of God and humiliation for those who had nothing. As a result he said, 'it is not the Lord's Supper that you eat'. Division and inequality within the body had made the meal a parody of what it ought to be.[27]

Controversies about eucharistic commensalism have wracked the church from that day to this. Many churches (like my own) for centuries 'fenced the tables' in order to exclude from the communion public offenders and people of bad repute – precisely the kind of people Jesus welcomed to his table! And intercommunion between all Christian denominations is still a distant goal. The example of Jesus' table fellowship has not yet led to eucharistic commensalism among Christians, although some progress has been made, particularly in a deeper shared understanding of the eucharist in documents such as the World Council of Churches Faith and Order Commission's landmark convergence statement, *Baptism, Eucharist and Ministry* (1982). Yet still there is not intercommunion or eucharistic commensalism among Christians.

Indeed, social divisions have sometimes reinforced and created barriers to intercommunion. It was reluctance to share the communion with those of another race that led to the division of the Dutch Reformed Church in South Africa into a white, a black and a 'coloured' church. Perennial problems arose in various contexts about whether those of high status might receive communion separately from, or before, those of lower status. In other contexts the question was raised whether slaves could receive communion with their masters. Did not the communion of the Lord's Table highlight a discrepancy between their status as slaves and masters and their status as equals in the sight of God?

In India there were constant arguments as to whether those of different castes might receive the eucharist together. And in a context such as the Indian caste system, the status of the clergyman who dispenses communion was also of vital importance to many. Few Christians of low caste origin were ordained for many years, and those who were, frequently were not accepted by Christians of high caste origin, particularly as ministers of the eucharist. When, in 1739, it was proposed in South India to ordain one Rajanaiken, a catechist of low caste origins, some of the SPCK/Lutheran missionaries protested: 'Rajanaiken is very useful and successful as a catechist ... But we should greatly hesitate to have the Lord's Supper administered by him, lest it should diminish the respect of the Christians of the higher castes for the Sacrament itself'.[28] The sacramental elements, in their view, would be polluted by the hands of a low caste person, however valid his ordination. In similar manner, in many cases arrangements were made for Christians of pure and impure caste origins to be segregated in church. In one church in South India walls were erected so that the priest could go to the altar in a kind of tunnel, and neither group could see the other even when receiving communion at the altar rails!

The eucharist was thus a trigger for controversies which involved the meeting of very different understandings not just of social order and customary behaviour, but of human beings and social ethics. It was as if the eucharist expressed a view of human equality and of the proper relationships between people which came into sharp conflict with hierarchical social structures, and in particular with the idea that some people by virtue of their birth were profane while others were inherently pure. A critique of the system of purity and pollution which lay at the heart of the caste system crystallized around the eucharist, which carried within itself, as it were, a social ethic sharply at variance with that of caste.

The implications of commensalism

There continued to be a pervasive unease among the more articulate and educated Indian Christians about the contrast between the missionaries' demand for an explicit practical renunciation of the caste-related inhibitions on interdining and the missionaries' own prohibition of intercommunion with Christians of other denominations. There is, I think, little doubt that this was a factor in the movement for church union, in which South India gave the lead. If Christianity was really concerned with the overcoming of divisions and the creation of an inclusive community, if the caste system, and in particular its exclusion of vast categories of people from table fellowship was wrong, then surely the denominational differences among Christians, particularly at the Lord's Table, must be overcome if the gospel was to have full effect.[29]

Just as many Indian Christians recognized that there was no difference in principle between the refusal of communion between the various churches and the prohibition of commensalism between Brahmin and Pariah, so they also increasingly recognized that the racism that led many Europeans, including some missionaries, to avoid eating with 'natives' was little different from the caste practices they had learned to scorn. Some missionaries did not allow Indian

Christians beyond their verandas. One of those who identified this issue most clearly was C. F. Andrews. 'It would be sad' he wrote, 'if the Church which condemns caste in the Indian Christian were to condone it in the English. Yet ... caste was originally nothing but racial exclusiveness'.[30] Indeed, Andrews saw racism as a central aspect of the moral challenge that India presented to Britain.[31] And Indian Christians such as Fakirbhai made similar points:

> Another thing which greatly surprised me was that if any high caste person accepted the Christian Faith the Indian Christians and the missionaries would tell him that he must entirely give up caste discrimination – and they made him do it! Yet nobody told the missionaries to give up their colour discrimination. Everyone assumed that the missionaries belonged to a different caste, and so there was no need for them to have relations of intermarriage with Indian Christians. It seemed that there was very little difference between our caste-discrimination and this kind of colour discrimination.[32]

The missionary insistence on interdining as an irreversible break with caste inevitably raised the general question of social equality, and how far this was an implication of the Christian gospel. Most missionaries, however, shared one assumption in common – that social class as experienced in Europe was a secular or civil institution which could sit perfectly happily alongside Christian faith and practice. No anomaly was involved if the squire and his poorest farm labourer received communion together in church, but were separated by a vast social distance outside, so that eating together at the common table would be regarded as unthinkable.

It was precisely this assumption that European forms of hierarchy were in no way in tension with the gospel which was challenged by a few Indian Christians and missionaries who rightly divined the radical and far-reaching implications of the opposition to caste. 'The West', wrote C. F. Andrews, 'must not try to pull the mote out of India's eye while the beam remains in its own eye.'[33] The church, he argued, can only succeed if she refuses to harbour within herself the racial and caste evils from which India is longing to be free.[34] Andrews and like-minded missionaries and Indian Christians believed that the Christian critique of caste was also a critique of class, and of the degradation and division engendered by a great gulf between rich and poor, upper and lower class. They drew attention to the fact that class had frequently been sacralized in the Christian West, and they also pushed the argument one stage further, suggesting that even a desacralized class, like caste as a 'civil order', still raised ethical issues for the Christian and could not sit totally at ease with the Christian gospel.

Eating and drinking and the way they are arranged have a very central place in Christian faith and life, as in most other religious systems. The practice and the theology of the eucharist cannot be separated from its ethical content, and that is very centrally egalitarian. When Christians gather to celebrate the Lord's Supper they are not only presenting a challenge to racism, class and caste in the church, but very centrally to the inequalities of the world.

A community of equals

Even in its brokenness and lack of faith, with its own assimilation of emphases upon ranking and status, with its arrogance and its authoritarianism, with its patriarchy and discrimination, the church is still palpably a fellowship of equals, striving to be faithful to the call to discipleship. It finds it hard to be indeed an inclusive, welcoming community, open to outsiders, and in particular to the poor, and marginalized folk for whom Jesus had a special care. It is bold to understand itself as an anticipatory community, prefiguring and anticipating something of the life of the Reign of God that is yet to come in its fullness, and it struggles to be an exemplary or paradigmatic community as explained by Stanley Hauerwas:

> The task of the church [is] to pioneer those institutions and practices that the wider society has not learned as forms of justice. (At times it is also possible that the church can learn from society more just ways of forming life.) The church, therefore, must act as a paradigmatic community in the hope of providing some indication of what the world can be but is not ... The church does not have, but rather is a social ethic. That is, she is a social ethic inasmuch as she functions as a criteriological institution – that is, an institution that has learned to embody the form of truth that is charity as revealed in the person and work of Christ.[35]

The church, that is, is called to pioneer egalitarian community, and is in fact such a community in as far as she is faithful to her Lord and gives glory to the triune God.

I have been exploring in this chapter the struggle of the church to *be* the church, a special kind of inclusive community with the child, representing the weak, and the poor in the midst, a community that affirms and expresses the equal worth of all human beings. The church, that is, is called to be a kind of experiment in egalitarian community, and a demonstration why equality is important, and that equality can work. The church is entrusted with powerful symbols, or sacraments, of equality, particularly the eucharist, which I have discussed in some detail, and baptism, which deserves fuller treatment that can be given here. There is always the problem of the church succumbing to empty ritualism, so that the significance of what is done and said is obscured or forgotten. One can sing the Magnificat, delighting in the beauty of the music, but deaf to the challenge it contains and expresses. But this is not inevitable.

The local congregation matters. In its worship, in the way it takes decisions, in its deployment of its material and human resources it can manifest egalitarian community in which the worth of each is affirmed – or it can be sucked into reflecting, reinforcing and even sanctifying the inequalities with which it is surrounded. But the church as a denomination, and the church as international, ecumenical and transcultural organization are also important because they bring together into a community of discourse, of faith and of sharing some of the richest and most powerful people in the world, and some of the poorest and weakest. And the church in these broader senses has human and material resources whose use and deployment reflects the real operative theologies of these institutions.

At every level the church of Jesus Christ is faced with the challenge of William Temple, who said that the church is an organization which exists for the sake of those who never darken its doors. It is not only the equality of all church members that matters. The church is called to witness to the equal worth of all human beings. And this demands that it consider not only its own life, but that it plunges into complex issues of public policy.

Equality and the Politics of Inclusion

Only a society which can imagine the plight of its weakest members, and legislates for their inclusion into society rather than their virtual expulsion from it, can call itself a just or equal society.

Margaret Drabble[1]

The moral test of Government is how that Government treats those who are in the dawn of life, the children; those who are in the twilight of life, the elderly; and those who are in the shadows of life – the sick, the needy, and the handicapped.

Hubert Humphrey[2]

This chapter is concerned with ways in which a concern for human equality does or might work out in public policy. I start by discussing some languages which have been used recently in the discussion of implementing equality in public policy, and which may or may not cast light on matters. And then I explore the implications of a commitment to equality in a few policy areas, particularly health care and welfare.

I enter into the complex minefield of public policy discussions with caution, and an awareness of the limitations of a theologian's competence in this vast area.[3] But I am also mindful of R. H. Tawney's warning that to state a principle without its application is irresponsible, and leaves the principle at such a level of generality as to be vacuous and virtually unintelligible.[4] Theologians may not be makers and implementers of policy any more than social scientists are. But both theologians and social scientists have an important contribution to make to the formulation of policy; although they are not politicians or ministers responsible to the electorate for their actions, they are citizens. Indeed, theologians and Christians claim to have a *dual* citizenship that should enable them to make some distinctive and useful contributions to policymaking in the earthly city. They can suggest the kinds of policies which might express their principles and implement equality. Indeed, they are duty bound to do so. They, almost alone, can offer reasons and arguments suggesting why it is right to spend public money on the support of those who, like Munuswamy, can never make a productive contribution to the economy. They may suggest why the disabled, the weak and the poor must be honoured and respected in a decent society. This is their response to Blake's call: 'Let every Christian, as much as in him lies, engage himself openly and publicly before all the World in some mental pursuit for the building up of Jerusalem.'

Christians also believe in the reality of judgment. In the famous story of the sheep and the goats in Matthew 25 the judge is the Son of Man, a title regularly applied to Jesus. When he comes in his glory it is the nations (*ta ethne*), not individuals, who are called to account for whether they have fed the hungry, given drink to the thirsty, welcomed the stranger, clothed the naked, cared for the sick and visited those in prison. Bible translators in an individualist age have difficulty with the idea that collectivities and nations have responsibilities for which they are accountable to God. But it is surely the case that there are certain kinds of responsibility for the poor and needy which can only be properly exercised by governments and communities and nations acting together in their corporate capacity. This is their responsibility before God, their 'moral test' as a nation or a government, in Hubert Humphrey's terms.

The reality of social exclusion

Much contemporary discussion of social policy revolves around the issue of social exclusion – what it is, why it is damaging, and how it can be remedied so that we may move towards a more inclusive and just society.

Munuswamy, whom I first encountered in the 1960s, certainly suffers from social exclusion. He begs on the railway bridge in part because he would not be allowed by the porter to enter the gate into the college compound. And, at least in theory, he may not board a train or enter the station platform without a ticket, which he does not have the resources to buy. Because of his poverty and lowly status, he is not encouraged to go into the better shops. In the bazaar he is constantly being moved on by nervous stall keepers to whom he is an embarrass-ment. If he is sick, he cannot go to the local clinics because there you have to pay for medical care. In an emergency, he could be admitted to the government hospital, where he is likely to receive inferior treat-ment and attention. Almost all the doors of opportunity to better his position or enlarge his little circle of friends and associates are closed to him. He is marginal to much of the life that goes on around him, and most people who actually see him regard him as dispensable. A sur-prising number of people passing to and fro on the railway bridge do not actually *see* him. It is as if for them he does not exist. He is literally 'beneath their notice'; if you asked them afterwards whether they had seen a beggar on the bridge they would in all probability answer 'No'. Munuswamy constantly bears a dual stigma – as leper, and as beggar. Many people are actually frightened of him; they see him, if not as a physical threat, as a source of infection and uncleanness. This is social exclusion at its most radical and most degrading – not just to Munuswamy, but to everyone else involved.

I, on the other hand, although a stranger from a foreign land and a different culture, am welcomed almost everywhere I go in Madras. I receive embarrassingly lavish hospitality. People I have never met will bother to explain to me how to get a ticket on the suburban railway, how to find the house of the colleague I am visiting, or the significance and meaning of that strange ceremony in the little temple outside the railway station. I am invited to weddings, and to my students' family homes. Total strangers stop me in the street to ask if I am the new arrival from Scotland, and to welcome me. I feel surrounded with warmth and affection, and affirmation is not far to seek. I have rooms in a Hall specially designed to encourage community and to overcome social barriers. A colleague's two young sons call to give me some cakes their mother has just baked. To my amazement, students I have never met drop by to say how happy they are that I have come, and to tell me about the local cinema, and which are the best shops for this and that, and to practise their English. Still a bachelor, and far from home, I am deep down lonely and somewhat nervous. But I have been welcomed, and affirmed and included. And this inclusion makes me feel confident and content, despite knowing that I am still for a time excluded from the depths of the culture and the intimacies of relationships.

Or consider the following real situation: an Edinburgh schoolgirl, while in the last two years at a local comprehensive school, took part in a social service scheme. One of her tasks was to help a lone parent with three young children in a 'difficult' housing estate. Discovering that the oldest child, an eight-year-old girl, and her sister had never ventured into the heart of the city, or travelled in a train, the schoolgirl arranged to take them by bus down to Princes Street, and then to Glasgow and back by train. The whole experience was new to them. The expedition was fun, but it was also for them a somewhat intimidating adventure into unknown and alien territory. At the end they were quite exhilarated, but glad to get home, to the place where they belonged, where they felt secure and included, a place on the periphery of one of the great and beautiful cities of Europe. Their exposure to two big cities and to the railway for the first time had simply underscored for them that they did not belong there, that that was a world from which, largely for reasons of poverty, they were excluded.

Compare that with my situation in the same city, as a professor in Edinburgh University. Each day I walk up the Mound to my work, which I love, in New College. I look around at the superb urban landscape – the two art galleries in their symmetrical Greek temples; the castle looming over us on its great crag, Princes Street Gardens, resplendent with flowers, the Head Office of the Bank of Scotland, the ancient crown spire of St Giles' Cathedral peering over the high tenements clinging to the spine of the city, and the dour gothic architecture of New College, where I work. Almost every day I hug myself with delight: this is my city, I belong here, how wonderful to be part of this historic city, to be included in a splendid metropolis with such a rich history which is also in a real sense a community where you constantly meet varied friends. A significant source of my sense of belonging, of being included, is my economic security, and all that flows from that.

But there are those in Edinburgh, as the schoolgirl discovered, who are excluded from the community, who rarely if ever have my sense that they are at home here, that this is *their* city, that it belongs to them, that they are included, that they are attended to. And the commonest reason for their exclusion is poverty, in all its varied dimensions, exacerbated by a range of well-intentioned policies, including schemes of urban planning and regeneration in the 1960s.

A new language of equality?

In these last few paragraphs I have been testing to see if we can speak as well, or even better, of the central issues with which this book is concerned not in terms of inequality and poverty, but rather in the new language of social exclusion and social inclusion. Can we speak illuminatingly about the problem of my relationship to Munuswamy in the language of inclusion and exclusion rather than in terms of poverty and inequality? Does this new language help us to understand and respond to inequality and its outworkings in Edinburgh and Madras and elsewhere?

It has been suggested that the language of social exclusion was invented by social scientists with the European Union and UNESCO who felt that the old language of inequality and poverty had become tired, conventional and unilluminating.[5] An alternative origin has been suggested by Professor Tony Atkinson, who cites 'cynics' as suggesting that 'social exclusion was adopted by the European community to appease former Conservative governments of Britain who believed that there was no real poverty in the UK, and that in any case poverty and inequality were not proper concerns of the European Commission'.[6] This kind of use of the term 'exclusion' has been traced back to the French sociologist, René Lenoir, who spoke of the excluded as the one tenth or so of the French population who were unprotected by social insurance.[7] The language of social exclusion has certainly, for whatever reason, become very popular since the mid-1990s in the discourse of sociology and social policy. And today the language of social exclusion has come into common usage in a big way, so much so that the British Economic and Social Research Council established a Centre for Analysis of Social Exclusion in the London School of Economics in 1997, with the remit, according to the cynics, of finding out what the concept meant!

An argument runs that the old forms of social exclusion which were described and dealt with in terms of poverty, deprivation, welfare and redistribution have been replaced with new radical forms of exclusion which are in many ways the direct consequences of recent fundamental social and economic changes, particularly globalization. As Bill Jordan puts it:

The paradox of the present age is that economic globalization – the growth of world trade, international units of production and human mobility – has simultaneously increased interdependency between citizens of different states, and capacities for excluding marginal local individuals from previously shared goods. In a world where each person's welfare is closely related to the behaviour of individuals in distant countries (for instance, over resource depletion, pollution or international migration) it is far easier, through new technological means, to exclude consideration of one's neighbour's actions and opportunities from decisions about one's own.[8]

It is now, it appears, easier than ever before to exclude Munuswamy and his interests from our discussion! The new globalized situation may require not only a new language but new forms of treatment and new policies, according to Anthony Giddens:

> Social democrats today need to combat newer forms of exclusion – at the bottom and at the top. At the bottom, 5% or so of the population risks becoming detached from the wider society – some, such as those imprisoned in decaying tower blocks, are casualties of the welfare state. At the top, an equivalent proportion, consisting mostly of affluent managers and professionals, may threaten to opt out of the wider society, into 'ghettos of the privileged'.[9]

Discourse in the new language of social exclusion has met with mixed reactions. Some people are uneasy lest it is, or becomes, a way of *avoiding* talking about poverty and inequality and redistribution, which these critics regard as the really hard and difficult issues. Perhaps, they suggest, the new language itself is intended to avoid controversy by introducing a certain vagueness into the discussion. After all, everyone, more or less, is in favour of inclusion, at least as long as it has no price tab. Perhaps social inclusion is simply more politically-correct language, and will maintain its acceptability as a general goal for society as long as no one specifies the costly and demanding – and perhaps unpopular – policies that are required to achieve real social inclusion, the elimination of poverty, and major moves towards equality.

On the other hand, it is salutary to see the problem recognized as involving more than a simple lack of material resources. However important such a lack of resources may be, and however serious its ramifications, there are kinds of poverty and inequality which have rather little to do with lack of resources, with lack of wealth. Groups such as the disabled or the elderly may be excluded and rendered dependent, with little if any reference to whether they are poor or wealthy. Inequalities of power, of various sorts, are sometimes relatively independent of differences in wealth; and certain ways of responding emphasize the differences in power by suggesting that some people – the relatively powerless ones – are the problem while other, more powerful people may provide the solution.

Or is social inclusion simply an *alternative* way of speaking about poverty and inequality? It is notable how even documents like the Joseph Rowntree Foundation's *Monitoring Poverty and Social Exclusion* treat poverty, inequality and social exclusion as synonyms, or interchangeable terms.[10] On this approach, presumably it is felt that calling poverty or inequality 'social exclusion' draws attention to some important dimensions which have sometimes been neglected hitherto in the analysis of poverty and inequality, particularly the way poverty affects the relations between poor people, and creates barriers within poor communities, and separates poor communities from the rest of society. Furthermore, terms such as 'poverty' suggest a condition, something that just happens; exclusion implies a process that some people impose on others, a problem in the way groups of people relate to one another. But the term 'exclusion' tends to hide the fact that it is also subordination. Exclusion may be too bland a way of speaking about a process of separation, subordination, humiliation and sheer deprivation of the resources necessary to maintain a decent life.[11]

On the other hand, treating poverty and inequality as social exclusion does not seem to be entirely satisfactory. It does not recognize that among poor people – and that is the group that we most commonly regard as excluded – there is still often a particularly vivid and real sense of community, of mutual responsibility, of shared destiny. Such communities of poor people have often lessons about care and companionship, and tolerance to teach wealthier communities. And although characteristically they will defend themselves against outside interventions and threats, such communities of the poor are sometimes quite remarkably inclusive, generous and welcoming to outsiders. Their problem is not so much exclusion from vibrant community, as simple poverty and lack of resources.

To illustrate this point, I refer to a thesis I had the privilege of supervising, by Dr Stewart Gillan. Using participant observation techniques, he studied a community of South African Blacks who had been deported several decades ago by the apartheid government from their fertile traditional farm lands to a barren semi-desert tract many miles away so that the government might hand over their lands to white farmers. Here was social and economic exclusion at its most extreme, blatant and calculating. Stewart Gillan's field notes testified to their vibrant sense of belonging together in community, and to the strength of their attachment to their ancestral lands. Prominent among the reasons they gave for this was that the tombs of their forefathers were there, a sign that they had inhabited that land for generations. And they naturally resented having been displaced, 'excluded', and relocated without consultation, or any serious regard for their interests and feelings.

All this, of course, was natural and to be expected. But what was surprising and, to me, amazingly impressive were the answers that came when Stewart asked these displaced and poor blacks what should happen to the whites who were now occupying their farmland. The typical response from pastors, from leaders and from perfectly ordinary people who were often illiterate went along these lines: the whites have been there on our land for a number of decades. They too have buried their dead in the land, and this gives them some kind of traditional right of tenure. And then, most impressively of all, came statements that there is enough land for us both; we can live together as one inclusive community.

When I first looked at this material that Stewart had gathered, I was amazed. I had assumed that the kind of generosity of spirit and willingness to forgive and build a new kind of inclusive community to succeed the divisiveness and exclusions of apartheid was characteristic of Nelson Mandela, Desmond Tutu and other leaders, but that lower down there would be resentment, bitterness and a desire for revenge. Yet here was an example of how in conditions of great hardship and oppression, commitment to ideals of inclusive community which were rooted both in Christian faith and in aspects of traditional African culture flourished and flowered. The poverty of this Black community had been exacerbated by their exclusion and deportation from their ancestral lands. But poverty, exclusion and inequality had not in this situation destroyed a hospitable sense of inclusive community.

Older people are often familiar with instances where disadvantage, hard times and oppression have bred solidarity and a powerful sense of community and hope. There are notable instances of this happening in working-class neighbourhoods during the days of the Depression and high unemployment, and in city centre slums during the blitz. Kierkegaard pointed to this sort of phenomenon with characteristic vividness: 'Adversity doesn't just knit people together but elicits that beautiful inner community, as the frost forms patterns on the windowpane which the warmth of the sun then erases.'[12] One of the impressive things about my South African example is that 'the warmth of the sun' does not seem now to erase the sense of inclusive community. It retains the power to influence the broader society for good even after the end of apartheid and the return of the dispossessed to their ancestral lands. Contemporary discourse of exclusion and inclusion usually assumes that it is the poor and the weak who are excluded, and that the agents of inclusion can only be the more wealthy and powerful. In fact, it is often the opposite that is the case: the poor and weak demonstrate and practise inclusive community, and teach the more powerful the nature of community.

It may be that the language of social inclusion provides an appropriate framework for the broader consideration of the themes of poverty and inequality, relating it to other appropriate variables. Poverty, as I have argued elsewhere, is very difficult indeed to construe, and it is not easy to achieve the kind of grounded and resilient understanding which is necessary if appropriate responses are to be devised.[13] One of the commonest distortions in the understanding of poverty is to regard it as essentially the problem of poor people, usually concentrated in certain areas and often developing a 'culture of poverty' which tends to perpetuate the problem and make its resolution more difficult. In other words, poverty is seen as a problem 'out there', concentrated for identifiable reasons in particular areas and groups. An assumption is commonly built in that the non-poor, 'people like us', have the capacity to solve the problem of poverty, if we have the will. We, the non-poor, are not part of the problem, but we have the capacity to solve it – and that generally means little more than giving poor people the kind of lifestyle that we have, and perhaps welcoming them into our kind of community. This problem-solving approach becomes even more dominant if it is assumed that poverty is primarily or mainly a lack of material resources, because then redistribution of a fairly straightforward sort becomes the line of treatment to be followed. R. H. Tawney effectively challenged this line of reasoning when he pointed out that what for some is the problem of poverty is for others the problem of wealth, and in his constantly reiterated emphasis that equality is for the sake of fellowship, is necessary for the development of a healthy, and he might have added inclusive, society.

Tawney's point is that equality is a necessary but not a sufficient condition for a healthy community. And it is a particular kind of community that is in his view here, marked by equality and inclusiveness, rather than a community in which everyone knows their place and their relative worth – as in an old fashioned Oxbridge college!

Thought about poverty and inequality is often given a skew by misleading stereotypes. A common scenario treats poverty as essentially the *fault* of poor people, the result of their behaviour, their culture and their immorality. *They* are the problem. The solution sometimes proposed is to cajole and threaten them into performing the duties of their station in a hierarchical society which is itself beyond question. And such a society may be regarded as inclusive on condition that one accepts without question one's place and function in the social hierarchy. Policies of 'welfare to work' are significant in recognizing that employment is for most people a, or the, major instrument of social inclusion. But in as far as these policies suggest subtly that recipients of benefit are for the most part work-shy, and that even in areas of high unemployment they ought to be able to find a secure and fulfilling job if they search seriously enough, they are conveying a message which actually itself excludes and humiliates those who cannot for good and sufficient reasons find employment. Why, for instance, should lone parents be urged to entrust their children to government-financed child care and go out to work, rather than caring for their children while themselves on benefit?

Negative stereotypes of the poor were endemic in the nineteenth century in treatments of what was called 'pauperism'; they continue today in the work of such as Charles Murray and L. M. Mead.[14] Poverty is regarded as a spiritual and moral ailment, *not of society as such*, but of the poor, a disease which was to be cured by spiritual and

moral change on their part. The poor were divided into the deserving
and the undeserving, or those that can be helped and the unhelpable.[15]
It was as if the poor had a different, and inferior, human nature from
that of the more prosperous members of society. But the leaders in
church and state were on the whole assumed to be capable of rising
above their own selfish interests to embrace a wise and chastened concern for the welfare of all.

For this way of thinking, which seems to be having a renaissance
today, the inequalities of society are accepted without question. Both
the problem and its remedy are located squarely among the poor. The
victims are blamed for their condition, and the cure lies largely in their
hands. The society is assumed to be hierarchical and authoritarian, but
it is also in a real sense inclusive, for everyone has their place and no one
can survive for long in exclusion from society. Perhaps this should give
cause for some hesitation in pressing the concept of social inclusion too
far, or in assuming that the term inequality as the description of an
ailment of society has become redundant.

Social exclusion, inequality and poverty

The recent burgeoning of interest in social exclusion reflects a determination to have 'joined up policies', which pay attention to the linkages between various dimensions of a social problem, linkages which
are often mutually reinforcing. It is unabashedly a problem-solving
approach, assuming that social inclusion does not require a reform of
the society, but rather that individual problems may be dealt with
one by one. It also shows a desire to bridge the gap between social and
political theory on the one hand and policymaking on the other, so that
policymaking may benefit from academic rigour and from empirical
insights rather than being poorly co-ordinated responses to crises as
they arise, or 'throwing money at a problem' when there is public outrage. The work of the Centre for Analysis of Social Exclusion at the
London School of Economics provides a convenient opportunity to
assess the significance and usefulness of this new interest.

In an important paper published by the Centre in 1998, Professor
Brian Barry asks two questions, 'What is Social Exclusion?' and
'What's Wrong with Social Exclusion?'[16] Social exclusion, he says, is

more than a repackaging of poverty, but there is nonetheless a close association between exclusion and poverty. Exclusion can be based on other factors than inequality of wealth and income, although it tends to wither in the absence of economic inequality unless it is voluntarily chosen, or imposed for ideological and non-economic reasons. However, it is now commonly agreed that the forms of social exclusion that should cause most concern are those which are imposed upon people and groups so that they cannot participate as they would wish in the normal activities of the broader society in which they find themselves. Material inequality is not a necessary condition of social exclusion (or social isolation, to use Barry's preferred term), but a high level of inequality tends to significantly reduce the ability of the poor groups to participate in the broader life of the community. There is also increasingly commonly in a number of countries and contexts the exclusion of the majority by a minority who can make independent provision for themselves so that they do not need to participate in many of the institutions and processes that are used by the majority. This is well exemplified in the 'gated communities' that are becoming common in some parts of the United States, in which policing, security and many other services are provided separately for those who have chosen to exclude themselves from the broader and more variegated community.

What, then is wrong with social exclusion? Barry suggests that it conflicts with equality of opportunity and it is antidemocratic in as far as it excludes whole groups from effective participation in politics. It also – and this, I think, is the nub of his case and the point at which theological resonances are most clear – erodes solidarity, the sense of responsibility for one another and belonging together which are features of a decent and healthy society. Barry is well aware that poverty itself obstructs equal opportunity in education, but there are also broader considerations relating to social exclusion to keep in mind. Barry is one of the few people who takes seriously today the complex relationship between poverty, social exclusion and education:

A hungry or malnourished child is unlikely to be good at concentrating on school work. The lack of a quiet room in which to study at home (and, increasingly, a computer) makes homework unattractive and difficult ... The more closely the resources of a school district reflect its tax base, the more under-funded schools in poor areas will be … And it is the social homogeneity of schools created by social exclusion that is significant. An abundance of research suggests that children with middle class attitudes and aspirations constitute a resource for the rest. A school without a critical mass of such children therefore fails to provide equality of educational opportunity to its pupils.

The social homogenization of schools is greatly increased by the withdrawal of wealthy parents from the state system. Above the upper threshold of social exclusion, the same people live, work, play and marry together, and the perpetuation of privilege is smoothed by the public school/Oxbridge connection … thus, equality of opportunity is eroded from both ends: some have too few opportunities, others too many.[17]

Differences in political power tend to be self-perpetuating. Social exclusion also undercuts solidarity and can easily lead to policies which are in the interests of powerful and wealthy groups but discriminate against excluded – and often forgotten – minorities.

Barry argues that social exclusion is a reality distinct from poverty and from economic inequality. Nonetheless, he suggests 'there is an association between the dispersion of incomes and social exclusion, but it is not a straightforward one because the relationship is mediated by the experience of common fate, through the sharing of common institutions',[18] such as schools, health care, and transport. Barry concludes with an affirmation of the importance of reducing economic inequality and a suggestion of the need for measures of redistribution: 'for a society such as Britain, it seems plausible that to avoid the social exclusion of a minority it is necessary for nobody to have less than half the median income, and that to avoid the social exclusion of the majority it is necessary for only a few to have more than three times the median income.'[19]

Barry's approach is attractive in a number of ways. It represents a move towards 'joined up' social thinking, and 'joined up' policy-making. It does not isolate economic variables while recognizing the central importance of differentials in material resources. The nub of the argument is that poverty and inequality are destructive of healthy community, and this is surely significant. But I have two areas of unease. The first is that so little attention is given to the question of who excludes whom. Barry notes that there is much self-exclusion of the prosperous which has adverse effects on the poor, but he says little about the people and the processes that have led to social exclusion. Embarrassingly even some idealistic projects developed with the common good in mind – like peripheral housing estates in the big cities – have turned out to be instruments of social exclusion. This brings me to my second reservation. Barry says little about inequalities of power and the effects of this on social exclusion. Socially excluded communities and groups are commonly the objects of problem-solving projects on the part of people who think they know what is good for the excluded. This approach underscores and confirms differences in power. It is more difficult, but also more positive, to involve marginalized people from the beginning in the process of discussion and definition of the issue, and then planning and implementation of a response. Such a process in itself begins to address the question of inequality of power, and is inherently more democratic.

Another paper from the Centre for Analysis of Social Exclusion by Professor A. B. Atkinson on 'Social Exclusion, Poverty and Unemployment', and other papers in a book on *Exclusion, Employment and Opportunity*, illustrate the way thinking on social exclusion is going.[20] Atkinson notes at the beginning of his paper that 'People may be poor without being socially excluded; and others may be excluded without being poor ... Unemployment may cause social exclusion, but employment does not ensure social inclusion.'[21] Atkinson points out that in many continental countries large rises in unemployment have not led to corresponding rises in poverty.

Atkinson then addresses the tricky question of how to define social exclusion. It must always be relative to a particular context; no absolute and universal definition is possible. In social exclusion he acknowledges that there must be an agent or agents:

> People may exclude themselves in that they drop out of the market economy; or they may be excluded by the decisions of banks who do not give credit, or insurance companies who will not provide cover. People may refuse jobs, preferring to live on benefit; or they may be excluded from work by the actions of other workers, unions, employers, or government...In terms of failure to achieve the status of inclusion, we may be concerned not just with a person's situation,

but also the extent to which he or she is responsible. Unemployed people are excluded because they are powerless to change their own lives.[22]

A further aspect of social exclusion is what Atkinson calls *dynamics*, and I would prefer to call *hope*, or a belief that the future may be better. People who have few prospects for the future and are at present unemployed and poor are locked into a structure of exclusion which also constrains their children and severely limits their ability to improve their condition. Indeed it has been argued that this kind of hopelessness links the concepts of poverty and of exclusion. Atkinson quotes Robert Walker:

> When poverty predominantly occurs in long spells ... the poor have virtually no chance of escaping from poverty and, therefore, little allegiance to the wider community ... In such a scenario the experience of poverty comes very close to that of social exclusion.[23]

The relation between employment and social inclusion is equally complex. Employment best contributes to social inclusion when it restores a sense of being in control of one's life, when it provides some appropriate recognized status in the community, together with prospects for the future.[24] And the welfare system, too, can be exclusionary in as far as it stigmatizes recipients of income support and labels people receiving benefits as scroungers or dependent members of the community. Exclusion may be cumulative, these and other forms of exclusion being mutually reinforcing. At a time when government emphasizes very strongly that work is the primary avenue of social inclusion, Atkinson stresses the continuing importance of benefits, of 'collective provision' which 'seems essential to assure social integration'.[25] And he concludes that 'All policy proposals should be tested against the contribution that they make to promoting social inclusion.'[26]

In another paper from the Centre for Analysis of Social Exclusion, its Director, Professor John Hills, examines and assesses current policies.[27] He points out that the proportion of national income spent on welfare – roughly a quarter – is not high compared with other countries in Europe, nor has it grown over the last two decades. On the other hand 'inequality increased dramatically in the 1980s', as a consequence both of economic and social changes and specific government policies. And, alarmingly, 'Over the whole period from 1979 to 1995, the incomes of the poorest 10–20 per cent were little or no higher in real terms, despite overall income growth of 40 per cent.'[28] British government policy on welfare has recently borrowed heavily from American 'welfare to work' policies, and sees paid work as a major, if not the major, agency of social inclusion. This has led to a rather unbalanced emphasis on formal employment as against unpaid care of children or dependent relatives, which is both an important contribution to the life and welfare of the community and a significant saving on welfare budgets. Rather strangely, there is fiscal encouragement to lone parents to seek paid work and entrust the care of their children to paid carers. According to Tony Blair, the welfare system is to be rebuilt around work and security: 'Work for those who can; security for those who cannot', is the slogan. Overall, the Blair government is committed to raising the living standards of the poorest, and tackling social division and inequality. After a careful scrutiny of government priorities and performance so far, Professor Hills concludes that significant changes are under way in Britain, but these do not appear to be a 'break with the past' so much as further movement along a road on which the system has been travelling for some time.

The new interest in social exclusion and social inclusion is not to be understood as an escape from taking issues of poverty and inequality, and indeed redistribution, seriously. It is rather a serious attempt to put such issues in the broader social context so that we can see how various interlinked factors interact with one another, and one hopes make more effective policy responses. The broader frame is an understanding of the kind of society we should seek – a well-integrated community with a high degree of solidarity and responsibility for and to one another, a community of neighbours, in short, in which the weak and the poor are not shamed and relegated to the margins, but encouraged to play a full part in the life of the community, and those with greater endowments of one sort or another are not allowed to evade their responsibilities to the broader community by excluding themselves. Such an understanding of community requires a high degree of equality.

One crucial issue seems to be systematically avoided throughout the discussion: how not only to include and integrate but to *honour* those who are prevented from making the usual sort of contribution to the economic and general welfare of society by disablement or other factors. From a biblical and theological perspective such people have a privileged status and a decent society sees them as having a special contribution to make to the community flourishing together. But only too often they are systematically humiliated by the institutions of society and in day-to-day relationships. Poverty, inequality and social exclusion are also humiliating. Avishai Margalit is right to suggest that the decent society is 'a society which does not humiliate'.[29]

Building a welfare society

The welfare state as it emerged in Britain and most other Western industrial democracies in the 1940s was a project of building an inclusive, just and equal society on the basis of the solidarities which had been forged in the days of the Depression and in the War. It was not simply a reaction against the individualistic excesses of the nineteenth century. Out of the experiences of the Depression and the Second World War there emerged a new awareness of shared suffering and shared joys, together with a determination that the sacrifices of the hard years of unemployment and hunger marches and of the War should not be wasted, but that a better Britain free from William Beveridge's five 'giants' –Want, Disease, Ignorance, Squalor and Idleness – should emerge. During the War, middle-class people who had been insulated from the worst horrors of the Depression came face to face with children evacuated from the slums of the cities, malnourished, unhealthy and unschooled. They saw what poverty and slum conditions did to children. Two nations met one another and felt in a new way responsibility for and to one another. As a result, hardly anyone questioned the need for cheap or free school meals and the provision of milk and orange juice and cod-liver oil for all children equally. The common goal of winning the War united all classes in a new quality of fellowship, which a huge majority of the population wished to see continue after the War.

Out of the War emerged a new and positive, if rather short-lived, vision of the state and its role in society, radically different from the view common in the 1920s and 1930s that the state was on the side of the owners and the managers and against the workers. The state was now seen as the genial guardian of the common good, helping to forge community and capable of looking after the weak and the vulnerable on behalf of the whole society. Few people for a time questioned that welfare was best provided for everyone on behalf of the whole community by the state, which had shown that it could deliver welfare on a just and acceptable basis in time of warfare. In peacetime it could surely do the same, or so people confidently hoped. The state, political leaders, civil servants and professionals were on the whole trusted to behave altruistically.

Although there were some who thought of welfare as primarily a safety net for the poorest, or even wished to go back to the old poor law style of provision, the overwhelming consensus for a time was that the welfare state was not just a way of meeting the needs of the weak and poor, but a way of restructuring society to make it more humane, caring and equal.[30] There was a commitment to democracy, participation and freedom as well as an acceptance of compassion and equality as core values. The understanding of citizenship was enlarged to include responsibility for one's fellow citizens, and the right to expect the community as a whole to respond to one's need. The state was generally trusted to take the initiative and to monitor welfare provision, but the intention was to create a more fraternal, just and caring society. And a principal tool for this purpose was to be redistribution.[31] According to David Thomson, 'The idea of the welfare state is the apotheosis of a couple of centuries of political activity guided by the ideal of human equality and social justice.'[32]

What went wrong? It is necessary, I think, first of all to remember that much went right, that much good happened as a result of the workings of the new welfare institutions and procedures. But after the initial euphoria, by the mid 1950s poverty was 'rediscovered', and it gradually became clear that the equalizing impact of the welfare state was far less than had been hoped. Welfare schemes turned out often to do more for those already prosperous than for the poor.[33] The one thing that now seems almost universally agreed is that there must be reform and change; the present situation is unsustainable, and current systems for the delivery of welfare are not coping effectively with poverty and deprivation. The poorest and most needy often are not helped in ways that encourage self-respect and actually engage with the underlying issues that cause poverty and social exclusion. The costs of welfare provision constantly go upwards (although the UK's percentage of GDP spent on welfare is not high compared with other European countries), and there is abundant evidence of large scale corruption and misuse of funds. There was a widespread suspicion that massive welfare projects like the British welfare state or the American war on poverty have not 'succeeded', and might in some cases have made the situation worse, together with a common feeling that at the root of present problems with welfare might lie misunderstandings of human nature, motivation, behaviour and character. Something clearly must be done, but what?

The earliest and strongest critiques of established forms of welfare provision came from the right wing. For example, David Marsland, a British neo-conservative academic, saw the welfare state as corrupting the nation, and wished to replace it with Victorian self-help. He regards the welfare state as 'a lethal threat to our freedom' which has 'made the British people a nation of greedy wastrels and an ungovernable mob, bereft of values and scornful of rules'. Welfare, he says, damages the economy, creates an underclass, fails to help the needy, and destroys the dynamism necessary for a healthy and prosperous society. We don't need the welfare state, we can't afford it, it doesn't work, and it 'inflicts damaging levels of moral and psychological harm on its supposed beneficiaries'. It is, in fact, he concludes, 'an enemy of society'.[34]

More moderate forms of such arguments are now being used by left-of-centre figures, and sometimes there is explicit reference to the need for religious notions to illuminate the situation and inform policy, even in a radically secularized society. For example, Frank Field, has urgently affirmed recently the need for an adequate and *truthful* account of human nature to undergird policy. And this leads to a new concern in the framing of welfare policy with issues of character and behaviour – matters which in Britain were virtually taboo for several decades.

Frank Field affirms the simple point so long ignored, that human nature underpins all political activities, and must become, he argues, a central determining force in the political debate on welfare's reconstruction.[35] An effective welfare system must be founded on 'a realistic view of human nature' which is unambiguously Christian, for,

We are less than perfect creatures and it is partly because of this most fundamental aspect of each of us that a distinction has continually to be drawn between where we are now and our destiny, on the one hand, and what might ideally be hoped for now in the bosom of the family and what can operate in the wider public arena, on the other.[36]

He suggests that a Christian account of human nature provides a far more adequate foundation for welfare provision than a one-sided stress on altruism because it takes into account the depths as well as the heights of which humans are capable, is hopeful without being naïve, and realistic without becoming cynical. 'Self-interest', Field argues, 'is the most powerful motivating force in each of us.'[37] Self-interest, not altruism, is humankind's main driving force.[38] He writes:

Part of the necessary moral order is not to do with decrying or thwarting self-interest, but with attempting to satisfy it in a way which is consistent with the public good. The most deadly charge which can be made against Britain's welfare state is that it increasingly ignores this cardinal principle.[39]

In welfare, as in other issues of public policy, the task is 'setting a legal framework where natural decent instincts guided by self-interest are allowed to operate in a manner which enhances the common good'.[40]

Particularly through means-testing, the older form of welfare provision was profoundly corrupting; a reformed welfare system, Field suggests, is capable of contributing effectively towards the remoralization of society. There are feckless, dishonest and idle welfare claimants, as in all social groups. But much dishonesty and 'scrounging' is a rational response to the welfare framework which has been imposed from on high by politicians. A properly designed and realistic welfare system is 'one of the great teaching forces open to advanced societies' and a way of affirming right conduct and discouraging wrong conduct.[41]

Field has, I suggest, a rather selective reading of Tawney. It is true that Tawney sees human beings as capable of great evil – but also as capable of generosity and altruism, as sinners called to salvation, in short. Tawney is more explicitly egalitarian than Field in his account of human nature, and he roots his egalitarianism, as we have seen, in his Christian faith. Tawney saw welfare provision as a way of creating greater equality, and he emphasized the inevitability of confronting the structures of power which sustain inequality. He regarded inequality and poverty as essentially structural matters, and resisted the tendency which has once again come into fashion to blame the poor for poverty, and the unemployed for their lack of work.

A rather different account of what has gone wrong with the British welfare state, and critique of lines of reform being advocated at present comes from Bob Holman[42] As always, he argues on an unashamedly Christian basis, and his experience as a community worker in Easterhouse, at the sharp end, grounds his critique in the social reality of deprivation. There is today, Holman suggests, a basic equivocation about equality. It is affirmed as a basic value, but in practice policies which might directly reduce income differentials are ignored in favour of policies which increase opportunities. Instead of addressing the issue of income inequality, which is the cause or reinforcement of so many social ills, the incomes of the poorest have not been improved, redistribution and increased taxation are rejected, and no attempt is made to control escalating top incomes. Most important of all, perhaps, there is no serious effort at the redistribution of power, significantly expressed in the participation of poor people in shaping the policies which will affect them so deeply. Greater equality

> entails not just lessening income differentials, but also ensuring that those in what Will Hutton calls the bottom 30 per cent of society, those with the lowest incomes, those who live in the inner cities and the council estates, have greater influence and power within society.[43]

The voice of poor people, unemployed people, people from deprived estates is not heard in the policymaking process which still is dominated by the powerful and well educated who often have no direct experience at the sharp end of the issues for which they are planning policy responses. In short, he says, 'the Social Exclusion Unit has excluded the excluded'. Because egalitarian principles are not applied to individual lifestyles, policymakers are distanced from the deprived areas and from people on low incomes, and the gap between policy and the individual lifestyle of key players invites charges of hypocrisy. Empowerment needs to be taken much more seriously if we are to move towards greater equality.

The welfare state as originally established in Britain represented a sustained attempt to realize understandings of community and mutual responsibility which were both learned 'from below', from the experience of ordinary people, particularly in the Depression and in wartime, and affirmed strongly by the Christian churches of Britain. It was, and is, I believe, an experiment that has proved its worth and its value as a central moral institution in society. There have also, of course, been disappointments and failures which require to be addressed. It requires reform. The lines that that reform should take are not yet clear. There will probably be little further movement down the Thatcherite road, with a pared-down welfare state as little more than a safety net for the poorest. Most people think that the present situation has so many defects that radical change is necessary, but the rhetoric of the present government in this area is still amazingly vague. The Green Paper on welfare reform spoke of a '"third way" promoting opportunity instead of dependence, with a welfare state providing for the mass of the people, but in new ways to fit the modern world'.[44] But that is hardly a visionary, lucid or challenging remark.

A national health service

The National Health Service as established in Britain after the Second World War was the flagship of the new welfare state. It was fundamentally committed to equal provision according to need rather than in relation to desert, wealth or social standing. For the first time ever there was to be universal provision of high quality health care for everyone, and treatment was not to depend on the size of the patient's purse, or indeed on the constraints of budgets allocated to GPs and to hospitals. In principle, the best treatment available was a possibility for everyone. Aneurin Bevan in 1952 outlined the philosophy of the young NHS:

> It asserts that the resources of medical skill and the apparatus of healing shall be placed at the disposal of the patient, without charge, when he or she needs them; that medical treatment and care should

be a communal responsibility; that they should be made available to rich and poor alike in accordance with medical need and by no other criteria.[45]

From the beginning, despite some opposition from the medical establishment and from right-wing groups,[46] the National Health Service has been immensely popular; and it maintains its popularity as a national institution despite major problems, some of which I shall discuss shortly. It caused no surprise when Bishop David Jenkins in 1990 spoke of the NHS as 'a kind of practical sacrament of the sort of society we believe to be both desirable and possible', an institution 'of immense symbolic significance, a sort of touchstone about the way we regard citizenship, its responsibilities, duties and rights'. As the 'keystone' of the welfare state, the original intention, in Jenkins's words, was 'to put the NHS at the centre of what I would call a set of humane messages'. These 'wider messages of the NHS about mutual caring, aiming at fair shares in what caring there is, and devising corporate and institutional means of this', need to be 'reiterated, reinforced and practically followed up' today.[47]

Another Anglican bishop, Dr Stephen Sykes, has argued that the National Health Service is a, or perhaps the, major institution of an emerging civil religion, which is of profound significance as providing social cohesion in an increasingly plural society. It is also a major institution of moral education. The operation of the National Health Service, according to Sykes, is a kind of ritual of civil religion, an articulation of a collective conscience, and an agency of moral education and the formation of citizens who believe that they have a responsibility to care for one another. Sykes notes 'the sheer durability of ideas and values embodied in, and promulgated by institutions as compared with the arguments of preachers, propagandists and philosophers.' The idea that misfortunes such as ill health, sickness and accidents which are suffered by individuals should be responded to collectively and caringly is both a conviction rooted deep in the Jewish and Christian traditions, and something that in relation to health care at least a huge majority of the British people warmly endorse.

The NHS, then, according to Sykes, 'embodies a moral idea':

The idea of the NHS is that the obligation to be present remains even if there is no family to fulfil it, whether through circumstance or through dereliction of duty; and that the obligation is accepted collectively by the state on behalf of all its citizens. It is a direct extension of the moral basis of family obligation to the whole population, the unlimited care during an incalculable period of an incalculable number of persons, to a standard determined only by the requirements of the individual case and the changing capacities of modern medical practice.[48]

The NHS provides us, argues Sykes, with a shared 'normative moral universe' and an exceptionally significant institution for moral teaching:

> If we come across an injured victim in the streets we know, not merely that we ought to help her, but that we are related to her as to one for whom we have already fulfilled a primary obligation. The victim and we belong to one moral system. In bringing this about we have already established the linkage between self-interest and the collective good. We do not have to ask ourselves whether the victim deserves medical attention, in terms of her likely past or future contribution to the economic success of society. Nor is there a strenuous calculation to be made about our self-interest in landing ourselves with expensive obligations. Our task is simply to get to the nearest telephones and summon the help we have already provided. The NHS has put in place the 'obligation of community', and to the extent has answered the question, 'And who is my neighbour?'[49]

This kind of morality hovers somewhere between being a public philosophy and a civil religion or civil theology. Sykes is as aware as I am how traditionally this understanding of moral obligation has been rooted in and nourished by the Christian faith. It is an open question how solidly it can be sustained without drawing upon the distinctive resources of that tradition. But in a plural society Christian insights must continue to be offered with modesty and openness.

Sykes presses his argument about the significance of the NHS one further, vitally important, stage. If the NHS is indeed an example of moral good possessed by the citizens of a particular nation – in this case Britain – is it legitimate to confine its benefits to the citizens of one nation? And if it is shown, as it has been, that standards of health care are better and the proportion of the Gross Domestic Product spent on health care is higher in neighbouring countries is there not an imperative to move towards greater equality in health care?[50] Do we not have to consider that the universality and equality of the provision of care is the moral lesson taught by the NHS? The public philosophy or civil religion represented by the NHS takes on 'a prophetic and eschatological dimension' when it notes that 'in due course it becomes inescapable that all human life is included in the vision, and that there is no sound reason why international politics should be conducted so as to exclude the marginal'. Thus the moral argument inevitably presses towards addressing as matters of immense moral seriousness inequalities in health, both internationally and internally in any one nation.

The National Health Service is not only, as Sykes argues a profoundly moral institution and a significant component of a generalized civil religion; it is also established on thoroughly Christian and egalitarian principles, as its history demonstrates. Christians, therefore, should be prepared to defend it as a public embodiment of principles which are integral to Christian faith. This does not, of course, involve turning a blind eye to the problems and the difficulties which the NHS periodically manifests in times of crisis. Affirming the principles of the NHS does not involve believing that its operation and structures are beyond improvement – far from it. Like all other institutions, the NHS has inbuilt tendencies to degenerate, and health professionals and administrators are, like the rest of us, sinners capable of acting selfishly at the expense of patients and of the common good. Structures of care and of accountability need constantly to be monitored and it is necessarily a constant struggle to ensure some kind of equality of provision both geographically and according to social group. But Christians should, I suggest, resist any suggestion that the National Health Service is founded on wrong principles, or that it has failed in a general sense. In terms of the proportion of GDP devoted to health care, the quality of care, and the statistics of morbidity and mortality, Britain does not compare very well with many other European countries with rather similar health care systems. But when the comparison is with the United States, where there is deeply entrenched opposition to any form of what they call 'socialized medicine', the British National Health Service is both a great deal cheaper, delivers much better overall results, and does not systematically discriminate against poor people.[51]

Care of the elderly

In industrial societies with an ageing population there is an increasingly acute problem of how to care for the elderly. Few families now have adults who can afford to stay at home without employment and care for elderly relatives; and types of close community which in the past often cared effectively for old people among them who did not have relatives to look after them are rare. The increasing number of elderly people in the community means a major increase in the ailments most associated with old age, and this in its turn puts great pressure on health care provision, and also requires a large increase in nursing homes and residential forms of sheltered accommodation for frail elderly people. The problem of resources is intractable, and present levels and forms of provision in Britain and other similar societies are generally agreed to be inadequate.

Issues of justice and equality also arise in a striking form. There is massive poverty among elderly people, mostly the kind of genteel poverty that is as far as possible hidden from public view. In Britain nearly two-thirds of those over the age of seventy are among the poorest 40% of the population, and they are only half as likely as the average of other age groups to be among the richest 40% of the population. The poverty among elderly people explains the difficulty felt by so many in providing for their own long-term care. Residential homes run by local authorities or voluntary agencies are sometimes unsatisfactory partly because of serious and persistent underfunding. Elderly people who purchase care from their own resources are often sucked by this drain on their finances into poverty, selling their houses and running down their savings. Because of pressure to achieve performance targets, hospitals often return elderly people to their homes more quickly than is desirable.

With these and other associated intractable problems in mind, the British government in 1997 established a Royal Commission on long-term care of the elderly with Professor Sir Stewart Sutherland as Chair. The remit of the Commission was as follows:

To examine the short and long term options for a sustainable system of funding of Long Term Care for elderly people, both in their own homes and in other settings, and, within 12 months, to recommend how, and in what circumstances, the cost of such care should be apportioned between public funds and individuals ...[52]

The Commission consulted widely and reported in 1999. Two of the thirteen members of the Commission dissented from major aspects of the financial recommendations of the Report. In introducing the Report, Stewart Sutherland indicated that the Commission was seeking 'just and socially inclusive provision' for old age, which would involve a sharing of responsibilities between the individual and the state in a way that would be fair and transparent. Everything should be done to preserve the dignity of those in need of long-term care through a set of proposals 'which would give due weight to fairness, efficiency and effectiveness, human practice as observed, real costs, and the acceptance of responsibility for self and others'.[53] A fundamental value of the Commission was that 'old age should be seen as the opportunity that it really is', and the dignity of the elderly should be affirmed in the way society provides for their needs.[54]

The Report divided the costs of long-term care into three categories: living costs, housing costs and personal care. Its broad conclusion was that personal care should be provided according to need without means testing. In other words, care should be provided for elderly people suffering from ailments or frailties characteristic of old age according to a foundational principle of the National Health Service – care provided free at the point of need. Living and housing costs, on the other hand, should be shared between the individual and the state after some appropriate kind of means testing. There should be public support for the costs of care underwritten out of general taxation.

The two dissenting members of the Commission argued that personal care should not be free at the point of need, but also subject to means testing like living costs and housing costs; the state should simply provide a safety net. This dispute within the Commission raises important moral issues. The Commission identified three possible ways of funding. The state could leave the decision as to whether to take out private insurance to the individual, possibly providing some kind of safety net for the very poorest. Or, secondly, the state could compel as many citizens as possible to take out insurance, making crisis provision for those who refuse to do so, or who are refused cover by the insurance companies. And thirdly, the final option, that which the majority of the Commission supported:

> The state could decide to provide some form of collective provision or insurance against the risk of long-term care, on the grounds of the universality of the risk, the unequal ability of citizens to make provision for themselves, and the inability of the [insurance] industry to produce universally affordable or effective products ...[55]

In technical insurance language, this 'spreads the risk' over the entire population. In non-technical language, it means that everyone contributes so that those in need can have the care they require when they need it. In biblical language it is a practical way of caring for the needy neighbour whom one does not know, as for oneself. It is essentially egalitarian in its distributional effect especially as a form of redistribution across the generations. The justification for universality is, as in the NHS, that the danger of a two-tier system providing poor services for poor people can only so be avoided, and in addition wealthier people contribute more through the taxation system in any case. This proposal would, the Commission argued, overcome a serious anomaly and injustice:

> At present, if a person receives nursing care – that is care which involves the knowledge or skills of a qualified nurse, either in a nursing home, or a home which is registered to provide both nursing and residential care – he or she has to pay for the nursing care as part of the home's fees (subject to means testing). If, however, comparable nursing care is delivered in a hospital or community setting it is completely free to the user. This state of affairs is not justified or defensible.[56]

But above all it is a way for society to affirm the dignity and equal worth of elderly people who no longer make a productive contribution to society, and have become dependent for longer or shorter periods of time.

The Note of Dissent argued along lines which would logically

involve the dismantling of the National Health Service and its replace-
ment by a largely insurance based health care system. 'Universal welfare provision', they claim, 'discourages thrift and self-reliance'.[57] The
signatories were alarmed at the financial implications of the Commission's Report, and instead recommended that 'the state must
estimate and cost the minimum standards of care that it believes to be
acceptable and then fund these costs. Second, it must decide what is to
be funded by the state and what by elderly people themselves.'[58] A
minimalist system of care, it is proposed, is to be funded by the
government. The precedent and the principle represented by the NHS
are to be set aside. And sadly it has appeared since the lines of the
recommendations of the Report became known that the sympathies of
the government are with the Note of Dissent rather than with the
majority recommendations.

Inequalities in health

Why should we be concerned about inequalities in health? The answer
must be largely in terms of justice. A just society must be concerned
about a situation in which some citizens have a far lower life expectancy
and worse health than other groups of citizens. But health is also a
major social value, as expressed impressively by Michael Wilson:

> We do not compete for health the way we compete for hygiene.
> Health is not for the rich to give to the poor. Health is a quality of life
> they make together. Neither can possess health apart from the other,
> nor steal health from the other without robbing himself … Health is
> non-competitive.[59]

In 1977 David Ennals, at that time Secretary of State for Health and
Social Security, set up a Working Group on Inequalities in Health
under the chairmanship of Sir Douglas Black, the chief Scientist at the
Department of Health and Social Security.[60] The Working Group was
to examine differences in health status between the social classes and
the causes of these differences, to compare the situation in Britain with
that in other industrial countries, and to explore the implications of
their findings for policy.

The government of the day was clearly deeply concerned at the obvious serious disparities in health standards and provision, and in the uptake of health care between the different classes. The evidence on which Julian Le Grand's book, *The Strategy of Equality* (1982) was based was already becoming known, and it was realized that the middle classes benefited disproportionately from the National Health Service.[61] 'The first step towards remedial action', said the minister concerned, David Ennals, 'is to put together what is already known about the problem ... It is a major challenge for the next ten or more years to try to narrow the gap in health standards between different social classes.'[62] The Group found that despite more than thirty years of a National Health Service committed to equal care for all, there remained 'a marked class gradient in standards of health'. Put baldly, the poorer sections of the community tended to die earlier and suffered from a notably higher incidence of sickness, disability and mental illness than the more prosperous groups, and in addition poor people had markedly greater difficulty than richer people in getting access to medical care, and the quality of care available to them was often inferior. Those who need the health service most, for a variety of reasons made less use of it. Inequalities in care were found to have been seriously exacerbated since the late 1970s by the considerable increase of the private medical sector. The Group stood foursquare behind the basic principles of the National Health Service – that health care of high quality should be available to everyone on an equal basis, according to need rather than ability to pay. But their enquiries revealed a worsening situation of acute inequalities in health and in medical provision which offended against the fundamental principles underlying the establishment of the National Health Service.

The remedy proposed by the Group was comprehensive and far-reaching. The health and social services should adopt three priorities: first, ensuring that children have a better start in life; secondly, improving the quality of life for disabled people, who commonly bear a heavy burden of cumulative ill-heath and deprivation, thereby reducing the need for institutional care; and, thirdly, an emphasis on preventative and educational action to encourage good health. But the Group also affirmed that, while the health and social services should play a major role, serious and offensive inequalities in health could not be removed without a significant reduction in differences in standards of living. In particular, the Group called for a comprehensive anti-poverty strategy, recognizing that poverty, like its frequent associate, unemployment, generates much ill-health. In other words, a radically unequal society which tolerates a high level of poverty cannot expect to avoid unacceptable disparities in health, medical care and quality of life.

The Black Report was received by the incoming Conservative Government with at least as much embarrassment as had greeted the Beveridge Report from certain right-wing circles some decades earlier. At first the Report was not printed; only 260 duplicated copies were run off, and circulation was accordingly severely limited, even within the National Health Service. Patrick Jenkin, the Secretary of State for Social Services at the time, noted that 'it will come as a disappointment to many that over long periods since the inception of the NHS there is generally little sign of health inequalities in Britain diminishing and, in some cases they may be increasing'.[63] He then stated firmly that the government could not endorse the Group's proposals, on the ground that they involved too much additional expenditure.

But there were certainly other grounds as well for the government's rejection of the report. The argument so effectively presented by the Working Group that inequalities in health will only be overcome in a more equal society directly conflicted with the view, still influential in some quarters, that equality is an undesirable thing,[64] and that a high level of economic, and by implication also health, inequality can be good for society as a whole. For today's anti-egalitarians there is nothing wrong as such with unequal provision. But the report's meticulously documented demonstration of what inequality in health means for individuals, families and communities was a direct challenge to the new vision of an economically dynamic, competitive and increasingly unequal society, unconcerned about the fair distribution of health care or anything else for that matter, and stressing the need for positive incentives at the top and negative incentives at the foot of the social pile.

Here two conflicting visions met head-on. The Black Report was a product of the best of the old egalitarian consensual vision which had framed the welfare state; Patrick Jenkin was the spokesman for a revived Victorian vision of society which is explicitly against equality, and unconcerned about inequalities unless they are very extreme and threaten social stability and order. The Government reacted to the

Black Report with some embarrassment and attempted to suppress it.
No serious effort was made to meet its arguments or propose an alternative way of responding to the problem, perhaps because it was not
recognized as a problem at all. Patrick Jenkin simply used the disturbing evidence contained in the Report to suggest that the NHS had
been radically unsuccessful in achieving some of its principal stated
objectives – but he blandly refused to endorse these goals, or to suggest
better ways of meeting them.

The Black Report not only demonstrated convincingly that in
Britain there was a 'health divide' which ran directly counter to the
original aims of the National Health Service and was unacceptable to
most people, but that there was a need for much more detailed
research, and regular updating of the data to monitor trends. In 1987 an
update, *The Health Divide: Inequalities in Health in the 1980s* by
Margaret Whitehead was published.[65] The picture was still of a quite
unacceptable level of inequalities in health within Britain, and there
was a continuing conviction that material deprivation played a major
role in sustaining the health divide, so that the reduction of deprivation
and poverty along with improved health services seemed to be the
appropriate response. However there was now a growing conviction
that the precise reasons for the health divide represented a major
challenge to empirical research. Between them the Black Report and
Dr Whitehead's *Health Divide* stimulated a major debate and a substantial amount of fresh research.

The 1998 report of the Independent Inquiry into Inequalities in
Health under Sir Donald Acheson, *The Widening Gap: Health
Inequalities and Policy in Britain* revealed a worsening situation. But it
was warmly welcomed by the Government as a guide to priorities in
Health Service planning and resource allocation. Among the alarming
details the Acheson Report revealed were these:

- The worst mortality rate, in Glasgow Shettleston, is 2.3 times the
  national average and more than 3.4 times that of the healthiest area
  (Wokingham, Berkshire).

- Infant mortality rates in Salford are twice as high as those in South
  Suffolk.

- If the infant mortality rate of babies born in the 'best health' constituencies was applied nationally, some 7,500 infants would not have died between 1991 and 1995.

- In the 1990s the mortality rate for deaths under 65 were 2.6 times higher in some areas, such as Manchester Central than in others, such as Sheffield Hallam.

- There are now 2.8 times as many people with long-term limiting illness in Glasgow Govan than in Wokingham.

Researchers suggest that these are closely related to increasing inequality of wealth and income, as well as other social and economic factors.

- The average household income in the worst health areas is 70 per cent of that in the best health areas.

- There are 4.2 times as many households with children in poverty in the worst health constituencies than in the best health constituencies.

- In areas with the best health there are 9.1 times more households with three or more cars and 6.5 times as many households with seven or more rooms in their homes than in the worst health areas.

- GCSE failure rates are 1.5 times higher in the worst health areas than in the best health areas.

- There are 3.6 times as many people not working in the worst health areas than in the best health areas.[66]

The most striking and important outcome of this research effort was not, however, simply the more detailed documentation of the widening health divide, or even the demonstration of alarming trends. It was in terms of an explanation of the social causation of the health divide, particularly pioneered by Dr Richard Wilkinson and his colleagues.[67]

Their discovery, carefully documented, was that it was not absolute poverty as much as inequality which caused ill health. Relative income is important very largely as an index of one's standing in relation to others, 'of where they place you in the overall scheme of things, and ... the impact this has on your psychological, emotional and social life.'[68] Surprisingly, at first glance, 'differences in medical care make a negligible difference to health inequalities'.[69] A study in the US discovered that at most ages death rates in Harlem, in one of the richest cities in the world, were higher than in rural Bangladesh, one of the poorest countries in the world. Domestically the differences are extreme: Wilkinson quotes a recent study showing that in a survey of nearly 700 electoral wards in the North of England, death rates were four times as high in the poorest 10 per cent of wards as they were in the richest 10 per cent.[70] It has been demonstrated that in most Western societies, each level in the social hierarchy has worse health than that immediately above it. As is well known, the differences are particularly striking and disturbing in cities where you have a wealthy and healthy middle class suburb a mile or two distant from a run-down housing estate with much poverty and a concentration of social problems. Almost instinctively people feel that in the same city things should not be like that.

By careful comparisons of a large number of societies, Wilkinson and his colleagues have been able to demonstrate that more egalitarian societies with smaller differences between rich and poor tend to have better health and increased longevity. 'In the developed world,' Wilkinson writes, 'it is not the richest countries that have the best health, but the most egalitarian'.[71] Unequal societies seem to generate more stress and unease which has direct effects on health. More integrated societies in which the worth of each member is affirmed and recognized have less stress and a distinctly better health record: 'the quality of the social life of a society is one of the most powerful determinants of health, and this in its turn, is very closely related to the degree of income equality'[72]. Our health, that is, depends on the quality of social relations within the community; human beings need respect, they need to be valued. Numerous examples have been studied to show that 'societies which are unusually egalitarian and unusually healthy were also unusually cohesive'.[73] More equal societies are likely to have stronger supportive social networks, and to be freer from stress and social conflict. People flourish and are more likely to be healthy in conditions of friendship, for 'Friendship is about mutuality, reciprocity, and the recognition that the needs of friends are needs for us. In contrast, hierarchy, dominance, and subordination is a pecking order based on power, coercion and access to resources regardless of the needs of others.'[74] And as one piece of economics research concluded, human beings need both to give and receive love – something theologians have been saying for centuries![75]

This chapter has of necessity been highly selective in the policy areas it has discussed. I have concentrated almost entirely on issues of care and social security because these areas show up most clearly whether a society is really concerned for the weakest, the most vulnerable and the excluded. But I could, almost as relevantly, have concentrated on taxation and redistribution, education and employment, transport, housing, human rights, racial equality or almost any other policy area. If a society really believes in equality it makes a fundamental difference right across the range of policy, for that society seeks to order its life in such a way as to affirm the equal dignity and claim of all its citizens. A belief in human equality, the equal worth of human beings, suggests the need for an integrated approach to the different, interlocking forms of inequality – economic, political, cultural, gender, and so forth. There is a need for democratic change in the power structures of society as well as decent benefits, fair taxes, and redistribution.

The evidence seems to show that human beings are more likely to flourish and thrive, to be healthy and content in a more equal society than in a society marked by deep and wide social and economic divisions. Human beings are made to love and to be loved. And in a good, just and equal society love is enabled and encouraged, and the appetite is whetted for the fuller love that will be found in the coming age. Governments and nations are tested by how they respond to the needs of the world, particularly the weak and poor and vulnerable. For that judgment they stand at the tribunal of the Son of Man.

Epilogue

Dr Dives and Poor Lazarus

In this book I have been exploring the conviction that equality is a good and important thing, and arguing that its roots are in the soil of the Judaeo-Christian tradition, and that it has a distinctive shape which is determined by that tradition. Gerry Cohen is, I believe, right in suggesting that what we need in these matters is 'the strength of conviction that depends on the depth of convictions'.[1] Philippe van Parijs introduces a powerful book by suggesting that he holds two convictions particularly strongly: that our societies are 'replete with unacceptable inequalities', and that 'freedom is of paramount importance.'[2] This is surely much preferable to suggesting that social theory is nothing more than the reflection of widely held opinions or prejudices. Convictions are not, of course, simply arbitrary assumptions which cannot be explained, defended or commended. They have roots, and they relate to other convictions about reality, about God, and human beings, and community. They do not stand alone, in isolation, but they are shaped by our beliefs and assumptions and theories about how people and societies ought to behave, about the nature and destiny of human beings. The soil in which our convictions about human equality are rooted is, whether we ourselves are religious people or not, permeated with Judaeo-Christian faith and assumptions; the distinctive shape of modern understandings of equality is also derived from the Judaeo-Christian tradition.

Most modern discussions of equality claim to be entirely secular, and rarely relate seriously to the history or roots of the conviction – dare one say 'faith'? – that human beings are of equal worth. Roots are important in sustaining a plant in being and enabling it to flourish; they give it nourishment. What if modern secular accounts of equality are like a daffodil that has been plucked from its bulb? It can flourish in water for a time, and look beautiful, but it soon fades and it certainly cannot seed or fruit. I agree with Louis Pojman, who argues that we need a metaphysical explanation to ground the doctrine of equal worth, and that historically all such explanations have been religious. If we can no longer take the religious roots of equality seriously, he continues, 'then it would seem perhaps we should abandon egalitarianism and devise political philosophies that reflect naturalistic assumptions, theories which are forthright in viewing humans as differently talented animals who must get on together'. He adds:

> The question is whether the kind of democratic ideals that egalitarians espouse can do without a religious tradition. If it cannot, then egalitarians may be living off the borrowed interest of a religious metaphysic, which (in their eyes) has gone bankrupt. The question is: Where is the capital?[3]

This book, in the assumption that socially-relevant religious faith is not bankrupt, is an attempt to offer and explore the resources that religious faith might have to sustain and shape the conviction that human beings are of equal worth, and are entitled to be treated as such, not because people are of equal merit, or achievement, or ability, but because God loves us equally regardless of desert, and commands us to love our neighbours as we love ourselves.

Much contemporary social theory, and much theology, is remarkably remote from questions of policy and practice. There is much in Gerry Cohen's view that depth of conviction 'comes from theory that is too fundamental to be practicable in the direct sense'.[4] But it is dangerous when social theory and theology become highly abstract and hardly related to possibilities of political or personal action. David Miller laments 'the huge gap that exists between the conceptions of social justice defended by political philosophers, particularly those we might describe as egalitarian liberals, and the kind of policy changes it is feasible to propose for the liberal societies of today'.[5] He is rightly, I think, concerned about 'the way in which theorizing about social justice has become detached from questions about political feasibility'. I do not argue that there is, or should be, a quick and easy movement between theory and reflection on the one hand, and policy and practice on the other. But social thought and theology can easily become word games without serious relation to the way things go, or any obvious bearing on the relationship between Munuswamy and me. The bridge between theory and practice must have two-way traffic; I have tried to open up the two carriageways a little, for the benefit, I hope, of theology, and perhaps even for social theory.

Miller, like many secular liberal theorists, seeks to root his principles of justice and equality in unspecified 'popular beliefs'; he is nervous about the utopian, but believes that social theory can have a 'sharp critical edge' which 'will guide us toward making substantial changes in our institutions and practices'.[6] Perhaps one of the contributions that theology might make today is the rehabilitation of a realistic utopianism which is aware both of the fallenness of things and of the need for hope. H. Richard Niebuhr was telling only half the truth when he said that 'Man's task is not building utopias but ... eliminating weeds and tilling the soil so that the kingdom of God may grow'.[7] In this generation it may be that it is left to theology to 'rekindle utopian energies', to nurture a vision of God's future, to call on people to seek equality with eagerness and commitment. For without utopias the present with its inequalities tends to be absolutized, and hopes are deprived of substance or motivating power. And theology has the advantage that it is linked to a community, the church, that is called to anticipate the Reign of God and provide proleptic manifestations of the festive conviviality of an equality of grace and love.

R. H. Tawney was right when he argued that equality is essential for community. Søren Kierkegaard saw clearly that equality is rooted in God's gracious equal love for us, and is an implication of the divine command to love the neighbour as oneself. He knew, as every Christian theologian should, that love and justice are two sides of the one reality. So it all comes back to the relation between Munuswamy and me, and how to overcome the varied barriers of inequality – structural, institutional, individual – that keep people apart and humiliate and degrade women and men made in the image of God.

I end, as I started, with the relationship between Munuswamy and me, but this time explored in the light of a story Jesus told, the parable of Lazarus who sat, like Munuswamy, outside the gate of the rich man – let us call him Dr Dives, for he stands for me and for most of my readers.

Dr Dives was largely unconscious that a great chasm had been fixed between his college and the poverty and deprivation which lay beyond the college gates. Poor Lazarus he had never really seen or heard; much of the time he did not believe that Lazarus still existed, out there beyond the college. If Lazarus did lurk there, his poverty, Dr Dives suspected, must be largely the fruit of his own fecklessness. Dr Dives, a Christian and a charitable man, tended to agree with Leslie Stephen, who wrote: 'We can only say to Lazarus, "You are probably past praying for, and all we can do is to save you from starving by any means which do not encourage other people to fall into your weaknesses".'[8]

Lazarus no longer lies, as once he did, publicly at the gate of the college. He has been moved out of sight, up back streets that Dr Dives never visits, to housing estates far from the centre of the city, or to distant lands. He is invisible, excluded, rarely heard. His complaints do not feature in the correspondence columns of *The Times* or the *Daily Telegraph*, and the theological journals rarely make reference to him.

Dr Dives would have been rather surprised and disturbed at the suggestion

- that Jesus Christ might be there, outside the college gates, at the margin of things, excluded with Lazarus, rather than in the splendid tabernacle in the college chapel;

- that the Christian should go out to meet him there; that Lazarus become his friend might welcome him into the heavenly habitations;

- that theology has a responsibility for articulating the cry of Lazarus as the voice of God;

- that the gospel and the church are centrally concerned with bridging the chasm between Dr Dives and poor Lazarus, making them friends.

And a friend deserves more than the crumbs from the theological high table.

Dr Dives could have done something to reach over the chasm, to stand where he could see Lazarus, to recognize and respond to Lazarus as an equal, to begin spinning the fragile strands of friendship. For friendship is embodied and expressed in the sharing of material, tangible and useful things, in bodily presence and in signs which affirm the other as a person of worth and dignity and significance. And friendship involves sharing pain and fear and anger. Slipping a small coin to a beggar to ease our conscience, or grudging and inadequate relief alike demean and degrade.

The crumbs from Dr Dives' table were all that Lazarus wished for. But crumbs are not enough for friends. Friends dine at the same table. Which is why the church down the ages has struggled to welcome as equals to the one Lord's Table Jew and Gentile, rich and poor, black and white, alien and citizen, scholar and the person with severe learning difficulties, Munuswamy and me, and you.

As so often, in this parable that I am exploring, there is an unexpected twist. At the start it seems that it is Lazarus who is in the problematic situation; Dr Dives is the one who has the resources to identify and resolve the problem, to establish friendship, feed Lazarus and dress his sores. But by the end, it is clear that it is Dives who is in trouble. At the start, if he had only known, he needed Lazarus as much as Lazarus needed him, but in a different way. At the end, it is too late to bridge the gap; Lazarus is now impeded from helping Dives. No longer can they together in friendship find the resolution of their problems. The time for that is past. Now Dives is the problem, has the problem.

Just a century or so ago, a real-life Dr Dives, Benjamin Jowett, Master of Balliol, used to say to the brightest and best of his students, 'Go and find your friends among the poor.' And they went to the East End of London, and the slums of Manchester and of Glasgow, and they worked in settlements and slum parishes, they established youth clubs, they worked with unemployed people, they helped provide medical care for malnourished children with rickets, they taught in adult education classes. They got to know poor people.

But when they tried to make friends, they found great problems. An ugly ditch of inequality seemed to be set between their world and the world of the poor. They were excluded from each other's lives. Individual idealistic efforts, however strenuous, were not enough to span the chasm. Good intentions did not seem adequate to bridge the gap. Friendship proved difficult. They went to the poor, but could not find a friend. Lazarus was still excluded from their lives. Rage and fear and shame are not easily shared. Structures of inequality – of poverty, and class and education – kept them apart. It was not easy to make friends, gathered at the one table.

Striving to make friends with the poor and generous charitable activity both attract plaudits. But that is not enough, as Archbishop Helder Camara famously highlighted long after when he said: 'If I give bread to a poor person, they call me a saint. If I ask *why* he is poor, they say I am a communist.'

And then, some decades after Jowett, another Master of Balliol, Edward Caird, called three students, three of the brightest and best, and said to them, 'Go to the East End of London, and find out what poverty is, and why in Britain there is so much grinding poverty alongside great wealth, and work out what can be done about it.' The three young men were Richard Tawney, William Beveridge and William Temple. They went to the East End and they worked there. They were appalled at what they found. Their consciences were pricked by poverty visible, audible, smellable. They grew angry and confused as they began in a little way to share the pain of poverty.

They realized now that there were great *structural* obstacles to friendship. By going out to Lazarus they saw that they must put the poor at the heart of their concern, that they must speak for the dumb, that they must work to make Britain a place where friendship was possible, the forces that corrode, corrupt or impede friendship removed. They went through a kind of intellectual and emotional conversion.

- Tawney, throughout the 1920s and 1930s denounced the mammon-worship which condemned multitudes to poverty and degradation and despair. He called for a fraternal society, a community of friends, in which the equal worth of Dives and Lazarus, of every human being before God is fully recognized.

- Beveridge in the 1940s sounded the call to do battle with the five 'giants' – Squalor, Idleness, Want, Disease and Ignorance – which stood in the way of a more Christian and a more caring Britain, in which friendship between Dives and Lazarus would be possible. When Beveridge's Report was published, the Archbishop of Canterbury said, 'This is the first time that anyone has set out to embody the whole spirit of the Christian ethic in an Act of Parliament'!

- Temple, as Archbishop of York and then of Canterbury, recruited

Christian intellectuals to share in the task of reshaping the social order, and mobilized church support for a more just, equal and fraternal Britain. His little book, *Christianity and Social Order*, has aptly been described as one of the foundation piers of the welfare state.

Out of the endeavours of such people, and many others, to fulfil their varied responsibilities before God as Christians, and as intellectuals, out of their leaving the security of the quadrangle to sit with Lazarus outside and feel what poverty and exclusion mean, emerged the vision and the blueprint for an equal society in which Dives and Lazarus might be friends and care for one another's needs, a society in which the great gulf between the rich and the poor was bridged.

These people all found out that a personal change and a personal commitment were important, but they were not enough. The structures and processes which caused poverty and impeded friendship had to be unmasked, confronted, reformed or replaced. Structures that enabled and expressed friendship had to be established. The nation, not just individuals, was under judgment.

And this is true today. Still a great ugly ditch is fixed between Dives and Lazarus, between me and Munuswamy, between comfortable Britain and poor Britain. This is a chasm which cannot be bridged by those who wish to help the poor, but do not know the poor, who are not friends with the poor, who have not been challenged in the depths of their being by the pain of poverty. It cannot be bridged only by individual action, or by charity, or by changes of lifestyle – important and desirable as these things are.

In the present debate about equality, it is the nation, and its economic and social structures, that stand under judgment. For we are considering the kind of society we want to have. We are considering how we may enable Dives and Lazarus to be friends, how we may love another and do justice to one another.

In that strange story of the sheep and the goats in Matthew 25 many readers do not notice that it is the *nations*, *ta ethne*, that are called to judgment before the Son of Man in his glory. It is not individuals. It is not believers. It is not disciples. It is the nations, the Gentiles, collectivities that are judged as to whether they have fed the hungry, given drink to the thirsty, welcomed the stranger, clothed the naked, helped the sick, and visited those in prison. In this story of the judgment of the nations the righteous cared for the needy simply because it was the right thing to do, not to gain a reward, or recognition, or applause. They did not understand the deeper significance of what they had done, that it was service to the Lord himself when they helped and befriended one of the least, one of those whom people did not wish to bother about.

Nor did the unrighteous, like Dr Dives, plumb the gravity of their inaction, until it was too late.

Appendix

Erica's Diary[1]

Erica's story, in her own words, reproduced here on pages 22-9 is supplemented by a diary she kept which gives important details about her family life, and how she coped.

The only problem we have now is the same as always and that is MONEY. I show this by keeping a diary.

Monday

I got up and got the kids dressed for school and gave them some tea and toast. Charlotte went to the post office to collect the child benefit. I gave Deidre £2.80 for two days' bus fares to school and back. Went to shop and spent money like this.

0.69	5 lb potatoes
0.69	loaf
5.00	gas token
5.03	cigs, tobacco, cig papers
0.60	2 tins beans
0.22	soap
0.49	washing-up liquid

Had a quick nap before I started on the kids' tea. When they came home from school, Gilbert and Mary needed money for school Christmas trips but I don't have it to give to them. I can't even start thinking about Christmas presents for the kids. I can't go to the DHSS because I already owe them so much. We watched some TV then we all went to bed.

Tuesday

Got the kids up and to school. Spend money on

0.69	potatoes
0.60	2 tins beans
0.69	bread
5.03	cigs, tobacco, cig papers
0.73	2lb sugar
1.98	soap powder
1.77	2 packets of toilet towels
0.67	packet of toilet rolls
1.40	ticket for Deidre for tomorrow

I am left with £31.00. I get a letter from the Water Board, they say that they are going to cut me off. I keep the £31 for the kids so they can get some sweets from the shops. It is not much but it will keep them happy for a little while. Made the tea, watched TV, then we all went to bed early.

Wednesday

Got up with the kids. Made them tea and toast and got them off to school. Peace at last. Charlotte went to the post office to get our social money. £74.49. Spend money on

10.00	gas token
10.00	electric
5.00	water token
4.87	cigs and tobacco
5.18	milk
0.69	bread
0.69	potatoes
0.49	marg
1.96	2 packets of Scotch pies
0.60	2 tins beans
1.40	Deidre's bus ticket

I have spent £40.96 and have £33.53 left. Gilbert is off school at the moment because he needs new shoes and that is £10. I can't afford them just now so I will have to wait and see what I can do for him. The kids come home from school. Thank God they get a meal at school.

Ivor is making the tea while I get the kids ready for bed. Deidre and Charlotte are going out with some friends. So me and Ivor are on our own at last for the first time in ages. The kids come back and we all went to bed.

Thursday

Up with kids again. No rest for the wicked. It is Halloween tonight. I can't afford to get things in so I will keep the door locked when other kids knock. I hate to do it but I have no option. The kids want to go out for the night, but I don't like the idea that they are taking from people and I can't give in return. But they keep going on and on so I told them to do what they want. So they are off to school now. Me and Charlotte are doing the housework, it is all I seem to do. Ivor got up for about ten minutes and went back to bed. Charlotte went to the shops for tea and bought

0.69	loaf
0.69	potatoes
2.97	cigarettes
1.28	1 doz eggs
0.60	2 tins beans
1.98	packet of sausages
1.40	bus ticket

I have £23.92 left.

The kids are home from school so I am making the tea and Charlotte is getting them ready to go out. Mary is a witch and Gilbert is a woman and they look good dressed up. So me and Ivor have the whole house to ourselves for a couple of hours. We listened to some music and played draughts. Then the kids came home, got washed and into bed. They said they had fun so they went right to sleep. Ivor and me watched some TV then went to bed.

Friday

Up with the kids, made them tea and toast, off to school. Got on with the cleaning and housework. Ivor is depressed today, a bit more than usual, so he is staying in bed all day. Charlotte went to the shops and got

0.69	bread
0.69	potatoes
0.49	marg

1.09	10 frozen hamburgers
0.60	2 tins beans
0.23	soap
1.40	ticket for Deidre

I have £18.73 left. Kids came home from school. I'll make a tea of hamburgers, chips and beans. Kids and me play cards and draughts and then we watch TV for a while then off to bed with them. That leaves me on my own so I am off for a bath and then bed.

Saturday

We all had a bit of a sleep in this morning then I made them some toast. The kids went out to play. I have a bit of a headache and feel sick but I can't go back to bed because someone has to look after the kids so I just have to soldier on. I sent Charlotte for the tea things:

0.69	bread
0.69	potatoes
5.00	electric token
2.93	cigs
0.60	2 tins beans
1.77	3 tins meat balls
1.98	box soap powder

I've got £5.07 left. I need another gas token because it is so cold in this house, but I can't afford it this week. I lay on the couch for a bit but it did not last long because there is some cleaning to do. Tea time again. We are having mashed potatoes and meat balls in gravy. Then we did the washing up and we all sat and watched a film on TV. We all went to bed early.

Sunday

I didn't want to get up today because I felt so fed up with my life. It's the same thing day-in, day-out. I don't get to go out with Ivor or on my own because we can't afford it. I don't know the last time we went out together. We don't get to go on holiday. The last time we went away was when we lived in Easterhouse with the Salvation Army to Butlin's holiday camp. That was seven years ago. Enough of my moaning. The kids are running about mad wanting their tea and toast. Charlotte goes to the shops.

0.69	bread
0.69	potatoes
1.38	2 tins corned beef
0.60	2 tins beans
1.50	10 cigarettes

I have 21p left. The kids have been out playing while I got their school clothes washed and make tea. Then it is into the bath for them for school tomorrow and off to bed.

I am sitting on my own again and I said a little prayer asking for a little guidance. Then I went to bed.

Monday

Up with kids for school. Made tea and toast for them. Gilbert is still off school because he has no shoes. I can't help it but on Wednesday I'll go round the second-hand shops to see what I can do because I must get him back to school quick. Mary and Deidre are off to school and Mary needed 80p for school. Charlotte is off to the post office to get the child benefit which is £28.61. She then went to the shop for me.

0.69	bread
0.89	tea bags
0.73	sugar
0.49	marg
0.69	potatoes
0.60	2 tins beans
1.38	dozen eggs
5.03	cigarettes, tobacco and cig paper
5.00	gas token, at last
1.40	bus ticket for Deidre

I have £10.21 left. The kids came home from school. They went to play in the back yard while I make the tea, chips and eggs and beans. They ate their tea and then got ready for bed and they watched TV with me and we went to bed.

Tuesday

Up for school again. Made the kids tea and toast and sent them to school. Charlotte and me cleaned out the house. Then we had a rest before she went to the shop for some things.

    0.69 bread
    0.60 *2* tins beans
    0.69 potatoes
    2.93 cigs
    1.40 2 tins hot dogs
    1.40 Deidre's bus fares

I now have £2.90 left. Sitting on my own for a bit watching the afternoon TV. Dozed off, woke up with a very sore head, but the kids are due in from school any minute. Mary is watching cartoons. Deidre is listening to music. Gilbert is cleaning his room. Charlotte is helping me do the tea. Ivor is in his bed. Tea is over, the kids are getting ready for bed. I am washing-up. We are going to watch TV then it's off to bed for the kids. Now I am on my own. It's a bit boring because all you can hear is lots of fireworks and bangers. It is November 5th. I am off to bed.

Wednesday

Got up. I get the kids dressed. I feed the kids breakfast and I send Ivor's up to him in bed because he spends most of his time in bed with his sore back plus he suffers from very bad depression. He ended up in hospital once with it. So most of the time I am on my own with the kids. Charlotte went to the post office for me. The hill to the post office is too much for me. I have two books. One is reserved for the money-lenders because I owe a lot and so I don't see any of that. Charlotte comes back with my money from the other book. It is £74.49. I spend

    10.00 gas token
    10.00 electric
     5.00 water
     4.40 cigarettes and tobacco
     0.69 loaf
     0.49 marg
     0.69 half a dozen eggs

I am left with £43.22. The kids are out playing with friends because they are off school for ten days. I am doing a bit of housework. Now I am reading some magazines I got from the day centre.

Charlotte has to go to town, £1.60 bus fare. She is back and she is going to the shop to get some dinner. I need quite a lot.

0.69	5lb potatoes
0.69	loaf
0.73	2lb sugar
1.92	soap powder
0.60	2 tins beans
0.86	tea bags

I have £36.13 left. Now I'll make the kids some dinner, which is beans on toast. Nothing to do but sit and watch TV. Tea time. Send for some fish fingers and beans which cost £2.56 so I've got £33.57. I make the kids their tea and get them ready for bed and watch some more TV. Ivor comes down for about an hour with us then back to bed for him. Then it's time for the kids' bed. Now I am on my own again so I go out to the path and stand for about five or ten minutes, come in and watch more TV. Now it's time for my bed.

Thursday

Up with the kids again. Send to the shops for bread to make the kids some tea and toast for breakfast. Sent some up to Ivor. Get the kids ready.

0.69	bread

Now left with £32.88. The kids are out to play, then they sit and watch TV with me. Dozed off for about half an hour then woke up with the kids fighting amongst themselves. I feel ill, I go to see the doctor at the day centre. I have to get the bus, which costs £1.60.

0.69	loaf
1.80	tobacco for Ivor
0.89	box of 12 frozen hamburgers

I have £27.90 left.

I came home and had to clean up after the kids because the place was in a hell of a mess. A woman's work is never done. So to tea, chips and burgers, then washing-up. I get the kids ready for bed. Not seen Ivor today, he's been in bed all this time, I'll have a bath then off to bed. I have to go and see a social worker tomorrow because I want to start looking for my son who was adopted out when he was two years old and I was just seventeen.

Friday

Got up and sent for some bread and marge. Made the kids some toast. Got ready to go to the social workers. Spent

0.69	bread
0.49	marge
1.90	tobacco
0.20	cig papers
0.69	5lb potatoes
5.18	milkman
1.80	bus fare to social work

I have £16.95 left. After I came home I cleaned up and Ivor got up for a little while and we talked about how I got on at the social services. I told him that if I want to register with the adoption agency I have to find £27 to register. But I don't have that kind of money and there is no one left to help me because I owe them a lot as it is. So I will just have to wait and see what happens with my adopted son.

I made some tea for the kids, sent for a dozen eggs and some beans, which came to £2.58 so leaving £14.37. Deidre came in with her friend and asked if she could go to the disco, but I had to tell her no because the money is tight. She was not pleased but she had to go along with it. Then we all sat and watched a film on TV before we went to bed.

Saturday

Got up as usual but my head hurts so bad. The kids are running about mad so I had to shout at them, so they were not pleased with me at all. Made them some toast. I had to send for bread plus some cigs. Must have my cigs or I can't get through the day. I hate it that people say that because you are on social security you shouldn't smoke. But it's like Valium, it calms me. I wish I could give it up. I have tried and failed.

0.69	bread
2.93	cigs
5.00	electric token

I have £5.75 left. I have asked the kids to help clean up for me. They moaned but they did it. We all sat and watched TV. The TV set is on its last legs and I don't know what I'd do without it.

The kids asked for some bread. I could only give them one slice each because it is all that was left. Ivor has not got up today.

Me, Deidre and Charlotte had a game of cards and I won. The kids went to bed.
I wanted to go for a bath but I have to keep the hot water for Sunday for the kids.
We had mashed potatoes and meat balls for tea.

0.69   potatoes
0.98   two tins meat balls

I have £4.08 left. I am off to bed now

Sunday

Got up with the kids as usual. From the shop got

0.69   bread
0.35   salt
0.69   5lb potatoes
0.60   2 tins beans
1.58   2 tins chopped ham

Just a few pence left. I need some gas but I don't have enough so we will just have
to put up with the cold till morning. It is quite cold in the house.

The kids look for their school clothes so that I can wash them. We just sit and
watch TV till it's time for tea. Charlotte helps to make the tea which is a big help,
and then we wash up together and she puts things away while I run the bath. In
goes Mary then Gilbert and off to bed for them.

Ivor got up for a couple of hours, so we watched TV and played cards then we
went to bed.

Notes

Prologue

1. J. Habermas, 'The New Obscurity and the Exhaustion of Utopian Energies' in Habermas (ed.), *Observations on the Spiritual Situation of the Age*, Cambridge, MA: MIT Press 1984.
2. This is not the place for a discussion of the theology of disability, but it might be important to note quite simply that in the Letter to the Hebrews Christ is spoken of as bearing the stigma for us, and believers are urged to share his bearing of stigma, and also that the term 'cretin', of course, originally meant Christian.

Chapter One

1. J. Habermas, *The Theory of Communicative Action I: Reason and the Rationalization of Society*, Boston: Beacon Press 1984, p. 287.
2. Ciran Cronin, in Translator's Introduction to J. Habermas, *Justification and Application: Remarks on Discourse Ethics*, Cambridge, MA: MIT Press 1993, p. xviii.
3. J. Forester, *Planning in the Face of Power*, Berkeley: University of California Press 1989, p. 118.
4. Consider, for example, Emmanuel Le Roy Ladurie's remarkable study of Cathars and Catholics in a fourteenth-century French village (*Montaillou*, Harmondsworth: Penguin 1980), which is based largely on the transcripts of the Inquisition, and (more recently and closer to home) James Hunter, *The Making of the Crofting Community* (new edn., Edinburgh: John Donald 2000), which draws heavily both on oral history and on the records of evidence to government commissions.
5. Prov. 31.8–9.
6. D. B. Forrester and Danus Skene (eds), *Just Sharing: A Christian Approach to the Distribution of Wealth, Income and Benefits*, London: Epworth Press 1988.
7. This is a process which reminds us of David Hume's famous saying, 'Reason is, and ought to be, the slave of the passions.' But we are suggesting particular kinds of passion that reason should serve.

8. For an example of this, see Ralph Glasser's account of how, as a poor Jewish scholarship boy from the Glasgow Gorbals he was received by the Oxford Fabians as no more than a 'prize working-class exhibit', without his opinions or his experience being taken seriously. Ralph Glasser, *Gorbals Boy at Oxford*, London: Pan 1990, esp. chs 3 and 5.

9. Cited in Amartya Sen, *Development as Freedom*, Oxford: Oxford University Press 1999, p. 174.

10. Cecil Woodham-Smith, *The Great Hunger*, New York: Old Town Books 1989, pp. 156, 171.

11. Cited from Adam Smith, *The Wealth of Nations* (1776), Vol. 2, Book 5, ch. 2, in Sen, *Development as Freedom*, p. 73.

12. Avishai Margalit, *The Decent Society*, Cambridge, MA: Harvard University Press 1996, pp. 1, 41.

13. Catharine Howarth, Peter Kenway, Guy Palmer and Cathy Street, *Monitoring Poverty and Social Exclusion*, York: Joseph Rowntree Foundation 1998.

14. Alissa Goodman, Paul Johnson and Stephen Webb, *Inequality in the UK*, Oxford: Oxford University Press 1997.

15. Family Policy Studies Centre, *Family Briefing Paper 15*, June 2000.

16. David Donnison, 'Don't Make Me Beg for a Decent Wage', *The Observer*, 15 March 1998, p. 16.

17. Goodman, Johnson and Webb, *Inequality in the UK*, pp. 64–6.

18. Reported in *The Herald*, 11 September 2000.

19. Bob Holman, with Carol, Bill, Erica, Anita, Denise, Penny and Cynthia, *Faith in the Poor*, Oxford: Lion 1998, pp. 56–78.

20. Amartya Sen, *Inequality Re-examined*, New York: Oxford University Press 1992, p. 12.

21. See Albert Weale, 'Equality' in *Dictionary of Ethics, Theology and Society*, London: Routledge 1996, p. 296.

22. On this see especially Robert Veatch, *The Foundations of Justice: Why the Retarded and the Rest of Us have Claims to Equality*, New York: Oxford University Press 1986. G. A. Cohen, *Self-ownership, Freedom and Equality*, Cambridge: Cambridge University Press 1995, pp. 224–5, suggests that 'we cannot address the claims of the radically disadvantaged as long as we stay with the contractarian standpoint of mutual advantage'. But where does the impulse to altruism come from?

23. But the belief that justice demands that people should be treated equally according to their deserts is not universal. As we shall see in detail later, in traditional Indian caste society penalties and rewards varied widely according to the caste status of the parties involved.

24. See the compelling discussion of this issue in Veatch, *The Foundations of Justice*.

25. I discuss this in more detail in my *Christian Justice and Public Policy*, Cambridge: Cambridge University Press 1997, ch. 5.

26. P. T. Bauer, *Equality, the Third World and Economic Delusion*, London: Weidenfeld & Nicolson 1981, p. 8.

27. John Plamenatz in J. R. Pennock and J. W. Chapman (eds), *Equality* [NOMOS IX]. New York: Atherton Press 1967, p. 83.

28. R. H. Tawney, *Equality*, London: Allen & Unwin 1964, p. 168.

29. See, particularly, Sen, *Development as Freedom*.

30. Douglas Rae, *Equalities*, Cambridge, MA: Harvard University Press 1981.

31. On self-ownership see Cohen, *Self-ownership, Freedom and Equality*.

32. Christine Koggel, *Perspectives on Equality: Constructing a Relational Theory*, Durham, MD: Rowman & Littlefield 1998.

33. Ralf Dahrendorf, 'Liberty and Equality' in *Essays in the Theory of Society*, London: Routledge 1968, pp. 211–14: 'Equality is a condition of the possibility of liberty whenever it relates to the rank of human existence, but ... it constitutes a threat to the possibility of liberty wherever it relates to the modes of human existence.'

34. H. J. Laski, cited in Lee Rainwater (ed.), *Social Problems and Public Policy: Inequality and Justice*, Chicago: Aldine 1974, p. 31.

35. See Amartya Sen, *Choice, Welfare and Measurement*, Oxford: Blackwell 1982 [for essay on 'Equality of What?']; *Inequality Re-examined*; *On Economic Inequality*, expanded edn, Oxford: Oxford University Press 1997.

36. Veatch, *The Foundations of Justice*, p. 127.

37. Plato, *Laws*, VI 757 in B. Jowett, *The Dialogues of Plato*, Oxford: Oxford University Press 1892, Vol. V, pp. 137–8.

38. Tawney, *Equality*, pp. 49–50.

39. In Richard B. Brandt (ed.), *Social Justice*, Englewood Cliffs, NJ: Prentice–Hall 1962, p. 41.

40. Rae, *Equalities*, pp. 131, 133.

41. Sen, *Inequality Re-examined*, p. x.

42. Michael Rustin in David Miller and Michael Walzer, *Pluralism, Justice and Equality*, Oxford: Oxford University Press 1995, p. 26.

43. Shakespeare, *The Merchant of Venice*, Act III, Scene 1.

44. Elizabeth Wolgast, *Equality and the Rights of Women*, Ithaca, NY: Cornell University Press 1980, p. 14.

45. Mary Midgely, *Beast and Man*, Ithaca: Cornell University Press 1978, p. 330n., cited in Wolgast, *Equality and the Rights of Women*, p. 15.

46. Charles Taylor et al., *Multiculturalism: Examining the Politics of Recognition*, Princeton: Princeton University Press 1994, p. 25, as cited by Nancy Fraser, *Justice Interruptus: Critical Reflections on the 'Post-socialist' Condition*, New York: Routledge 1997.

47. Taylor et al., *Multiculturalism*, p. 95.

48. Axel Honneth, 'Integrity and Disrespect: Principles of a Conception of Morality Based on the Theory of Recognition', *Political Theory* 20/2, 1992, p. 195.

49. Fraser, *Justice Interruptus*, pp. 3, 6.

50. See Michael Walzer, *Spheres of Justice*, New York: Basic Books 1983; Miller and Walzer, *Pluralism, Justice and Equality*.

51. Isaiah Berlin, 'Equality', *Proceedings of the Aristotelian Society* LVI, 1956, p. 320.

52. Harry G. Johnson, 'Some Micro-economic Reflections on Income and Wealth Inequalities', *Annals of American Academy of Political and Social Science* 409, 1973, p. 54.

53. Søren Kierkegaard, *Papers and Journals: A Selection*, trans. and ed. Alastair Hannay, Harmondsworth: Penguin 1996, p. 271.

54. John E. Coons and Patrick M. Brennan, *By Nature Equal: The Anatomy of a Western Insight*, Princeton: Princeton University Press 1999, pp. 6, 39, 46, 321.

55. Steven Lukes, *Individualism*, Oxford: Blackwell 1979.

56. This controversy has been explored by Philip Green in *The Pursuit of Inequality*, Oxford: Robertson 1981.

57. J. Rawls, *A Theory of Justice*, Oxford: Oxford University Press 1972, pp. 504–12.

Chapter Two

1. Cited from *The New York Review of Books* 30, 21 July 1983, pp. 43–6, by W. Werpehowski, 'Political Liberalism and Christian Ethics: A Review Discussion', *Thomist* 48, 1984, p. 93.

2. Rom. 7.18–25.

3. In Andrew R. Morton (ed.), *The Future of Welfare*, Edinburgh: Centre for Theology and Public Issues 1997 (Occasional Paper 41), p. 150.

4. Rawls's statement that 'Enlightenment Liberalism ... historically attacked orthodox Christianity' and is in this respect quite different from what he calls 'political liberalism' is quite misleading. John Rawls, *The Law of Peoples, with 'The Idea of Public Reason Revisited'*, Cambridge, MA: Harvard University Press 1999, p. 176.

5. J. R. Pole, *The Pursuit of Equality in American History*, Berkeley: University of California Press 1978, p. 51, n.83 and Coons and Brennan, *By Nature Equal*, pp. 3–4.

6. Ronald Dworkin, 'Why Liberals should Care about Equality' in *A Matter of Principle*, Cambridge, MA: Harvard University Press 1985, p. 205.

7. Bruce A. Ackerman, *Social Justice in the Liberal State*, New Haven: Yale University Press 1980, p. 11.

8. Ackerman, *Social Justice in the Liberal State*, p. 18.

9. Ackerman, *Social Justice in the Liberal State*, p. 111.

10. Dworkin, 'Why Liberals should Care about Equality', p. 206.

11. Dworkin, 'Why Liberals should Care about Equality', p. 205.

12. For a perceptive critique, see A. Weale, 'The Impossibility of Liberal Egalitarianism', *Analysis* 40, 1980.

13. I have discussed Rawls in more detail in my *Christian Justice and Public Policy*, ch. 5.

14. John Rawls, 'Justice as Fairness: Political not Metaphysical', *Philosophy and Public Affairs* 14/3, 1985, p. 223.

15. John Rawls, *Political Liberalism*, New York: Columbia University Press 1993.

16. Rawls, *The Law of Peoples*.

17. Rawls, *The Law of Peoples*, pp. 131–2.

18. Rawls, *The Law of Peoples*, pp. 132–3.

19. Rawls, *The Law of Peoples*, pp. 134–5.

20. Rawls, *The Law of Peoples*, p. 150.

21. Rawls, *The Law of Peoples*, p. 158.

22. Rawls, *The Law of Peoples*, p. 175.

23. I discuss these Pastoral Letters more fully in *Beliefs, Values and Policies*, Oxford: Clarendon Press 1989. See also Jeremy Waldron, 'Religious Contributions in Public Deliberation', *San Diego Law Review* 30, 1993, pp. 817–48 for a 'secular' political theorist's examination of the significance of the Pastoral Letters, and religious contributions to public debate in a liberal society.

24. Bernard Crick in Andrew R. Morton (ed.), *Justice and Prosperity: A Realistic Vision? A Response to the Report of the Commission on Social Justice*, Edinburgh: Centre for Theology and Public Issues 1995, p. 50.

25. Commission on Social Justice, *Social Justice: Strategies for National Renewal*, London: Vintage 1994, p. 397.

26. *Social Justice*, p. 13.

27. Matthew Arnold, 'Stanzas from the Grande Chartreuse'. Gramsci is credited with similar words, 'the old is dying and the new cannot be born' in Colin Hay, 'Labour's Thatcherite Revisionism: Playing the Politics of "Catch-Up"', *Political Studies* 42/3, 1994, p. 707.

28. In Jane Franklin (ed.), *Equality*, London: Institute for Public Policy Research 1997, p. 32.

29. Commission on Social Justice, *The Justice Gap*, London: Institute for Public Policy Research 1993, pp. 4, 19.

30. In Franklin (ed.), *Equality*, p. 31.

31. On this see the comments of Adrian Sinfield and Morag Gillespie in Morton (ed.), *Justice and Prosperity*, pp. 31–2, 40.

32. *Social Justice*, p. 17.

33. *The Justice Gap*, p. 4.

34. *The Justice Gap*, pp. 13, 19.

35. Wilf Stevenson, *Equality and the Modern Economy: Seminar 5*, London: The Smith Institute 1999.

36. Anthony Giddens, *The Third Way and Its Critics*, Cambridge: Polity 2000; *The Third Way: The Renewal of Social Democracy*, Cambridge: Polity 1998; and 'Why the Old Left is Wrong on Equality', *New Statesman*, 25 October 1999, pp. 25–7.

37. Giddens, 'Why the Old Left is Wrong on Equality'.

38. M. Walzer, 'Pluralism and Social Democracy', *Dissent*, Winter 1998, cited in Giddens, *The Third Way and Its Critics*, p. 85.

39. G. A. Cohen, 'Equality, Equality of Opportunity, and the Labour Party', typescript 1999, p. 4.

40. Patricia Hewitt, 'How an Egalitarian Can Be an Elitist', *New Statesman*, 21 February 2000.

41. Hewitt, 'How an Egalitarian Can Be an Elitist', p. 26.

42. Waldron, 'Religious Contributions in Public Deliberation', p. 846.

43. Waldron, 'Religious Contributions in Public Deliberation', p. 848.

44. Veatch, *The Foundations of Justice*.

Chapter Three

1. George P. Fletcher, 'In God's Image: the Religious Imperative of Equality under the Law', *Columbia Law Review* 99, 1999, pp. 1608–29, p. 1615.

2. So Hans Frei and others.

3. Alasdair MacIntyre, *Three Rival Versions of Moral Enquiry: Encyclopaedia, Genealogy, and Tradition*, Notre Dame: University of Notre Dame Press 1990, p. 19.

4. MacIntyre, *Three Rival Versions of Moral Enquiry*, p. 179.

5. See Fletcher, 'In God's Image', p. 1613: 'One of the peculiar features of American political theory is the way in which committed egalitarians totally ignore the theological foundations of American thinking about equality.'

6. Sanford Lakoff, *Equality in Political Philosophy*, Cambridge, MA: Harvard University Press 1964, p. 180; Herbert Spiegelberg, 'A Defence of Human Equality', *Philosophical Review* LIII, 1944, pp. 101ff., p. 101.

7. Johnson, 'Some Micro-economic Reflections on Income and Wealth Inequalities', p. 54.

8. Keith Joseph and Jonathan Sumption, *Equality*, London: John Murray 1979, pp. 4–5; John Charvet, *A Critique of Freedom and Equality*, Cambridge: Cambridge University Press 1981, p. 2.

9. See E. Troeltsch, *The Social Teaching of the Christian Churches*, ET London: Allen & Unwin 1931, pp. 199, 902; Spiegelberg, 'A Defence of Human Equality', p. 107. And now see Douglas A. Hicks, *Inequality and Christian Ethics*, Cambridge: Cambridge University Press 2000; Coons and Brennan, *By Nature Equal*.

10. W. Brueggemann, 'Trajectories in Old Testament Literature and the Sociology of Ancient Israel' in Norman K. Gottwald and Richard A. Horsley (eds), *The Bible and Liberation: Political and Social Hermeneutics*, rev. edn. Maryknoll: Orbis 1993, pp. 201–26.

11. Norman K. Gottwald, *The Tribes of Yahweh: A Sociology of the Religion of Liberated Israel*, London: SCM Press 1979.

12. Brueggemann, 'Trajectories in Old Testament Literature', p. 215.

13. George V. Pixley, *God's Kingdom*, London: SCM Press 1981.

14. Gen. 2.23.

15. Gen. 3.16; cf. Gerhard von Rad, *Genesis*, rev. edn. London: SCM Press 1972, pp. 93–4.

16. Gen. 1.26–27.

17. 'By God's will, man was not created alone but designated for the "thou" of the other sex. The idea of man, according to P, finds its full meaning not in the male alone but in man and woman.' Von Rad, *Genesis*, p. 60.

18. See David Cairns, *The Image of God in Man*, rev. edn. London: Fontana 1973, ch. 18.

19. On this see Cairns, ch. 2, and G. Kittel (ed.), *Theological Dictionary of the New Testament*, Grand Rapids: Eerdmans 1965, Vol. 3.

20. John 5.18.

21. Phil. 2.6.

22. Lord Eustace Percy, *The Heresy of Democracy*, London: Eyre & Spottiswoode 1954, p. 29.

23. W. F. Webster (ed.), *Rig-Veda Sanhitá*, London: Tübner 1888, pp. 252–3 (X.xc.xix.11–13).

24. W. F. Webster (ed.), *Rig-Veda Sanhitá*, London: Tübner 1888, pp. 252–3 (X.xc.xix.11–13).

25. In George L. Abernethy (ed.), *The Idea of Equality: An Anthology*, Richmond, VA: John Knox Press 1959, p. 65.

26. On this see now Don S. Browning et al., *From Culture Wars to Common Ground: Religion and the American Family Debate*, Louisville: Westminster John Knox 1997, esp. ch. 5: 'Honor, Shame and Equality in Early Christian Families'.

27. Mal. 2.10.

28. See especially Elisabeth Schüssler Fiorenza, *Discipleship of Equals: A Feminist Critical Ekklesia-logy of Liberation*, New York: Crossroad 1984.

29. I am indebted for this point to Dr J. I. H. McDonald. He cites Arius Didymus: 'A man has the rule of the household by nature, for the deliberative faculty in a woman is inferior, in children it does not yet exist, and in the case of slaves, it is completely absent.'

30. Job 31.13–28.

31. Deut. 15.11.

32. Deut. 15.

33. Lev. 25.

34. Lev.19.33–34

35. Amos 5.21, 23–24.

36. Or, 'by you all the families of the earth shall bless themselves', Gen. 12.3. Cf. Gen. 18.18; 22.18; 26.4; Acts 3.25; Gal. 3.8.

37. Ps. 72.1, 2, 4.

38. 2 Sam 12.

39. 1 Kings 21.

40. Emanuel Rackman, 'Judaism and Equality' in Pennock and Chapman (eds), *Equality*, p. 154 says that although it emphasized equal dealing, biblical Hebrew had no word for 'equality'.

41. Lev. 19.14–15.

42. Max Müller (ed.), *Sacred Books of the East*, Oxford 1886, pp. 301–2.

43. On apocalyptic see especially Christopher Rowland, *Radical Christianity*, Cambridge: Polity 1988, ch. 3; *Revelation*, London: Epworth Press 1993; and 'Revelation' in *The New Interpreter's Bible*, Vol. 12, Nashville: Abingdon 1998.

44. Cited from *No Rusty Swords*, London: Collins 1965, pp. 324–5 in Rowland, 'Revelation', p. 508.

45. Phil. 2.5–11.

46. Matt. 20.25–28.

47. Luke 22.27.

48. 2 Cor. 5.21.

49. Eph. 2.14.

50. Luke 15.2.

51. Philip F. Esler, *Community and Gospel in Luke-Acts*, Cambridge: Cambridge University Press 1987, has a fine discussion of the issue of table-fellowship between Jews and Gentiles in Luke and Acts, but oddly says hardly anything at all about the scandal caused by Jesus' open table, to which all sort of 'impure', unrespectable and suspect people were welcome.

52. But in some passages it is suggested that there is rank and degree in heaven: Matt. 5.19; 10.41f.; 11.11; 19.28; 20.23; 25.19ff.; Luke 19.17, 19.

53. Matt. 23.12.

54. Gerd Theissen, *A Theory of Primitive Christianity*, London: SCM Press 1999, pp. 71ff.

55. Theissen, *A Theory of Primitive Christianity*, p. 71.

56. Theissen, *A Theory of Primitive Christianity*, p. 75.

57. Luke 1.51–53.

58. Schüssler Fiorenza, *Discipleship of Equals*.

59. Matt. 20.1–16.

60. See Theissen, *A Theory of Primitive Christianity*, pp. 64–71.

61. Matt. 22.37–40.

62. Matt. 25.31–46; I John 4.20–21.

63. Cited from S. Kierkegaard, *The Point of View, etc.*, London: Oxford University Press 1939, p. 120 in Daniel Jenkins, *Equality and Excellence*, London: SCM Press 1961, p. 39.

64. Luke 4.18–19. On wealth and poverty in Luke-Acts see especially Esler, *Community and Gospel in Luke-Acts*.

65. Luke 16.19–31.

66. Gal. 3.28. Cf. Col. 3.11; I Cor. 12.13; Rom. 10.12.

67. Eph. 2.13–16.
68. Acts 10.28.
69. Acts 17.22–33.
70. Luke 13.29; Matt. 8.11–12.
71. I Cor. 12.12–27; Rom. 12.4–5; Eph. 4.16
72. Rom. 12.5; Eph. 4.25.
73. Robert M. Grant, *Early Christianity and Society: Seven Studies*, London: Collins 1978, pp. 36–8; J. A. T. Robinson, *The Body*, London: SCM Press 1952.
74. I Cor. 12.24–26.
75. 2 Cor. 8.13–14; I Cor. 16.1ff.
76. Acts 2.44–45; 4.34–35.
77. See Theissen, *A Theory of Primitive Christianity*, p. 69.
78. I Cor. 11.20.
79. Acts 4.32, 34–35. Cf. Acts 2.44–45.
80. Apol. 39.11, cited in Grant, *Early Christianity and Society*, p. 101.
81. Rom. 2.11; Acts 10.34–35.
82. James 2.1–6.
83. Max Weber, *The Religions of India*, Glencoe: Free Press 1958, pp. 37–8.
84. I am indebted for these points on slavery to J. I. H. McDonald's forthcoming commentary on Colossians.
85. Rev. 13.
86. I Cor. 7.20.
87. See especially J. I. H. McDonald's treatment of the 'household tables', in his forthcoming commentary on Colossians.
88. Eph. 6.5–9. Cf. Col. 3.22–25; I Cor. 7.21–24.
89. Gal. 3.28.
90. Philemon 15–17.
91. I Cor. 7.21–24. See also J. A. and R. W. Carlyle, *A History of Medieval Political Thought in the West*, Edinburgh: Blackwood 1927, Vol. 1, pp. 86–8.
92. Aristotle, *The Politics*, trans. Stephen Everson, Cambridge: Cambridge University Press 1988, pp. 6–9.
93. R. Bultmann, *Theology of the New Testament*, London: SCM Press 1952, Vol. 1, p. 309.
94. Troeltsch, *The Social Teaching of the Christian Churches*, p. 61.

Chapter Four

1. Michael Walzer, *Thick and Thin: Moral Arguments at Home and Abroad*, Notre Dame: Notre Dame Univesity Press 1994, pp. 12–13, cited in Miroslav Volf, *Exclusion and Embrace: A Theological Exploration of Identity, Otherness, and Reconciliation*, Nashville: Abingdon 1996, p. 200.
2. Dahrendorf, *Essays in the Theory of Society*, p. 152.

3. Louis Dumont, *Homo Hierarchicus*, Paris: Gallimard 1966; ET London: Weidenfeld & Nicolson 1970, rev. edn. Chicago: University of Chicago Press 1980.

4. Irving Kristol, 'Equality as an Ideal', *International Encyclopaedia of the Social Sciences*, New York: Macmillan 1968, Vol. 5, p. 108.

5. David Thomson, *Equality*, Cambridge: Cambridge University Press 1949, p. 13.

6. Acts 17.28.

7. Coons and Brennan, *By Nature Equal*, pp. 30 and 200.

8. Seneca, *On Benefits*, 20, cited in Abernethy (ed.), *The Idea of Equality*, p. 56.

9. John Plamenatz in Lyman Bryson et al. (eds), *Aspects of Human Equality*, New York: Conference on Science, Philosophy and Religion in Their Relation to the Democratic Way of Life, Inc. 1956, p. 85.

10. Henry S. Maine, *Ancient Law*, 14th edn. London: John Murray 1891, p. 93.

11. Charles Avila, *Ownership: Early Christian Teaching*, London: Sheed & Ward 1983, p. 43.

12. Grant, *Early Christianity and Society*, pp. 107–9, and Avila, *Ownership*, p. 37.

13. Avila, *Ownership*, p. 50.

14. Grant, *Early Christianity and Society*, pp. 115–16.

15. Avila, *Ownership*, p. 66.

16. Grant, *Early Christianity and Society*, pp. 104–7; Abernethy (ed.), *The Idea of Equality*, pp. 68–9; Carlyle and Carlyle, *A History of Medieval Political Theory in the West*, Vol. 1, pp. 111–19.

17. Pennock and Chapman (eds), *Equality*, p. 101.

18. Grant, *Early Christianity and Society*, p. 38.

19. Cited in Arthur O. Lovejoy, *The Great Chain of Being*, New York: Harper & Row 1960, p. 64.

20. Carlyle and Carlyle, *A History of Medieval Political Theory*, pp. 121–3, 206–9.

21. G. R. Owst, *Literature and Pulpit in Medieval England*, Oxford: Oxford University Press 1961, quoted in David Miller, *Social Justice*, Oxford: Clarendon Press 1976, p. 282.

22. Emmanuel le Roy Ladurie, *Carnival in Romans*, Harmondsworth: Penguin 1981, pp. 282ff.

23. Cited in Pennock and Chapman (eds), *Equality*, p. 140.

24. Cited in Norman Cohn, *The Pursuit of the Millennium*, New York: Oxford University Press 1970, p. 199. See also Brian Bird, *Rebel Before His Time: A Study of John Ball and the English Peasants' Revolt of 1381*, Worthing: Churchman 1987.

25. Cited from *Chronicon Angliae* in Bird, *Rebel Before His Time*, p. 65.

26. See Troeltsch, *The Social Teaching of the Christian Churches*, pp. 370–1; Cohn, *The Pursuit of the Millennium*, pp. 199–203.

27. Cited in Cohn, *The Pursuit of the Millennium*, p. 200.

28. Luther, *Reply to the XII Articles*, cited in Lakoff, *Equality in Political*

Philosophy, p. 33; cf. Pennock and Chapman (eds), *Equality*, p. 128.

29. Joshua Mitchell, 'The Equality of All under the One in Luther and Rousseau: Thoughts on Christianity and Political Theory', *The Journal of Religion* 72, 1992, pp. 351–65.

30. See Rowland, *Radical Christianity*; Cohn, *The Pursuit of the Millennium*, pp. 234–51; Owen Chadwick, *The Reformation*, Harmondsworth: Penguin 1964, p. 189.

31. Cohn, *The Pursuit of the Millennium*, pp. 261–80; Chadwick, *The Reformation*, pp. 190–2.

32. Bryson et al. (eds), *Aspects of Human Equality*, p. 223; Rowland, *Radical Christianity*.

33. Abernethy (ed.), *The Idea of Equality*, p. 101.

34. Cited in David Marquand, 'The Paradox of Tony Blair', *New Statesman*, 20 March 2000, pp. 25–7.

35. Thomas Hobbes, *Leviathan*, ed. Michael Oakeshott, Oxford: Blackwell no date, ch. 13.

36. On Hobbes and theology see especially F. C. Hood, *The Divine Politics of Thomas Hobbes: An Interpretation of 'Leviathan'*, Oxford: Clarendon Press 1964; and A. P. Martinich, *The Two Gods of 'Leviathan': Thomas Hobbes on Religion and Politics*, Cambridge: Cambridge University Press 1992.

37. John Dunn, 'From Applied Theology to Social Analysis: The Break between John Locke and the Scottish Enlightenment' in Istvan Hont and Michael Ignatieff (eds), *The Shaping of Political Economy in the Scottish Enlightenment*, Cambridge: Cambridge University Press 1983, p. 119. See also John Dunn, *The Political Thought of John Locke*, Cambridge: Cambridge University Press 1969; and John Marshall, *John Locke: Resistance, Religion and Responsibility*, Cambridge: Cambridge University Press 1994.

38. Jeremy Waldron, *Christian Equality in the Thought of John Locke*, Oxford University: Carlyle Lectures 1999 [typescript], pp. 38–9. Cf. Waldron, 'Religious Contributions in Public Deliberation', p. 844.

39. Waldron, *Christian Equality*, p. 210.

40. Richard Baxter, *Chapters from a Christian Directory*, selected by Jeannette Tawney, London: G. Bell 1925.

41. Baxter, *Chapters from a Christian Directory*, p. 26.

42. Baxter, *Chapters from a Christian Directory*, pp. 28–9.

43. Joshua Mitchell, 'The Equality of All'.

44. J. J. Rousseau, *The Social Contract and Discourses*, London: Dent 1913, p. 160.

45. Rousseau, *The Social Contract*, p. 42.

46. Coons and Brennan, *By Nature Equal*, p. 116.

47. Cited in André Béteille (ed.), *Social Inequality: Selected Readings*, Harmondsworth: Penguin 1969, p. 16.

48. In Peter Laslett and W. G. Runciman (eds), *Philosophy, Politics and Society*, second series, Oxford: Blackwell 1962, p. 116.

49. Rousseau, *The Social Contract*, p. 42.

50. Alexis de Tocqueville, *Democracy in America*, London: Oxford University Press 1946, p. 1.

51. Tocqueville, *Democracy in America*, p. 13.

52. Tocqueville, *Democracy in America*, p. 599.

53. Cited in Joshua Mitchell, 'The Equality of All', from Tocqueville, pt 2 ch. 9.

54. Cited in Abernethy (ed.), *The Idea of Equality*, p. 185.

55. Cited in Fletcher, 'In God's Image', p. 1612.

Chapter Five

1. Veatch, *The Foundations of Justice*, pp. 111–12.

2. Veatch, *The Foundations of Justice*, pp. 111–12.

3. Kierkegaard, *Papers and Journals: A Selection*, pp. 491–2.

4. J. M. Winter and D. M. Joslin, *R. H. Tawney's Commonplace Book*, Cambridge: Cambridge University Press 1972, p. 53. On Tawney as a Christian thinker see especially, Simon J. Robinson, 'R. H. Tawney's Theory of Equality: A Theological and Ethical Analysis', unpublished Edinburgh PhD thesis 1989.

5. Alan Wilkinson, *Christian Socialism: Scott Holland to Tony Blair*, London: SCM Press 1998, p. 98.

6. Norman Dennis and A. H. Halsey, *English Ethical Socialism: Thomas More to R. H. Tawney*, Oxford: Clarendon Press 1988, p. 149.

7. Cited in Ross Terrill, *R. H. Tawney and His Times*, Cambridge, MA: Harvard University Press 1973, p. 64.

8. Wilkinson, *Christian Socialism*, p. 106.

9. Ronald Preston, 'R. H. Tawney as a Christian Moralist' in *Religion and the Persistence of Capitalism*, London: SCM Press 1979, p. 100.

10. Winter and Joslin, *R. H. Tawney's Commonplace Book*, pp. 53–4.

11. Winter and Joslin, *R. H. Tawney's Commonplace Book*, pp. 53–4.

12. Winter and Joslin, *R. H. Tawney's Commonplace Book*, pp. 67–8. Italics mine.

13. R. H. Tawney, *'The Attack' and Other Papers*, London: Allen & Unwin 1953, p. 182.

14. Tawney, *'The Attack' and Other Papers*, pp. 182–4.

15. See Miroslav Volf, '"The Trinity is our Social Program" : The Doctrine of the Trinity and the Shape of Social engagement', *Modern Theology* 14.3, July 1998, pp. 403–23 and *After Our Likeness: The Church as the Image of the Trinity*, Grand Rapids: Eerdmans 1998; Jürgen Moltmann, *The Trinity and the Kingdom of God*, London: SCM Press 1981; Leonardo Boff, *Trinity and Society*, Maryknoll: Orbis 1988.

16. Rae, *Equalities*, p. 82.

17. Terrill, *R. H. Tawney and His Times*, pp. 124–36.

18. Tawney, *Equality*, p. 56.

19. Tawney, *Equality*, p. 118.
20. Tawney, *Equality*, p. 105.
21 Tawney, *Equality*, p. 105.
22. Tawney, *Equality*, p. 164.
23. Winter and Joslin, *R. H. Tawney's Commonplace Book*, pp. 53–4.
24. Tawney, *Equality*, p. 56.
25. Søren Kierkegaard, *Philosophical Fragments*, trans. David Svenson, Princeton: Princeton University Press 1962, p. 33.
26. Kierkegaard, *Philosophical Fragments*, p. 39.
27. Søren Kierkegaard, *For Self Examination*, Princeton: Princeton University Press 1974, p. 5.
28. Søren Kierkegaard, *Works of Love*, trans. D. F. Swenson, with an Introduction by D. V. Steere, London: Oxford University Press 1946, p. 73. I have, however, used the translation of this passage cited in P. L. Quinn, 'Kierkegaard's Christian Ethics' in A. Hannay and Gordon D. Marino (eds), *The Cambridge Companion to Kierkegaard*, Cambridge: Cambridge University Press 1998, p. 359.
29. Kierkegaard, *Works of Love*, p. 72.
30. Kierkegaard, *Works of Love*, p. 50.
31. Tawney, *'The Attack' and Other Papers*, p. 189.
32. Tawney, *Equality*, p. 145.
33. Tawney, *'The Attack' and Other Papers*, p. 181.
34. Wilkinson, *Christian Socialism*, p. 26.
35. Wilkinson, *Christian Socialism*, p. 60.
36. Wilkinson, *Christian Socialism*, p. 103.
37. Kierkegaard, *Papers and Journals: A Selection*, pp. 599–600.
38. Cited from the *Papirer* in Alastair Hannay, *Kierkegaard*, London: Routledge 1982, p. 276.
39. Hannay, *Kierkegaard*, p. 385.
40. Cited in Hannay, *Kierkegaard*, p. 297.
41. Veatch, *The Foundations of Justice*, p. viii: 'Those within the major Western religious traditions who think they are discovering moral truths tend to support a more egalitarian theory of justice in which the least well off have special claims on the rest of society.'
42. G. Gutiérrez, 'The Task and the Content of Liberation Theology' in C. Rowland (ed.), *The Cambridge Companion to Liberation Theology*, Cambridge: Cambridge University Press 1999, p. 25.
43. G. Gutiérrez, cited in R. Gibellini (ed.), *Frontiers of Theology in Latin America*, London: SCM Press 1980, p. x.
44. Cited in Stephen J. Pope, 'Proper and Improper Partiality and the Preferential Option for the Poor', *Theological Studies* 54, 1993, p. 243.
45. G. Gutiérrez, *A Theology of Liberation*, London: SCM Press 1974, p. 308.
46. Jorge Pixley and Clodovis Boff, *The Bible, the Church and the Poor*, London:

Burns & Oates 1989, p. 3. The Introduction to this book, 'Who Are the Poor Today, and Why?' is a classic statement of the liberationist position.

47. J. Míguez Bonino, *Revolutionary Theology Comes of Age*, London: SPCK 1975, p. 148.

48. Pixley and Boff, *The Bible, the Church and the Poor*, p. 5.

49. Pixley and Boff, *The Bible, the Church and the Poor*, p. 115.

50. Pixley and Boff, *The Bible, the Church and the Poor*, p. 124.

51. Pixley and Boff, *The Bible, the Church and the Poor*, p. 87.

52. *Lumen Gentium*, 1b.

53. Pixley and Boff, *The Bible, the Church and the Poor*, p. xii.

54. Pixley and Boff, *The Bible, the Church and the Poor*, p. 219.

55. On this see Hicks, *Inequality and Christian Ethics*, p. 144; and Pope, 'Proper and Improper Partiality'.

56. Oscar Romero, *Voice of the Voiceless*, Maryknoll: Orbis 1985, p. 184, cited in Pope, 'Proper and Improper Partiality', pp. 249–50.

57. Cited in Pope, 'Proper and Improper Partiality', p. 242.

58. *Instruction on Christian Freedom and Liberation*, par. 68. See Peter Hebblethwaite's excellent article, 'Liberation Theology and the Roman Catholic church' in Rowland (ed.), *The Cambridge Companion to Liberation Theology*, pp. 179–98.

59. See especially Thomas Nagel, *Equality and Partiality*, Oxford: Oxford University Press 1991; Eric Rakowski, *Equal Justice*, Oxford: Clarendon Press 1991; and Brian Barry, *Justice as Impartiality*, Oxford: Clarendon Press 1995.

60. Pope, 'Proper and Improper Partiality'.

61. Drew Christiansen, 'On Relative Equality: Catholic Egalitarianism after Vatican II', *Theological Studies* 45, 1984, pp. 651–75.

62. The similarities to Tawney's emphasis that equality was for the sake of fellowship are striking.

63. Christiansen, 'On Relative Equality', p. 657.

Part Three: Introduction

1. MacIntyre, *Three Rival Versions of Moral Enquiry*, p. 80.

2. Tawney, '*The Attack*' and Other Papers, p. 178.

3. 2 Cor. 10.5.

Chapter Six

1. Dag Hammarskjöld, *Markings*, London: Faber & Faber 1964.

2. Rom. 7.18–19, 21–25.

3. Luke 10.25–37. My account of the parable is influenced by Karl Barth's treat-

ment in *Church Dogmatics*, Vol. I/2, Edinburgh: T. & T. Clark 1956, pp. 411–52.

4. Luke 18.18–30. Cf. Mark 10.17–21.

5. See the discussion of Law and Love in the story of the Good Samaritan in Andrew R. Morton (ed.), *Beyond Fear: Vision, Hope and Generosity*, Edinburgh: St Andrew Press 1998, pp. 96–9.

6. Luke 18.22.

7. Theissen, *A Theory of Primitive Christianity*.

8. Robert Holman, *Poverty: Explanations of Social Deprivation*, London: Martin Robertson 1978.

9. Bob Holman, *Towards Equality: A Christian Manifesto*, London: SPCK 1997, p. 94.

10. Holman, *Towards Equality*, p. 96.

11. Margaret Drabble, *The Case for Equality*, London: Fabian Society, Tract 527, 1988, p. 8. Cited in Holman, *Towards Equality*, p. 72.

12. In Bob Holman, Helen Stanton and Stephen Timms, *Joined-up Writing: New Labour and Social Inclusion*, pamphlet, London: Christian Socialist Movement 1999, p. 15.

13. Holman, Stanton and Timms, *Joined-up Writing*, p. 16.

14. This section is indebted to Forrester and Skene (eds), *Just Sharing*, pp. 116–18.

15. *The Letter to the Commonalty* in Roger A. Mason (ed.), *John Knox on Rebellion*, Cambridge Texts in the History of Political Thought, Cambridge: Cambridge University Press 1994, pp. 124–5.

16. Tawney, *Equality*, pp. 144–5.

17. In Forrester and Skene (eds), *Just Sharing*, pp. 4–5.

18. Iris M. Young, *Justice and the Politics of Difference*, Princeton: Princeton University Press 1990, p. 27.

19. Tawney, '*The Attack*' *and Other Papers*, p. 27.

20. D. Donnison in Forrester and Skene (eds), *Just Sharing*, pp. 2–6. Reproduced by kind permission of David Donnison.

21. David Donnison, *The Politics of Poverty*, Oxford: Martin Robertson 1982.

22. The details have been taken from the Quaker Tax Witness Fund brochure.

Chapter Seven

1. Kenneth Leech, *The Social God*, London: Sheldon Press 1981, p. 129.

2. See especially Engels's treatment of Owenite experiments in his tract, *Socialism: Utopian and Scientific*, published in many editions and taken from Engels Anti-Dühring, London: Lawrence & Wishart 1934.

3. Alasdair MacIntyre, *After Virtue*, London: Duckworth 1981, p. 245.

4. Sheldon Wolin, *Politics and Vision: Continuity and Innovation in Western Political Thought*, London: Allen & Unwin 1961, pp. 96–7.

5. Michael Mann, *The Sources of Social Power*, Vol. 1, Cambridge: Cambridge University Press 1986.

6. A. D. Nock, *Early Gentile Christianity and its Hellenistic Background*, New York: Harper & Row 1964, p. 102.

7. Mann, M., *Sources of Social Power*, p. 325.

8. *Lumen Gentium*, 1.1.

9. Ross Terrill, *The Uppsala Report, 1968*, Geneva: WCC 1968, p. 17.

10. This paragraph is much indebted to G. Gassmann, 'The Church as Sacrament, Sign and Instrument' in Gennadios Limouris (ed.), *Church, Kingdom, World: The Church as Mystery and Prophetic Sign*, Geneva: World Council of Churches 1986.

11. See especially Moltmann, *The Trinity and the Kingdom of God*; Volf, *After Our Likeness*; '"The Trinity is our Social Program"'; and *Exclusion and Embrace*.

12. I am grateful to Nicholas Sagovsky for helping to clarify my mind on this matter.

13. John Zizioulas, *Being As Communion: Studies in Personhood and the Church*, Crestwood, NY: St Vladimir's Seminary Press 1985, p. 224.

14. Volf, *After Our Likeness*, p. 236.

15. Boff, *Trinity and Society*, pp. 236–7.

16. Cited in Volf, *Exclusion and Embrace*, p. 54.

17. Luke 15.2.

18. For a detailed discussion see Esler, *Community and Gospel in Luke-Acts*, ch. 4.

19. Fernando Belo, *A Materialist Reading of the Gospel of Mark*, Maryknoll: Orbis 1981. See also Michel Clevenot, *Materialist Approaches to the Bible*, Maryknoll: Orbis 1985.

20. Matt. 11.19; Luke 13.29–30.

21. Norman Perrin, *Rediscovering the Teaching of Jesus*, London: SCM Press 1967, pp. 102–3.

22. J. I. H. McDonald, *The Resurrection: Narrative and Belief*, London; SPCK 1989, p. 100.

23. Eph. 2.11–22.

24. Acts 10.

25. Acts 15; Gal. 2.11–21.

26. Weber, *The Religions of India*, pp. 37–8.

27. On this see especially Gerd Theissen, *The Social Setting of Pauline Christianity*, Edinburgh: T&T Clark 1982, pp. 145–74. And on the significance of meals in the ancient world as a context for eucharistic development see Dennis E. Smith and Hal E. Taussig, *Many Tables: The Eucharist in the New Testament and Liturgy Today*, London: SCM Press 1990.

28. Cited in M. E. Gibbs, *The Anglican Church in India, 1600–1970*, Delhi: ISPCK 1972, pp. 20–1.

29. It is surprising that this issue does not feature in Bengt Sundkler, *Church of South India: The Movement towards Union, 1900–1947*, London: Lutterworth

1954, nor does caste appear in the index. There are a few oblique references to the matter in R. D. Paul, *The First Decade: An Account of the Church of South India*, Madras: CLS 1958, pp. 14ff. It is a strange fact that no one to my knowledge has yet made a serious attempt to contextualize the development of the ecumenical movement in India.

30. C. F. Andrews, *The Renaissance in India*, London: United Council for Missionary Education 1912, p. 172. Cf. pp. 181–3.

31. C. F. Andrews, *India and Britain: A Moral Challenge*, London: SCM Press 1935.

32. Cited in R. H. S. Boyd, *Manilal Parekh, 1885–1907; Dhanjibhai Fakirbhai, 1895–1967; A Selection*, Madras: Christian Literature Society 1974, p. 41.

33. C. F. Andrews, *The True India: A Plea for Understanding*, London: Allen & Unwin 1939, p. 151.

34. C. F. Andrews, *The Renaissance in India*, London: United Council for Missionary Education 1912, pp. 188–9.

35. Stanley Hauerwas, *Truthfulness and Tragedy*, Notre Dame: Notre Dame University Press 1977, pp. 142–3.

Chapter Eight

1. Drabble, *The Case for Equality*, p. 8.

2. Cited in *With Respect to Old Age: Long Term Care – Rights and Responsibilities*, Report of the Royal Commission on Long Term Care, London: The Stationery Office 1999, p. xv.

3. I have discussed the movement from principle to policy in my *Beliefs, Values and Policies*.

4. Tawney, '*The Attack' and Other Papers*, p. 189.

5. See Giddens, *The Third Way and Its Critics*, p. 104.

6. Tony Atkinson, 'Social Exclusion, Poverty and Unemployment' in A. B. Atkinson and John Hills (eds), *Exclusion, Employment and Opportunity*, London: LSE Centre for Analysis of Social Exclusion 1998, p. 9.

7. Atkinson, 'Social Exclusion', p. 18.

8. Bill Jordan, *A Theory of Poverty and Social Exclusion*, Cambridge: Polity 1996, p. 81.

9. Jordan, *A Theory of Poverty and Social Exclusion*, p. 53.

10. Howarth et al., *Monitoring Poverty and Social Exclusion*.

11. I am grateful to Andrew Morton for suggesting these points.

12. Cited by Bernard Williams from Kierkegaard, *Papers and Journals: A Selection*, p. 39, in Franklin (ed.), *Equality*, p. 55.

13. See my *Christian Justice and Public Policy*, ch. 4.

14. See, for example, L. M. Mead, *Beyond Entitlement: The Social Obligations of Citizenship*, New York: Basic Books 1986; and C. Murray, *Losing Out: American Social Policy, 1950–1980*, New York: Basic Books 1984.

15. The undeserving were described in the late nineteenth century by Helen Bosanquet, one of the leading lights of the Charity Organisation Society thus: 'The Residuum displayed all the defects of character which rendered it industrially incompetent: absence of foresight and self-control; recklessness; aimless drifting; self-indulgence; an insuperable aversion to steady work; low intellect; degradation of the natural affections to animal instincts; a disposition unfavourable to the acquisition of skill and many other vices of similar kinds.' Cited by Alan Deacon in Morton (ed.), *The Future of Welfare*, p. 121. For a recent defence of the COS, see A. W. Vincent, 'The Poor Law Reports of 1909 and the Social Theory of the Charity Organisation Society' in David Gladstone (ed.), *Before Beveridge: Welfare Before the Welfare State*, London: IEA 1999, pp. 64–85.

16. Brian Barry, *Social Exclusion, Social Isolation and the Distribution of Income*, London: LSE Centre for Analysis of Social Exclusion 1998.

17. Barry, *Social Exclusion*, pp. 13–14.

18. Barry *Social Exclusion*, p. 21.

19. Barry, *Social Exclusion*, p. iv.

20. Atkinson, 'Social Exclusion'.

21. Atkinson, 'Social Exclusion', p. v.

22. Atkinson, 'Social Exclusion' p. 14.

23. Atkinson, 'Social Exclusion', p. 14 citing Robert Walker, 'The Dynamics of Poverty and Social Exclusion' in G. Room (ed.), *Beyond the Threshold*, Bristol: Policy Press 1995, p. 105.

24. Atkinson, 'Social Exclusion', p. 17.

25. Atkinson, 'Social Exclusion' , p. 22.

26. Atkinson, 'Social Exclusion' p. 22.

27. John Hills, *Thatcherism, New Labour and the Welfare State*, London: LSE Centre for Analysis of Social Exclusion 1998.

28. Hills, *Thatcherism, New Labour and the Welfare State*, p. 18.

29. Margalit, *The Decent Society*, p. x.

30. Cf. The comment of David Miliband, head of the Prime Minister's policy unit: 'The core aim of the welfare state has never been the creation of equality, but instead the abolition of poverty.' In *Fabian Review* 111/4, Winter 1999, p. 11.

31. See Albert Weale, 'Equality, Social Solidarity and the Welfare State', *Ethics* 100, April 1990, pp. 473–88; and 'The Welfare State and Two Conflicting Ideals of Equality', *Government and Opposition* 20, 1985, pp. 315–27.

32. Thomson, *Equality*, p. 220.

33. This point has been classically made by Julian Le Grand in his *The Strategy of Equality: Redistribution and the Social Services*, London: Allen & Unwin 1982, and in his subsequent writing.

34. D. Marsland, *Welfare or Welfare State? Contradictions and Dilemmas in Social Policy*, London: Macmillan 1966. Behind Marsland's position lies, of course,

the more temperate and measured thought of Charles Murray and Lawrence Mead; and attentive readers will not fail to notice echoes of the nineteenth century.

35. Frank Field, *How to Pay for the Future: Building a Stakeholders' Welfare*, London: Institute of Community Studies 1996, p. i.

36. Frank Field et al., *Stakeholder Welfare*, London: IEA 1996, p. 109.

37. Frank Field in Morton (ed.), *The Future of Welfare*, p. 143.

38. Field et al., *Stakeholder Welfare*, p. 19.

39. Field et al., *Stakeholder Welfare*, p. 20.

40. Field et al., *Stakeholder Welfare*, p. 144.

41. Field et al., *Stakeholder Welfare*, p. 111.

42. Holman, Stanton and Timms, *Joined-up Writing*; and 'Is This the Right Direction?, *Third Way* 21/9, 1998, pp. 24–6.

43. Holman, Stanton and Timms, *Joined-up Writing*, p. 15.

44. DSS (1998b), p. 19.

45. Quoted by Stephen Sykes in Morton (ed.), *The Future of Welfare*, p. 43.

46. For example, representatives of the Institute for Economic Affairs referred to the NHS as 'the main instrument for the creation of equality by coercion'.

47. In Centre for Theology and Public Issues, *The Market and Health Care*, Edinburgh: Centre for Theology and Public Issues 1990, pp. 2–13.

48. In Morton (ed.), *The Future of Welfare*, p. 45.

49. Morton (ed.), *The Future of Welfare*, p. 46.

50. The percentage of GDP spent on health care in the late 1990s in Britain was 6.9; in Switzerland 9.6; in Germany 9.5; in France 9.7; and in the Netherlands 8.8.

51. For further discussion, see my *Christian Justice and Public Policy*, pp. 160–4.

52. *With Respect to Old Age*, p. ix.

53. *With Respect to Old Age*, p. xi.

54. *With Respect to Old Age*, p. 3.

55. *With Respect to Old Age*, p. 27.

56. *With Respect to Old Age*, p. 62.

57. *With Respect to Old Age*, p. 116.

58. *With Respect to Old Age*, p. 114.

59. M. Wilson, *Health is for People*, London: Darton, Longman & Todd 1975, p. 63, cited in A. V. Campbell, 'Health, Justice and Community: A Theological View' in Alison J. Elliot (ed.), *Inequalities in Health in the 1980s*, Edinburgh: Centre for Theology and Public Issues 1988 (Occasional Paper 13).

60. My discussion of the Black Report is adapted from Duncan B. Forrester, *Christianity and the Future of Welfare*, London: Epworth 1985, pp. 81–4.

61. Le Grand, *The Strategy of Equality*.

62. Peter Townsend and Nick Davidson, *Inequalities in Health: The Black Report*, Harmondsworth: Penguin 1982, p. 14.

63. Townsend and Davidson, *Inequalities in Health: The Black Report*, p. 39.

64. For instance, Joseph and Sumption, *Equality*.

65. Margaret Whitehead, *The Health Divide: Inequalities in Health in the 1980s*, London: the Health Education Council 1987; see also Elliot (ed.), *Inequalities in Health in the 1980s*.

66. These bullet points derived from the Acheson Report are taken from *Poverty: Journal of the Child Poverty Action Group* 105, Winter 2000, p. 19.

67. See especially Richard G. Wilkinson, *Unhealthy Societies: The Afflictions of Inequality*, London: Routledge 1996; and Michael Marmot and Richard G. Wilkinson (eds), *Social Determinants of Health*, Oxford: Oxford University Press 1999.

68. Wilkinson, *Unhealthy Societies*, p. 113.

69. Wilkinson, *Unhealthy Societies*, p. 67.

70. Wilkinson, *Unhealthy Societies*, p. 53.

71. Wilkinson, *Unhealthy Societies*, p. 3.

72. Wilkinson, *Unhealthy Societies*, p. 5.

73. Marmot and Wilkinson, *Social Determinants of Health*, p. 261.

74. Marmot and Wilkinson, *Social Determinants of Health*, p. 262.

75. Marmot and Wilkinson, *Social Determinants of Health*, p. 213.

Epilogue

1. In Franklin (ed.), *Equality*, p. 31.

2. Philippe van Parijs, *Real Freedom for All*, Oxford: Clarendon Press 1995, p. 92.

3. Louis Pojman, 'On Equal Human Worth: A Critique of contemporary Egalitarianism' in Louis P. Pojman and Robert Westmoreland (eds), *Equality: Selected Readings*, Oxford: Oxford University Press 1997, p. 296.

4. In Franklin (ed.), *Equality*, p. 31.

5. David Miller, *Principles of Social Justice*, Cambridge, MA: Harvard University Press 1999, pp. x–xi.

6. Miller, *Principles of Social Justice*, pp. x–xi.

7. H. Richard Niebuhr, 'A Communication: The Only Way to the Kingdom of God', *The Christian Century* 49, 6 April 1932, p. 447, cited in Hicks, *Inequality and Christian Ethics*, p. 138.

8. Leslie Stephen, 'Social Equality', *International Journal of Ethics* 1, 1891, p. 288.

Appendix

1. Holman et al., *Faith in the Poor*, pp. 65–77.

Select Bibliography

Abernethy, George L. (ed.), *The Idea of Equality: An Anthology,* John Knox Press: Richmond, VA 1959

Acheson, D., *Independent Inquiry into Inequalities in Health Report,* London: The Stationery Office 1999

Ackerman, Bruce A., *Social Justice in the Liberal State,* New Haven: Yale University Press 1980

Ake, Christopher, 'Justice as Equality', *Philosophy and Public Affairs* 5, 1975–6

Atkinson, H. B., *Social Justice and Public Policy,* Brighton: Wheatsheaf 1983

Atkinson, H. B., *The Economics of Inequality,* Oxford: Clarendon Press 1975

Atkinson, Tony, 'Social Exclusion, Poverty and Unemployment' in A. B. Atkinson and John Hills (eds), *Exclusion, Employment and Opportunity,* London: LSE Centre for Analysis of Social Exclusion 1998

Audi, Robert and Wolterstorff, Nicholas, *Religion in the Public Square: The Place of Religious Convictions in Political Debate,* Lanham: Rowman & Littlefield Publishers 1997

Avila, Charles, *Ownership: Early Christian Teaching,* London: Sheed & Ward 1983

Barry, Brian, *Justice as Impartiality,* Oxford: Clarendon Press 1995

Barry, Brian, *Social Exclusion, Social Isolation and the Distribution of Income,* London: LSE Centre for Analysis of Social Exclusion 1998

Baxter, Richard, *Chapters from a Christian Directory,* Selected by Jeannette Tawney, London: G. Bell 1925

Bedau, Hugo A., *Justice and Equality,* Englewood Cliffs, NJ: Prentice–Hall 1971

Belo, Fernando, *A Materialist Reading of the Gospel of Mark,* Maryknoll: Orbis 1981

Benhabib, Seyla, *Situating the Self: Gender, Community and Post-modernism in Contemporary Ethics,* New York: Routledge 1992

Berlin Isaiah, 'Equality', *Proceedings of the Aristotelian Society* LVI, 1956

Béteille, André (ed.), *Social Inequality: Selected Readings,* Harmondsworth: Penguin 1969

Béteille, André, *Inequality among Men,* Oxford: Blackwell 1977

Béteille, André, *The Idea of Natural Inequality,* London: LSE 1980

Béteille, André (ed.), *Equality and Inequality,* Delhi: Oxford University Press 1983

Blackstone, W. T. (ed.), *The Concept of Equality*, Minneapolis: Burgess 1969

Boff, Leonardo, *Trinity and Society*, Maryknoll: Orbis 1988

Bonino, J. Míguez, *Revolutionary Theology Comes of Age*, London: SPCK 1975

Bouglé, C., *Les Idées Egalitaires: Etude Sociologique*, Paris: F, Alcan 1899

Bowlby, Ronald, 'Is there a Theology of Equality?', *The Modern Churchman*, New Series, xxxvi, 1983, pp. 3–15

Brueggemann, W., 'Trajectories in Old Testament Literature and the Sociology of Ancient Israel' in Norman K. Gottwald and Richard A. Horsley (eds), *The Bible and Liberation: Political and Social Hermeneutics*, rev. edn. Maryknoll: Orbis 1993, pp. 201–26

Byrne, Patrick H., 'Ressentiment and the Preferential Option for the Poor', *Theological Studies* 54, 1993, pp. 213–41

Cairns, David, *The Image of God in Man*, rev. edn. London: Fontana 1973

Centre for Theology and Public Issues, *The Market and Health Care*, Edinburgh: Centre for Theology and Public Issues 1990

Charvet, John, 'The Idea of Equality as a Substantive Principle of Society', *Political Studies* XVII, 1969, pp. 1–13

Charvet, John, *A Critique of Freedom and Equality* Cambridge: Cambridge University Press 1981

Christiansen, Drew, 'On Relative Equality: Catholic Egalitarianism after Vatican II', *Theological Studies* 45, 1984, pp. 651–75

Clevenot, Michel, *Materialist Approaches to the Bible*, Maryknoll: Orbis 1985

Cohen, G. A., 'On the Currency of Egalitarian Justice', *Ethics* 99, 1989

Cohen, G. A., *Self-ownership, Freedom and Equality*, Cambridge: Cambridge University Press 1995

Cohen, G. A., 'Equality, Equality of Opportunity, and the Labour Party', typescript 1999

Cohn, Norman, *The Pursuit of the Millennium*, New York: Oxford University Press 1970

Commission on Social Justice, *Social Justice in a Changing World*, London: Institute for Public Policy Research 1993

Commission on Social Justice, *Social Justice: Strategies for National Renewal*, London: Vintage 1994

Commission on Social Justice, *The Justice Gap*, London: Institute for Public Policy Research 1993

Coons, John E., and Brennan, Patrick M., *By Nature Equal: The Anatomy of a Western Insight*, Princeton: Princeton University Press 1999

Dahrendorf, Ralf, 'Liberty and Equality' in *Essays in the Theory of Society*, London: Routledge 1968

Dahrendorf, Ralf, *Class and Class Conflict in Industrial Society*, London: Routledge 1959

Dennis, Norman and Halsey, A. H., *English Ethical Socialism: Thomas More to R, H, Tawney*, Oxford: Clarendon Press 1988

Donnison, David, 'Liberty, Equality and Fraternity', *The Three Banks Review* 88, 1970, pp. 3–23

Donnison, David, 'Equality', *New Society*, 20 November 1975

Donnison, David, *The Politics of Poverty*, Oxford: Martin Robertson 1982

Dorr, Donald, *Option for the Poor: A Hundred Years of Catholic Social Teaching*, Maryknoll: Orbis 1992

Drabble, Margaret, *Case for Equality*, London: Fabian Society Tract 527, 1988

Dumont, Louis, *From Mandeville to Marx: The Genesis and Triumph of Economic Ideology*, Chicago: University of Chicago Press 1977

Dumont, Louis, *Homo Hierarchicus*, Paris: Gallimard 1966, ET London: Weidenfeld & Nicolson 1970, rev. edn. Chicago: University of Chicago Press 1980

Dunn, John, 'From Applied Theology to Social Analysis: The Break between John Locke and the Scottish Enlightenment' in Istvan Hont and Michael Ignatieff (eds), *The Shaping of Political Economy in the Scottish Enlightenment*, Cambridge: Cambridge University Press 1983

Dworkin, Ronald, 'What Is Equality?' Part 1, 'Equality of Welfare', *Philosophy and Public Affairs* 10/3, Summer 1981; 'What Is Equality?' Part 2 'Equality of Resources', *Philosophy and Public Affairs* 10/4, Fall 1981; 'What Is Equality?' Part 3, 'The Place of Liberty' 73/1 *Iowa Law Review* 1, 1987

Dworkin, Ronald, 'Why Liberals should Care about Equality' in *A Matter of Principle*, Cambridge, MA: Harvard University Press 1985

Elliot, Alison J., *Inequalities in Health in the 1980s*, Edinburgh: Centre for Theology and Public Issues 1988 (Occasional Paper 13)

Engels, F., *Socialism: Utopian and Scientific*, pamphlet published in many editions and taken from Engels Anti-Dühring, London: Lawrence & Wishart 1934

Esler, Philip F., *Community and Gospel in Luke-Acts*, Cambridge: Cambridge University Press 1987

Fletcher, George P., 'In God's Image: the Religious Imperative of Equality under the Law', *Columbia Law Review* 99, 1999, pp. 1608–29

Flew, A., *The Politics of Procrustes: Contradictions of Enforced Equality*, New York: Prometheus 1981

Forrester, Duncan B., *Christianity and the Future of Welfare*, London: Epworth 1985

Forrester, Duncan B., *Beliefs, Values and Policies*, Oxford: Clarendon Press 1989

Forrester, Duncan B., *Christian Justice and Public Policy*, Cambridge: Cambridge University Press 1997

Forrester, D. B., and Skene, Danus (eds), *Just Sharing: A Christian Approach to the Distribution of Wealth, Income and Benefits*, London: Epworth Press 1988

Frankfurt, Harry, 'Equality as a Moral Ideal', *Ethics* 98, 1987

Franklin, Jane (ed.), *Equality*, London: Institute for Public Policy Research 1997

Franklin, Jane (ed.), *Social Policy and Social Justice: The IPPR Reader*, Cambridge: Polity 1998

Fraser, Nancy, 'Social Justice and Identity Politics', *Centre for the Study of Democracy Bulletin* 7/1, 2000

Fraser, Nancy, *Justice Interruptus: Critical Reflections on the 'Post-socialist' Condition*, New York: Routledge 1997

Giddens, Anthony, *The Third Way: The Renewal of Social Democracy*, Cambridge: Polity 1998

Giddens, Anthony, 'Why the Old Left Is Wrong on Equality', *New Statesman*, 25 October 1999, pp. 25–7

Giddens, Anthony, *The Third Way and Its Critics*, Cambridge: Polity 2000

Goodman, Alissa, Johnson, Paul, and Webb, Stephen, *Inequality in the UK*, Oxford: Oxford University Press 1997

Gordon, David et al., *Inequalities in Health: The Evidence Presented to the Independent Enquiry into Inequalities in Health*, London: Policy Press 2000

Gottwald, Norman K., and Horsley, Richard A., eds, *The Bible and Liberation: Political and Social Hermeneutics*, rev. edn. Maryknoll: Orbis 1993

Grant, Robert, M., *Early Christianity and Society: Seven Studies*, London: Collins 1978

Green, Philip, *The Pursuit of Inequality*, Oxford: Robertson 1981

Gutiérrez, G., *A Theology of Liberation*, London: SCM Press 1974

Gutiérrez, G., 'The Task and the Content of Liberation Theology' in C. Rowland (ed.), *The Cambridge Companion to Liberation Theology*, Cambridge: Cambridge University Press 1999

Gutmann, Amy, *Liberal Equality*, Cambridge: Cambridge University Press 1980

Gutmann, Amy (ed.), *Multiculturalism: Examining the Politics of Recognition*, Princeton: Princeton University Press 1994

Habermas, J., 'The New Obscurity and the Exhaustion of Utopian Energies' in Habermas (ed.), *Observations on the Spiritual Situation of the Age*, Cambridge, MA: MIT Press 1964

Haksar, Vinit, *Equality, Liberty and Perfectionism*, Oxford: Oxford University Press 1979

Hannay, Alastair, *Kierkegaard*, London: Routledge 1982

Hannay, Alastair and Marino, Gordon D. (eds), *The Cambridge Companion to Kierkegaard*, Cambridge: Cambridge University Press 1998

Hauerwas, Stanley, *Truthfulness and Tragedy*, Notre Dame: Notre Dame University Press 1977

Hayek, F. A., *The Road to Serfdom*, London: Routledge & Sons 1944

Hayek, F. A., *The Constitution of Liberty*, London: Routledge & Kegan Paul 1960

Hayek, F. A., *Law, Legislation and Liberty*, London: Routledge & Kegan Paul 1982

Hebblewaite, Peter, 'Liberation Theology and the Roman Catholic Church' in C. Rowland (ed.), *The Cambridge Companion to Liberation Theology*, Cambridge: Cambridge University Press 1999, pp. 179–98

Hewitt, Patricia, 'How an Egalitarian Can Be an Elitist', *New Statesman*, 21 February 2000

Hicks, Douglas A., *Inequality and Christian Ethics*, Cambridge: Cambridge University Press 2000

Hills, John, *Thatcherism, New Labour and the Welfare State*, London: LSE Centre for Analysis of Social Exclusion 1998

Holman, Robert, *Poverty: Explanations of Social Deprivation*, London: Martin Robertson 1978

Holman, Bob, *Towards Equality: A Christian Manifesto*, London: SPCK 1997

Holman, Bob, with Carol, Bill, Erica, Anita, Denise, Penny and Cynthia, *Faith in the Poor*, Oxford: Lion 1998

Holman, Bob, Helen Stanton and Stephen Timms, 'Is This the Right Direction?', in *Third Way* 21/9, 1998

Holman, Bob, Helen Stanton and Stephen Timms, *Joined-up Writing: New Labour and Social Inclusion*, pamphlet, London: Christian Socialist Movement 1999

Honderich, Ted, 'On Inequality and Violence' in R. S. Teres (ed.), *Nature and Conduct*, London: Macmillan 1975

Honderich, Ted, 'The Question of Well-being and the Principle of Equality', *Mind* XC, 1981, pp. 481–504

Honderich, Ted, 'The Principle of Equality Defended', *Politics* 3/1, 1983, pp. 33–7

Honneth, Axel, 'Integrity and Disrespect: Principles of a Conception of Morality Based on the Theory of Recognition', *Political Theory* 20/2, 1992

Howarth, Catharine, Kenway, Peter, Palmer, Guy and Street, Cathy, *Monitoring Poverty and Social Exclusion*, York: Joseph Rowntree Foundation 1998

Hunter, James, *The Making of the Crofting Community*, Edinburgh: John Donald new edn., 2000

Jenkins, Daniel, *Equality and Excellence*, London: SCM Press 1961

Jordan, Bill, *A Theory of Poverty and Social Exclusion*, Cambridge: Polity 1996

Jordan, Bill, *Freedom and the Welfare State*, London: Routledge 1976

Joseph, Keith and Sumption, Jonathan, *Equality*, London: John Murray 1979

Kellner, Peter, 'Equality of Worth and the New Politics' in Matthew Taylor and Jim Godfrey (eds), *Forces of Conservatism*, London: Institute for Public Policy Research 1999

Kierkegaard, S., *The Point of View, etc.*, trans and ed. Walter Lowrie, London: Oxford University Press 1939

Kierkegaard, S., *Works of Love*, trans D. F. Swenson, with an Introduction by D.

V. Steere, London: Oxford University Press 1946

Kierkegaard, S., *Philosophical Fragments*, trans. David Svenson, Princeton: Princeton University Press 1962

Kierkegaard, S., *For Self Examination*, Princeton: Princeton University Press 1974

Kierkegaard, S., *Papers and Journals: A Selection*, trans. and ed. Alastair Hannay, Harmondsworth: Penguin 1996

Koggel, Christine, *Perspectives on Equality: Constructing a Relational Theory*, Durham, MD: Rowman & Littlefield 1998

Kristol, Irving, 'Equality as an Ideal', *International Encyclopaedia of the Social Sciences*, New York: Macmillan 1968, Vol. 5, pp. 108–11

Lakoff, Sanford, *Equality in Political Philosophy*, Cambridge, MA: Harvard University Press 1964

Lane, David, *The End of Social Inequality? Class Status and Power under State Socialism*, London: Allen & Unwin 1982

Laslett, Peter and Runciman, W. G. (eds), *Philosophy, Politics and Society*, second series, Oxford: Blackwell 1962 [Essays by B.Williams and Rawls]

Le Grand, Julian, 'How to Cage the Fat Cats', *New Statesman*, 26 July 1999, pp. 25–7

Le Grand, Julian, *The Strategy of Equality: Redistribution and the Social Services*, London: Allen & Unwin 1982

Leech, Kenneth, *The Social God*, London: Sheldon Press 1981

Letwin, W. (ed.), *Against Equality: Readings on Economic and Social Policy*, London: Macmillan 1983

Lovin, Robin, 'Equality and Covenant Theology', *Journal of Law and Religion* 2/2, 1984, pp. 241–62

Lukes, Steven, *Individualism*, Oxford: Blackwell 1979

MacIntyre, Alasdair, *Against the Self-Images of the Age*, London: Duckworth 1971

MacIntyre, Alasdair, *After Virtue*, London: Duckworth 1981

MacIntyre, Alasdair, *Three Rival Versions of Moral Enquiry*, Notre Dame: University of Notre Dame Press 1990

Margalit, Avishai, *The Decent Society*, Cambridge, MA: Harvard University Press 1996

Marmot, Michael and Wilkinson, Richard G. (eds,), *Social Determinants of Health*, Oxford: Oxford University Press 1999

Middlemass, Keith, 'Unemployment: the Past and Future of a Political Problem', *The Political Quarterly* 51, 1980

Midgely, Mary, *Beast and Man*, Ithaca: Cornell University Press 1980

Miller, David and Walzer, M., *Pluralism, Justice and Equality*, Oxford: Oxford University Press 1995

Miller, David, *Principles of Social Justice*, Cambridge, MA: Harvard University Press 1999

Miller, David, *Social Justice*, Oxford: Clarendon Press 1976

Mitchell, Joshua, 'The Equality of All under the One in Luther and Rousseau: Thoughts on Christianity and Political Theory', *The Journal of Religion* 72, 1992, pp. 351–65

Mitchell, Joshua, *Not by Reason Alone: Religion, History and Identity in Early Modern Political Thought*, Chicago: University of Chicago Press 1993

Moltmann, J., *The Trinity and the Kingdom of God*, London: SCM Press 1981

Morgan, George, Jnr., 'Human Equality', *Ethics* LIII, 1943, pp. 115–20

Morton, Andrew R. (ed.), *Justice and Prosperity: A Realistic Vision? A Response to the Report of the Commission on Social Justice*, Edinburgh: Centre for Theology and Public Issues 1995

Morton, Andrew R. (ed.), *The Future of Welfare*, Edinburgh: Centre for Theology and Public Issues 1997 (Occasional Paper 41)

Morton, Andrew R. (ed.), *Beyond Fear: Vision, Hope and Generosity*, Edinburgh: St Andrew Press 1998

Murray, C., *Losing Out: American Social Policy, 1950–1980*, New York: Basic Books 1984

Nagel, Thomas, 'Equality' in *Mortal Questions*, Cambridge: Cambridge University Press 1979

Nagel, Thomas, *Equality and Partiality*, Oxford: Oxford University Press 1991

Nussbaum M., and Sen, Amartya (eds), *The Quality of Life*, Oxford: Clarendon Press 1993

Okun, Arthur M., *Equality and Efficiency: The Great Trade-off*, Brookings Institution: Washington, DC 1975

Oppenheim, Felix E., 'The Concept of Equality', *International Encyclopedia of the Social Sciences*, New York: Free Press 1968, Vol. 5, pp. 102–8

Outka, Gene, 'Equality and Individuality: Thoughts on Two Themes in Kierkegaard', *Journal of Religious Ethics* 10/2, 1982, pp. 171–203

Outka, Gene, *Agape: An Ethical Analysis*, New Haven: Yale University Press 1972

Parijs, Philippe van, *Real Freedom for All*, Oxford: Clarendon Press 1995

Pennock, J. R., and Chapman, J. W. (eds), *Equality* [NOMOS IX], New York: Atherton Press 1967

Perry, Michael, *Religion in Politics: Constitutional and Moral Perspectives*, Oxford: Oxford University Press 1997

Phillips, Anne, *Which Equalities Matter?* Oxford: Polity 1999

Pixley, George V., *God's Kingdom*, London: SCM Press 1981

Pixley, Jorge and Boff, Clodovis, *The Bible, the Church and the Poor*, London: Burns & Oates 1989

Plamenatz, John P., 'Equality of Opportunity' in *Aspects of Human Equality*, Lyman Bryson et al. (eds), New York: Conference on Science, Philosophy and

Religion in Their Relation to the Democratic Way of Life, Inc. 1956

Plant, R., 'Democratic Socialism and Equality' in R. Lipsey and D. Leonard (eds), *Socialist Agenda: Crosland's Legacy*, London: Cape 1981

Pojman, Louis P., and Westmoreland, Robert (eds), *Equality: Selected Readings*, Oxford: Oxford University Press 1997

Pole, J. R., *The Pursuit of Equality in American History*, Berkeley: University of California Press 1978

Pope, Stephen J., 'Proper and Improper Partiality and the Preferential Option for the Poor', *Theological Studies* 54, 1993, pp. 242–71

Preston, Ronald, 'R. H. Tawney as a Christian Moralist' in *Religion and the Persistence of Capitalism*, London: SCM Press 1979, pp. 83–110

Rae, Douglas, *Equalities*, Cambridge, MA: Harvard University Press 1981

Rainwater, Lee (ed.), *Social Problems and Public Policy: Inequality and Justice*, Chicago: Aldine 1974

Rakowski, Eric, *Equal Justice*, Oxford: Clarendon Press 1991

Rawls, J., *A Theory of Justice*, Oxford: Oxford University Press 1972

Rawls, J., 'Justice as Fairness: Political not Metaphysical', *Philosophy and Public Affairs* 14/3, 1985, pp. 223–51

Rawls, J., *Political Liberalism*, New York: Columbia University Press 1993

Rawls, J., *The Law of Peoples, with 'The Idea of Public Reason' Revisited*, Cambridge, MA: Harvard University Press 1999

Raz, J., 'Principles of Equality', *Mind* vol. 87, 1978, pp. 321–42

Rees, John, *Equality*, London: Pall Mall Press 1971

Robinson, Simon, J., 'R. H. Tawney's Theory of Equality: A Theological and Ethical Analysis', Unpublished Edinburgh PhD thesis 1989

Robson, William A., *Welfare State and Welfare Society*, London: Allen & Unwin 1976

Roemer, John E, *Equality of Opportunity*, Cambridge, MA: Harvard University Press 1998

Romero, Oscar, *Voice of the Voiceless*, Maryknoll: Orbis 1985

Rowland, Christopher, *Radical Christianity*, Cambridge: Polity 1988

Rowland, Christopher, *Revelation*, London: Epworth Press 1993

Rowland, Christopher, 'Revelation' in *The New Interpreter's Bible*, Vol. 12, Nashville: Abingdon 1998

Royal Commission on Long Term Care, *With Respect to Old Age: Long Term Care – Rights and Responsibilities*, London: The Stationery Office 1999

Runciman, W. G., *Relative Deprivation and Social Justice: A Study of Attitudes to Social Inequality in Twentieth Century England*, London: Routledge 1966

Schüssler Fiorenza, Elisabeth, *Discipleship of Equals: A Feminist Critical Ekklesialogy of Liberation*, New York: Crossroad 1984

Sen, Amartya, *Choice, Welfare and Measurement*, Oxford: Blackwell 1982

Sen, Amartya, *On Ethics and Economics*, Oxford: Blackwell 1987

Sen, Amartya, *Inequality Re-examined*, New York: Oxford University Press 1992

Sen, Amartya, *On Economic Inequality*, expanded edn., Oxford: Oxford University Press 1997

Sen, Amartya, *Development as Freedom*, Oxford: Oxford University Press 1999

Sen, Amartya, *Reason Before Identity*, Oxford: Oxford University Press 1999

Shaw, Mary et al., *The Widening Gap: Health Inequalities and Policy in Britain*, London: Policy Press 2000

Smith, Dennis E., and Taussig, H., *Many Tables: The Eucharist in the New Testament and Liturgy Today*, London: SCM Press 1990

Smith, T. V., *The American Philosophy of Equality*, Chicago: University of Chicago Press 1927

Sobrino, Jon, *The True Church and the Poor*, London: SCM Press 1985

Sonjee, A. H., 'Individuality and Equality in Hinduism', in J. R. Pennock and J. W. Chapman (eds), *Equality* [NOMOS IX], New York: Atherton Press 1967

Spiegelberg, Herbert, 'A Defence of Human Equality', *Philosophical Review* LIII, 1944, pp. 101ff.

Stephen, Leslie, 'Social Equality', *International Journal of Ethics* I, 1891, pp. 201–88

Stephens, James Fitzjames, *Liberty, Equality, Fraternity*, ed. J. White, Cambridge: Cambridge University Press 1967

Stevenson, Wilf, *Equality and the Modern Economy: Seminar 5*, London: The Smith Institute 1999

Stevenson, Wilf (ed.), *Social Democrat and Social Liberal: Is There a Difference?* London: The Smith Institute 1999

Stevenson, Wilf (ed.), *Why Equality? What is Equality?* London: The Smith Institute 1999

Tanner, Kathryn, *The Politics of God: Christian Theologies and Social Justice*, Minneapolis: Fortress Press 1992

Tawney, R. H., *'The Attack' and Other Papers*. London: Allen & Unwin 1953

Tawney, R. H., *Equality*, London: Allen & Unwin 1964

Tawney, R. H., *The Acquisitive Society*, new edn. with Preface by Peter Townsend, Brighton: Harvester Press 1982

Taylor, Charles, et al., *Multiculturalism: Examining the Politics of Recognition*, Princeton: Princeton University Press 1994

Temple, William, *Christianity and Social Order*, Harmondsworth: Penguin 1942

Terrill, Ross, *R. H. Tawney and His Times*, Cambridge, MA: Harvard University Press 1973

Terrill, Ross, *The Uppsala Report, 1968*, Geneva: WCC 1968

Theissen, Gerd, *A Theory of Primitive Christianity*, London: SCM Press 1999

Theissen, Gerd, *The Social Setting of Pauline Christianity*, Edinburgh: T&T Clark 1982

Thomson, David, *Equality,* Cambridge: Cambridge University Press 1949

Tocqueville, Alexis de, *Democracy in America,* London: Oxford University Press 1946,

Townsend, Peter and Davidson, Nick, *Inequalities in Health: The Black Report,* Harmondsworth: Penguin 1982

Troeltsch, Ernst, *The Social Teaching of the Christian Churches,* London: Allen & Unwin 1931

Turner, Bryan S., *Equality*, London: Tavistock 1986

Vallely, Paul (ed.), *The New Politics: Catholic Social Teaching for the Twenty-first Century,* London: SCM Press 1998

Veatch, Robert, *The Foundations of Justice: Why the Retarded and the Rest of Us have Claims to Equality,* New York: Oxford University Press 1986

Volf, Miroslav, *Exclusion and Embrace: A Theological Exploration of Identity, Otherness, and Reconciliation,* Nashville: Abingdon 1996

Volf, Miroslav, *After Our Likeness: The Church as the Image of the Trinity,* Grand Rapids: Eerdmans 1998

Volf, Miroslav, '"The Trinity is our Social Program": The Doctrine of the Trinity and the Shape of Social Engagement', *Modern Theology* 14.3, July 1998, pp. 403–23

Waldron, Jeremy, 'Religious Contributions in Public Deliberation', *San Diego Law Review* 30, 1993, pp. 817–48

Waldron, Jeremy, *Christian Equality in the Thought of John Locke,* Oxford University: Carlyle Lectures, typescript, 1999

Walker, Robert, 'The Dynamics of Poverty and Social Exclusion', in G. Room (ed.), *Beyond the Threshold,* Bristol: Policy Press 1995

Walsh, Michael and Davies, Brian, *Proclaiming Justice and Peace: One Hundred Years of Catholic Social Teaching,* London: HarperCollins 1991

Walzer, Michael, *Spheres of Justice,* New York: Basic Books 1983

Walzer, Michael, 'In Defense of Equality', *Dissent,* Fall 1973, pp. 399–408

Weale, Albert, *Equality and Social Policy,* London: Routledge 1978

Weale, Albert, 'The Impossibility of Liberal Egalitarianism', *Analysis* 40, 1980

Weale, Albert, 'The Welfare State and Two Conflicting Ideals of Equality', *Government and Opposition* 20, 1985, pp. 315–27

Weale, Albert, 'Equality, Social Solidarity and the Welfare State', *Ethics* 100, April 1990, pp. 473–88

Weale, Albert, 'Equality' in *Dictionary of Ethics, Theology and Society,* London: Routledge 1996, p. 296

Werpehowski, W., 'Political Liberalism and Christian Ethics: A Review Discussion', *Thomist* 48, 1984

Whitehead, Margaret, *The Health Divide: Inequalities in Health in the 1980s,* London: Health Education Council 1987

Wilensky, Harold L., *The Welfare State and Equality*, Berkeley: University of California Press 1975

Wilkinson, Alan, *Christian Socialism: Scott Holland to Tony Blair*, London: SCM Press 1998

Wilkinson, Richard G., *Unhealthy Societies: The Afflictions of Inequality*, London: Routledge 1996

Williams, Bernard, 'The Idea of Equality' in Joel Feinber (ed.), *Moral Concepts*, London: Oxford University Press 1970, pp. 157–8

Wilson, John, *Equality*, London: Hutchinson 1966

Winter, J. M., and Joslin, D. M., *R. H. Tawney's Commonplace Book*, Cambridge: Cambridge University Press 1972

Wolgast, Elizabeth, *Equality and the Rights of Women*, Ithaca, NY: Cornell University Press 1980

Wolin, Sheldon, *Politics and Vision: Continuity and Innovation in Western Political Thought*, London: Allen & Unwin 1961

Wollheim, Richard, 'Equality', *Proceedings of the Aristotelian Society* LVI, 1956, pp. 281–309

Young, Iris M., *Justice and the Politics of Difference*, Princeton: Princeton University Press 1990

Zizioulas, John D., *Being As Communion: Studies in Personhood and the Church*, Crestwood, NY: St Vladimir's Seminary Press 1985

Index